Ethnic Profiling in the European Union: Pervasive, Ineffective, and Discriminatory

OPEN SOCIETY INSTITUTE

NEW YORK

ISBN: 978-1-891385-88-9

Published by
Open Society Institute
400 West 59th Street
New York, NY 10019 USA
www.soros.org

For more information contact:
Open Society Justice Initiative
400 West 59th Street
New York, NY 10019 USA
www.justiceinitiative.org

Cover designed by Judit Kovács | Createch Ltd.
Cover photo by Diether Endlicher | Associated Press
Text layout and printing by Createch Ltd.

Table of Contents

Acknowledgments

This report is the result of many contributions made over several years. It was written by Rachel Neild, based on input from many others. In particular, Lanna Hollo of Hollo Human Rights Consulting helped to shape the report's approach, and provided the bulk of the research for Chapters IV and V. The report would not have been possible without her research and expertise. James A. Goldston wrote the legal analysis and review of conceptual problems with profiling and Maxim Ferschtman provided additional legal analysis. Rebekah Delsol researched and wrote sections on U.K. practices. Indira Goris provided legal research on police powers and counterterrorism authorities in the European Union. Peter Rodrigues, of the Anne Frank Foundation, contributed supporting materials from the Netherlands.

The report was edited by David Berry, James A. Goldston, Diane Orentlicher, and Robert O. Varenik.

Stephen Humphries and Andrea Kriszan prepared a first version of the report in 2006 on the basis of research provided by Boyko Boev, Jeremie Gaulthier, Philip Gounev, Andras Pap Laszlo, Joel Miller, Daniel Wagman, and Gus Hosein. Misti Duvall, Ammar Abu Zayyad, Cathy Lull, Alina Finkelshteyn, Shamus Brennan and Sebastian Kohn assisted with additional research and fact checking.

Further research and legal assistance were provided by the law clinics at Harvard University and New York University. We are grateful to Jamie O'Connell, then of the Harvard Law School Human Rights Program and currently program officer, Boalt Hall Committee for International Human Rights Clinic at Berkeley Law (Boalt Hall) and to students Aren Adjoian, Gwen Gordon, Colleen Guilford, Emily Gumper, and Rahul Mukhi. We also wish to give great thanks to Jayne Huckerby and Smita Narula of the International Human Rights Clinic of NYU School of Law and to students Mana Barari, Jennie Kim, and Margie van Weerden.

Many thanks to participants at the May 2007 peer review meeting, and especially to Sara Silvestri and Elizabeth Collett of European Policy Centre for their cooperation in organizing and hosting the event.

Finally, we are particularly grateful to security officials in Germany's Ministry of the Interior and in the intelligence services and police of the Netherlands who took the time to review a pre-publication draft and meet with us to discuss it. We regret that French officials did not agree to a similar consultation. We also appreciate the time and consideration of staff at the U.K. Ministry of Justice and from the London Metropolitan Police Service who provided input and comments.

The Open Society Justice Initiative bears sole responsibility for the final version of this report, including any errors or misrepresentations.

I. Executive Summary and Recommendations

A. Executive Summary

Since the 9/11 attacks in the United States, 32 percent of British Muslims report being subjected to discrimination at airports. Police carrying machine guns have conducted identity checks on 11-year-olds at German mosques. Moroccan immigrants have been called *"moro de mierda"* ("Arab shit") by Spanish police. The personal data of 8.3 million people were searched in a massive German data mining exercise which targeted—among other characteristics—people who were Muslim, and which did not identify a single terrorist.

These are examples of ethnic profiling by police in Europe—a common, long-standing practice that has intensified in recent years. Evidence from countries across the European Union shows that police routinely use generalizations about ethnicity, religion, race, or national origin in deciding whom to target for identity checks, stops, and searches. Contemporary concerns about terrorism underlie a rising interest in ethnic profiling in Europe, which many see as an effective way to identify terrorist suspects.

It might be comforting to believe that police can spot terrorists and other criminals based on generalizations about ethnicity, race, national origin, or religion. But that is not the case. As this report demonstrates, ethnic profiling by police in Europe may be pervasive, but it is inefficient, ineffective, and discriminatory. Fortunately, better alternatives exist.

Defining Ethnic Profiling

The term "profiling" refers to a police practice in which a defined set of characteristics is used to look for and apprehend someone who has committed a crime (criminal profiling) or to identify people likely to engage in criminal activity (behavioral profiling). Criminal and behavioral profiling are accepted and lawful policing tools designed to allow the most efficient allocation of scarce law enforcement resources. As long as the profiles used by police are based on specific information about an individual or factors that are objective and statistically proven to be significant indicators of criminal activity, profiling is legal.

The term "ethnic profiling" describes the use by law enforcement of generalizations grounded in ethnicity, race, religion, or national origin—rather than objective evidence or individual behavior—as the basis for making law enforcement and/or investigative decisions about who has been or may be involved in criminal activity. Ethnic profiling is manifest most often in police officers' decisions about whom to stop, ask for identity papers, question, search, and sometimes arrest. Ethnic profiling may result from the racist behavior of individual police officers, or from the institutionalized bias ingrained in many police forces.

A host of bad outcomes stem from ethnic profiling, including stopping, searching, and even arresting innocent people; overlooking criminals who do not fit the established profile; undermining the rule of law and perceptions of police fairness; stigmatizing entire communities; and alienating people who could work with police to reduce crime and prevent terrorism.

Ethnic Profiling Is Pervasive—and Has Grown Since 9/11

Ethnic profiling did not emerge as a post-9/11 response to terrorism. Evidence clearly indicates that police across Europe have long engaged in ethnic profiling of immigrant and minority communities. Despite a dearth of quantitative information on policing and ethnicity in most of Europe, the data that exist indicate ethnic profiling is widespread.

Since the 9/11 attacks, interest in and use of ethnic profiling have grown sharply. Even if the European public may condemn high-profile abuses (such as rendition and torture) associated with the "war on terror," many see the profiling of Muslims as a matter of common sense. According to this argument, young Muslim men destroyed the World Trade Center in New York, blew up Madrid's Atocha train station, and bombed the London Underground, so they should be the targets of police attention. With so much at stake, ethnic profiling may seem like smart law enforcement.

Police in Europe seem to agree. In the United Kingdom (the only EU member state to systematically gather ethnic data on police practices), data show dramatic increases in stops and searches of British Asians following terrorist attacks: stops of persons of Asian descent conducted under counterterrorism powers increased three-fold following the 9/11 attacks, and five-fold after the July 2005 London Underground bomb attacks.[1] In Germany, police have used preventive powers to conduct mass identity checks outside major mosques. In France and Italy, raids on homes, businesses, and mosques—often lacking a basis in specific evidence—have targeted Muslims, particularly those considered religiously observant. Numerous studies since 2001 have documented "a growing perception among Muslim leaders and communities across Europe that they are being stopped, questioned, and searched not on the basis of evidence and reasonable suspicion but on the basis of 'looking Muslim'."[2]

Since 2001, the frequency of ethnic profiling in Europe has alternately increased and decreased in response to notorious crimes. Ethnic profiling has spiked in the immediate wake of terrorist attacks, then declined. A number of the ethnic profiling practices described in this report are less prevalent in mid-2009 than they were immediately following the March 11, 2004 Madrid and July 7, 2005 London bombings. In particular, the most overt forms of ethnic profiling, such as broad data mining and large-scale raids and mass identity checks outside places of worship, are now rarer.

The apparent decline in the more egregious forms of ethnic profiling underscores that, all too frequently, the practice is more of a public relations tool than a reasoned response to crime and terrorism. In this respect, it reflects a political reality that is subject to change. Although public concern has waned since the summer of 2006, another attack would almost certainly prompt political authorities and security agencies to revive the explicit and public targeting of Muslims.

Ethnic Profiling Is a Form of Discrimination

Ethnic profiling, although widespread, constitutes discrimination and thus breaches basic human rights norms. By relying on ethnic, racial, or religious stereotypes, ethnic profiling breaches one of the most fundamental principles of law: that each person must be treated as an individual, not as a member of a group. In employing physical appearance as code for criminal propensity, ethnic profiling turns the presumption of innocence on its head. Except where police use of ethnicity, race, or religion is limited to the characteristics contained in individual suspect descriptions, or based on concrete, trustworthy, and timely intelligence that is time- and/or place-specific, profiling is a violation of European and international law, which, for important reasons of history and logic, has placed strict limits on distinctions based on ethnicity, race, national origin, and religion.

The European Convention on Human Rights prohibits discrimination and guarantees the full and equal enjoyment of rights in respect of, inter alia, the administration of justice. The European Court of Human Rights has made clear that ethnic profiling, like other differences in treatment based "exclusively or to a decisive extent on a person's ethnic origin," is per se unlawful. The European Commission against Racism and Intolerance (ECRI) has repeatedly expressed concerns with ethnic profiling across a wide range of EU member states. In fact, ECRI has specifically addressed ethnic profiling by police, even in the context of counterterrorism measures. ECRI's *General Policy Recommendation Number Eight on Combating Racism while Fighting Terrorism* (2004) urges governments to "pay particular attention to...checks carried out by law enforcement officials within the countries and by border control personnel."[3] And yet, notwithstanding the overwhelming weight of European jurisprudence and legal organs, to date, ethnic profiling has not been expressly outlawed by the European Union or any European government.

European law on matters pertaining to ethnic profiling is a complex patchwork of protection and gaps. Article 29 of the Treaty on the European Union states that the Union's objective shall be "to provide citizens with a high level of safety within an area of freedom, security and justice by developing common action among the Member States in the fields of police and judicial cooperation in criminal matters and by preventing and combating racism and xenophobia." Although some suggest that the term "goods and services" that are addressed in the EU Racial Equality Directive should be understood to encompass policing within member states, most European authorities argue that under current regional treaties, the EU has competency only in matters of law enforcement cooperation between member states, not in regard to domestic law enforcement practices. On this basis, an increasing number of operational agreements have been developed to facilitate law enforcement cooperation and automated access to law enforcement information between member states in order to fight terrorism and serious crime.[4] Furthermore, the EU is rapidly building vast databases for immigration and border control and allowing law enforcement access to these resources to aid in fighting terrorism and crime.[5]

Operational capacity and cooperation are being developed at a pace that far outstrips the development of regional accountability standards and oversight mechanisms. It is troubling that these initiatives fall within the scope of EU action, but outside the scope of EU protections against discrimination. It is even more troubling when the inadequate state of data protection standards for law enforcement cooperation is added to the equation. The Framework Decision on the Protection of Personal Data in the context of law enforcement cooperation has been criticized as establishing lesser standards than those set out in the 2005 European Data Protection Directive. This is a disturbing trend that can and should be remedied through the creation of a regional norm that clearly defines ethnic profiling and establishes minimum safeguards that build on—rather than erode—the European Union's current non-discrimination and data protection law.

Ethnic Profiling Is Ineffective

There is no evidence that ethnic profiling stops crime or prevents terrorism. Separate studies in the United Kingdom, the United States, Sweden, and the Netherlands have all concluded that ethnic profiling is ineffective.[6] Stops and searches conducted under counterterrorism powers in Europe have produced few charges on terrorism offenses and no terrorism convictions to date.

In fact, profiling reduces security by misdirecting police resources and alienating some of the very people whose cooperation is necessary for effective crime detection. When law enforcement officers engage in ethnic profiling, they are, wittingly or not, contributing to a growing sense of marginalization in minority and immigrant communities. Ethnic profiling stigmatizes entire racial, ethnic, or religious groups as more likely to commit crimes and thereby signals to the broader society that all members of that group constitute a threat. If the police and government security agencies use ethnicity to determine who is a terrorist or a criminal, why should not local shopkeepers, restaurant owners, or airplane flight attendants?

Many law enforcement professionals understand these dangers. A senior U.K. police officer recently warned that "there is a very real risk of criminalizing minority communities" through "the counterterrorism label....The impact of this will be that just at the time when we need the confidence and trust of these communities, they may retreat inside themselves."[7]

Extensive research and the findings in this report indicate not only that ethnic profiling does not improve police efficacy, but that in all likelihood it reduces it, both in countering terrorism and addressing common crime. Numerous studies of policing show that when police operate on the basis of their personal judgments—that is, with a high level of discretion—they rely more on stereotypes and focus disproportionate attention on minorities, which reduces their effectiveness. With a plethora of crime and terrorist threats confronting Europe, it is critical that police resources be used as efficiently as possible.

Equally important, when police treat an entire group of people as presumptively suspicious, they are more likely to miss dangerous persons who do not fit the profile. Before the July 7, 2005 London attacks, the leader of the bombers "had come to the attention of the intelligence services as an associate of other men who were suspected of involvement in a terrorist bomb plot. But he was not pursued because he did not tick enough of the boxes in the pre-July profile of the terror suspect."[8] Ethnic profiling in fact creates a direct incentive for terrorist organizations to recruit persons who do not fit the profile.

Alternatives to Ethnic Profiling

It's not just that ethnic profiling is illegal and counter-productive; there are better ways of fighting crime and terrorism. The reform of the United States Customs Service (which searches travelers at U.S. borders for contraband) in the late 1990s demonstrates that profiling based on individual behavior is more effective than profiling based on race or ethnicity. In 1999, when the Customs Service abandoned a profile based on ethnicity and instead focused on behavior, its productivity and efficiency soared. The number of searches declined from 10,733 in the first quarter of 1999 (pre-reform) to 2,814 searches in the first quarter of 2000 (post-reform), but the percent of searches that yielded contraband leaped from 3.5 percent to nearly 11 percent.[9]

In 2007–2008, a pilot project undertaken by the Open Society Justice Initiative in collaboration with a municipal police force in Spain similarly reduced the disproportionate rate at which minorities were stopped, while increasing police efficiency. In Fuenlabrada, Spain, police achieved dramatic results by moving away from ethnic profiling and adopting new methods that emphasized the use of data and greater communication and cooperation with minority communities. In a four-month period, the number of stops declined from 958 per month to 396 per month, but the percentage of successful stops (i.e., stops that uncovered a crime or other infraction) rose from 6 percent to 28 percent.[10]

A key component of the Fuenlabrada success was the collaboration between police and minority communities—a factor central to effective law enforcement, but often overlooked by proponents of ethnic profiling. As leading counterterrorism experts have noted, one of the main elements of an effective counterterrorism policy is to "develop strong confidence-building ties with the communities from which terrorists are most likely to come or hide in."[11] This is possible, but only if those communities are not being alienated by race-based policing.

The threat of terrorist violence, like the everyday reality of ordinary crime, is genuine and must be addressed. The challenge is to do so in ways that enhance, rather than undermine, both security and individual rights. Ethnic profiling strikes at the heart of the social compact linking law enforcement institutions with the communities they serve. It wastes police resources, discriminates against whole groups of people, and leaves everyone less safe. Fortunately, alternatives exist. Ending the use of ethnic profiling by police does not mean doing nothing; rather, it means changing police practices to make them more effective. New practices can direct law enforcement resources more efficiently, based on intelligence rather than prejudice.

Abandoning accepted practices and implementing new ones is never easy. But until ethnic profiling is recognized as a problem, expressly banned in law, and addressed in practice, the damage it wreaks will only deepen. In a Europe under threat from terrorism and characterized by increasing xenophobia, it is essential that those entrusted to enforce the law do so with maximum effectiveness and full respect for the basic principle of equal justice.

B. Recommendations

To European Authorities:

- *Outlaw profiling at the European level.* The European Union should adopt a Framework Decision[12] defining ethnic profiling, making clear that it is illegal, and providing safeguards against it. Ethnic profiling should be defined as the use by law enforcement officers of generalizations grounded in race, ethnicity, religion, or national origin, rather than objective evidence or individual behavior, as the basis for making law enforcement and/or investigative decisions about who has been or may be involved in criminal activity.

- *Ensure that data mining does not rely on ethnic profiling.* Data mining—the process of extracting patterns or trends from large amounts of information—increasingly relies upon ethnic profiling. The European Commission and Council should provide guidelines for national authorities on adequate safeguards against ethnic profiling in data mining operations. Guidelines should reinforce the standard set forth in relevant data protection instruments of the Council of Europe, which prohibit the collection or use by law enforcement of data on individuals solely on the basis that they have a particular ethnic origin or religious conviction, except where "absolutely necessary for the purposes of a particular inquiry."[13] Among other safeguards, they must make clear that intrusive processing of sensitive personal data is permissible only when strictly necessary, for example when: a) such data are contained in an individual suspect description; or b) they are based on timely, concrete, and trustworthy intelligence that is specific to a place, time, and crime or crime pattern. Data mining should be limited to a specific inquiry, with access given on a case-by-case basis.

- *Support gathering of statistics on ethnicity and law enforcement practices.* The Working Party on the Protection of Individuals with regard to the processing of Personal Data (Article 29 Working Party) should issue an opinion providing guidance to member states which makes clear that the collection of anonymous statistical data on ethnicity and law enforcement is consistent with European data protection norms. When used properly and with appropriate safeguards, ethnic data are essential to detect, monitor, and address ethnic profiling practices.

- *Fund collaboration between police and minority communities.* The European Commission should provide financial support for pilot projects, research, and dissemination of best practices to address ethnic profiling and enhance law enforcement effectiveness. Such work may be conducted by national and local law enforcement authorities, civil society, academic bodies, and European regional entities such as the Fundamental Rights Agency. Collaborative projects between law enforcement and civil society groups, particularly those representing minority communities, have proven to be especially valuable in reducing ethnic profiling while increasing police efficiency.

- *Refine the EU's radicalization policy.* To combat radicalization, the European Union should continue to explore root causes of violent radicalization, including discrimination, exclusion, and racism; refrain from categorizations that rely on ethnic, racial, or religious stereotypes; avoid conflating nonviolent conservative religious practices with radicalization processes; and urge member states to pursue similar policies.

To National Elected Authorities and Policymaking Bodies:

- *Modify national legislation to incorporate an express prohibition against ethnic profiling.* Anti-discrimination legislation in most EU member states requires amendment to make clear that ethnic profiling is unlawful. In addition, laws and operational guidelines for law enforcement officers should expressly prohibit ethnic profiling and establish clearly the limited circumstances under which sensitive personal factors such as ethnicity and religion may be used in policing, including data mining: where there is either a specific suspect description or clear and reliable intelligence.

- *Establish a requirement of reasonable suspicion for all police stops.* National laws and police guidelines should set out clear and precise standards for initiating stops and making identity checks and searches based upon a reasonable suspicion standard. This legal standard should be supported with guidance and training that explicitly prohibit the use of ethnicity as a basis for identity checks and stop and searches.

- *Speak out against discrimination and ethnic profiling.* Make it clear that ethnic profiling is not an effective tactic in the fight against either terrorism or common crime and that, as a policy matter, it will not be tolerated.

- *Gather data on law enforcement and ethnicity.* Establish systems for gathering—with safeguards sufficient to comply with European data protection norms—statistical data on law enforcement and ethnicity that can determine whether, where, and why ethnic profiling is occurring and support measures to address it. Detecting and monitoring ethnic profiling require anonymized ethnic statistics (as opposed to ethnic data that can be traced to individual persons) that allow for comparison of minority and majority groups' experiences of law enforcement. Where ethnic profiling is found to be widespread, conduct a full audit of policy and practice to determine and correct the factors driving or permitting such profiling.

- *Establish clear oversight mechanisms.* Where they do not already exist, put into place judicial oversight and other supervisory mechanisms (such as parliamentary oversight) to assess the evidentiary basis for antiterrorism and investigative measures such as raids, surveillance and monitoring, and arrests. Charge oversight authorities with the duty to assure that all law enforcement measures under scrutiny meet tests of necessity and proportionality, and comply fully with European antidiscrimination norms.

- *Establish accessible complaints mechanisms.* Assure that civilians have information about and access to complaints mechanisms that are capable of investigating allegations of ethnic profiling, through examining individual complaints and analyzing patterns of complaints. Effective, independent accountability mechanisms are essential in all areas of security and law enforcement, including for intelligence agencies and counterterrorism operations.

- *Promote police outreach to minority communities.* Initiate policies to support police outreach to minority ethnic and religious communities and enhance mutual understanding and trust.

- *Avoid statements linking ethnicity, national origin, race, or religion to terrorism or criminal behavior.* Information provided to the media about law enforcement actions should refer to the ethnicity of the persons involved only when it is directly relevant and necessary to the public interest.

- *Improve legal and institutional tools to address hate crime.* Develop a clear definition of hate crimes, an accessible system for members of minority groups to report hate crimes, investigative capacity to address hate crimes, and a rapid response capacity for serious hate crimes.

To Law Enforcement Managers:

- *Assess the impact of law enforcement.* Establish measures to evaluate all anticrime and counterterrorism measures for both their law enforcement effectiveness and their impact on local communities. Assessments should consider both quantitative outputs and qualitative outcomes such as public satisfaction and police-community relations.

- *Monitor and supervise the use of discretionary powers such as identity checks and stops and searches.* Implement systems to monitor both the number and nature (quality) of officers' encounters with members of the public for use in discussions with local authorities and residents, and for police training and performance evaluation.

- *Implement strategies known to reduce ethnic profiling.* Ethnic profiling can be addressed through reducing officer discretion in the selection of individuals to stop. This can be achieved through increased supervision of patrol officers and scrutiny of stops and their outcomes, and increased reliance on intelligence and behavioral factors to direct the use of stop powers.

- *Provide clear and detailed operational guidelines and training for all law enforcement officers on the correct conduct of identity checks, stops, and searches.* This training should be practical, should address ethnic profiling, and should include managers, and, where possible, members of minority communities in design and delivery.

- *Base all antiterrorism measures—including raids, monitoring, and arrest—on factual evidence rather than religious or ethnic stereotypes.* When interrogating terror suspects, focus on material evidence of their involvement in the criminal acts under investigation and not on their religious beliefs or practices. Ensure that all law enforcement and counterterrorism actions fully respect religious and cultural practices as well as religious objects and places.

- *Require respectful treatment of all members of the public during encounters with law enforcement.* Establish explicit equal treatment standards in police codes of ethics, including a requirement that officers explain the reason for an identity check, stop, or search, and establish clear consequences for infractions.

- *Schedule regular meetings between police and community members.* Increase officers' accountability to the communities they are policing by holding meetings between police and community members, particularly those from minority or disadvantaged sections of the population. Take community concerns seriously and respond to them directly or by referring them to appropriate authorities or agencies.

- *Be transparent.* Provide information on the evidentiary basis for crime prevention and counterterrorism measures to the ethnic and religious minority communities that are affected, in order to allay perceptions of discriminatory targeting, while maintaining necessary investigative confidentiality and respecting personal privacy and judicial procedures.

- *Establish policies to recruit and retain minority law enforcement officers and staff.* Ideally, law enforcement agencies should look like the communities they serve. At a minimum, all police officers should have an understanding of the diverse communities in which they work.

To Civil Society:

- *Contribute to the movement away from ethnic profiling.* Advance knowledge and encourage good practice by researching, monitoring, and reporting on ethnic profiling and the policing of minority communities.

- *Conduct public education campaigns on rights and responsibilities in police-community relations.* Just as the police need to reach out to minority communities, communities may also need training and support to understand the law, the police and their powers, and the rights and responsibilities of community members.

- *Participate in and support police-community outreach efforts and community policing campaigns.* Support the capacity of local minority communities to organize and participate in dialogue and partnership with police.

II. Ethnic Profiling: What Is It and When Is It Unlawful?

A. Ethnic Profiling Defined and Described

"Ethnic profiling" is defined in this report as the use of generalizations grounded in ethnicity, race, national origin, or religion—rather than objective evidence or individual behavior—as the basis for making law enforcement and/or investigative decisions about who has been or may be involved in criminal activity. (Throughout this report, the term "ethnic profiling" is used to refer to profiling on any or all of these four grounds.) As used in this report, "ethnic profiling" refers to situations in which ethnicity, race, national origin, or religion is a determining criterion for law enforcement decisions—even if it is not the sole basis for such decisions.[14]

By its nature, ethnic profiling departs from a basic principle of the rule of law: that law enforcement determinations should be based on individual conduct, not on membership in an ethnic, racial, national, or religious group. Ethnic profiling uses and perpetuates stereotypes about criminal offenders and minority groups that are supposedly more prone to offend, effectively basing investigative decisions on group attributes rather than a potential suspect's behavior.

While ethnic profiling is inherently problematic, it has roots in widely used practices that are not racist or irrational, including actuarial risk-assessment methods and other ways to statistically categorize people according to identifiable group characteristics. Insurance companies, hospitals, and government agencies commonly base management and other decisions on data showing, for example, that individuals over the age of 60 are more likely than younger people to be susceptible to certain illnesses. Such generalizations can help save time, apportion resources appropriately, and inform management decisions.

Similar considerations apply to policing. Particularly in view of limited resources, police rightly seek to maximize their effectiveness in preventing, detecting, and investigating crime. The development of various types of profiles to support investigations is an accepted and permissible law enforcement strategy—provided the profiles do not cross the line that separates legitimate policing from discriminatory practices.

Ethnic Profiling Compared to Other Types of Profiling by Police

Accepted law enforcement tools include what is sometimes called "criminal profiling" or "offender profiling." A criminal profile is constructed by analyzing a crime—the nature of the offense and the manner in which it was committed—to develop guidance to help police identify an unknown perpetrator. The underlying theory is that certain types of crime can be studied and common factors analyzed to build an offender profile of some predictive value to aid police investigations. The serial killer profile is a classic example (and indeed, some trace the roots of profiling back to police attempts to identify the serial killer known as Jack the Ripper in Victorian London). In contrast to ethnic profiling, criminal profiling has not provoked public controversy[15] despite the considerable debate among criminologists as to its efficacy.[16]

Ethnicity is also frequently and validly used by police in compiling an individual suspect description, on the basis of victim or witness reports, in connection with a specific crime. Personal appearance, which almost invariably includes racial or ethnic characteristics, is a core component of a suspect description. For example, a suspect description might state that the suspect was a white male about six feet tall with a heavy build, that he was wearing a leather jacket, and had brown hair and blue eyes.

While a suspect description typically includes a valid, indeed necessary, use of ethnicity, it can be and has been used in ways that over-target individuals who appear to share the perpetrator's ethnicity. When a description is so vague that a large percentage of a given category of people fits it—a familiar example is "young, black men in athletic clothing"—police risk perpetuating stereotypes, alienating large numbers of individuals, and undermining their investigations. In Austria, following a series of brutal robberies committed by two dark-skinned men, the Vienna police were ordered to stop all black Africans traveling in pairs for identity checks; only when this provoked an outcry did they refine the suspect description to focus on black men, about 25 years old and 170 cm. tall, who had a slim build and were wearing light down jackets.[17] When police receive an overly general suspect description that features race, ethnicity, or similar characteristics, they should seek further specific operational intelligence to guide their investigations.[18] Otherwise, an overall general suspect description can cross the line into ethnic profiling.

Police may also legitimately use ethnicity and other personal factors when they have specific, concrete intelligence regarding future crimes "involving a particular group of potential suspects at a specific location, for a short, specified duration of time."[19] It is fairly common for police and criminal justice officials to create special, temporary task forces to address crime organizations with ties to people of a certain national origin or ethnicity. Immigration officers, customs officials, and border guards make similar use of profiles that include ethnicity and national origin in their efforts to detect drug smuggling and other forms of organized crime.[20]

Targeting an ethnic gang or nationality-based crime ring risks perpetuating harmful stereotypes while undermining police efficacy. Criminals often adapt to law enforcement practices in order to avoid detection; this is particularly easy to do when law enforcement is known to focus on specific groups. Thus when ethnicity is part of a profile of transnational or organized crime groups, it is critical that the profile be based on concrete, trustworthy and timely intelligence that is time- and/or place-specific, not deep-rooted stereotypes.

While there are few serious evaluations of how much police efficiency is enhanced through the use of organized crime profiles, in at least one case the U.S. Customs Service (now called the Customs and Border Protection Agency) found that the rate at which officers detected drugs doubled after they abandoned a "drug mule" profile that had focused on Caribbean and Latin American women.[21] Research conducted for this report shows that ethnic profiling is similarly likely to undermine rather than advance law enforcement efficiency.

Ethnic Profiling Practices

Ethnic profiling is used across a range of police operations and tactics, including stop-and-search tactics,[22] identity checks, and other exercises of police investigative powers used to detect or prevent crime.[23] As this report will explore, additional tactics—including raids, surveillance and monitoring practices, data mining, and arrests—may also be used in a discriminatory manner indicative of ethnic profiling.

Profiling can take many forms—some explicit, others indirect or even unintentional. Establishing that ethnic profiling has been used is straightforward when the practice is undertaken pursuant to explicit orders, as sometimes occurs with airport searches. But profiling frequently results from the cumulative effect of decisions by individual officers, some of whom may hold racist views but many of whom may be unaware of the degree to which generalizations and ethnic stereotypes are driving their subjective decision-making about which individuals to stop and check.

While racist individuals in law-enforcement institutions certainly contribute to ethnic profiling, the practice remains pervasive precisely because it is often the result of widely accepted, if not adequately acknowledged, negative stereotypes about racial or ethnic groups.[24] Ethnic profiling may result from institutional policies targeting certain forms of crime and/or certain areas without consideration of the disproportionate impact such policies and resource allocation have on the targeted communities.

Many of these practices would not be captured by a narrow definition of ethnic profiling as the use of ethnicity, race, religion, or nationality as the only basis for targeting suspicion. In practice, law enforcement decisions are rarely based on just one factor. Accordingly, this report defines ethnic profiling to encompass situations where ethnicity, race, national origin, or religion is a determining, even if not the exclusive, basis for making law enforcement and/or investigative decisions about persons who are believed to be or to have been involved in criminal activity.

B. Is Ethnic Profiling Legal?

The conceptual framework for this report's analysis of ethnic profiling derives from international and regional law, with a particular focus on the antidiscrimination guarantees set forth in the European Convention on Human Rights.[25] Article 14 prohibits discrimination in the enjoyment of rights protected by the Convention.[26] Convention rights that are particularly relevant to the practices addressed in this report include the rights to liberty and security of the person (Article 5(1)); fair trial rights associated with "the determination of [an individual's] civil rights" and of "any criminal charge against him" (Article 6(1)); the right to respect for privacy, family life, correspondence, and home (Article 8); freedom of religion (Article 9) and assembly (Article 11); and freedom of movement (Article 2, Protocol No. 4).

Protocol No. 12 broadens the European Convention's protections against discrimination by, among other things, prohibiting discrimination on any ground in respect of any right set forth in national law "by any public authority" (Article 1).[27] The Explanatory Report to Protocol No. 12 makes clear that this prohibition applies to discrimination "by a public authority in the exercise of discretionary power,"[28] which would include identity checks, stops and searches, and surveillance activities by law enforcement officers.

While the legal norm against discrimination is universal and fundamental, not all distinctions or differences in treatment by public authorities, including law-enforcement personnel, constitute discrimination. The European Court of Human Rights has ruled as follows: "A differential treatment of persons in relevant, similar situations, without an objective and reasonable justification, constitutes discrimination."[29]

The court has set forth the following test for determining when a distinction or difference in treatment amounts to discrimination:

[T]he principle of equality of treatment is violated if the distinction has no objective and reasonable justification. The existence of such a justification must be assessed in relation to the aim and effects of the measure under consideration, regard being had to the principles which normally prevail in democratic societies. A difference of treatment in the exercise of a right laid down in the Convention must not only pursue a legitimate aim: Article 14 is likewise violated when it is clearly established that there is no reasonable relationship of proportionality between the means employed and the aim sought to be realised.[30]

Applying this test to ethnic profiling as a tool of policing, there can be little doubt that the distinctions employed by police in their law enforcement activities pursue a "legitimate aim." Preventing, detecting, and investigating terrorism and ordinary crime are not only legitimate aims but core functions of the state. However, given its reliance on ethnic or racial criteria, it will rarely, if ever, be possible to show that ethnic profiling is objectively and reasonably justified. It cannot be said that a "reasonable relationship of proportionality" exists between the use of ethnic profiling and the fight against crime and terrorism.

In assessing the relationship between means and ends in respect of ethnic profiling three factors are paramount (several additional considerations, examined below, may also come into play):

- *Effectiveness*: In general, this report's analysis of specific ethnic profiling practices will consider a practice to be effective when it is based on an objective statistical link between the ethnic criteria employed and the probability that persons captured by the practice committed or planned to commit the offense in question. A high probability that the profiling criteria are capable of identifying criminals, including terrorists—beyond a general statistical link—is essential for ethnic profiling to be demonstrably effective as a means of preventing terrorist or other crimes.[31]

- *Proportionality*: It must be shown that the benefits derived from using ethnic profiling in terms of increasing law enforcement efficiency outweigh the harm done through the real or perceived discriminatory impacts of ethnic profiling on the targeted individuals or groups.[32]

- *Necessity*: The use of ethnic profiling is unnecessary if the same law enforcement results could have been achieved through an alternative, nondifferentiating approach.[33]

The practice of ethnic profiling has received its most intensive consideration by the European Court of Human Rights in the case of *Timishev v. Russia*.[34] The applicant had challenged Russian police officers' action in barring him from crossing an internal administrative boundary because of his Chechen ethnicity[35] pursuant to an official policy of excluding Chechens from that area.[36] Building on prior case law making clear that discriminatory treatment by law enforcement authorities can violate Article 14 of the ECHR,[37] the court held that the applicant had been subjected to different treatment in relation to his right to liberty of movement "solely" due to his ethnic origin and that the difference in treatment was not justified. Accordingly, it found a violation of Article 14 of the ECHR in conjunction with a violation of Article 2 of Protocol No. 4 (liberty of movement).[38] Notably, the court found that

> ... no difference in treatment which is based exclusively or to a decisive extent on a person's ethnic origin is capable of being objectively justified in a contemporary democratic society. ...[S]ince the applicant's right to liberty of movement was restricted solely on the ground of his ethnic origin, that difference in treatment constituted racial discrimination within the meaning of Article 14 of the Convention.[39]

Thus, if ethnicity constitutes an "exclusive" or "decisive" basis for law enforcement action, it almost certainly constitutes discrimination—and is therefore a violation of Article 14 of the European Convention. In other cases, the court has held that distinctions based on differences in religion or nationality will not generally survive judicial scrutiny.[40]

Domestic European jurisprudence makes clear that, in many cases, ethnic profiling is, as in *Timishev*, a form of direct discrimination that cannot be objectively justified.[41] Thus, in striking down the disproportionate denial of permission to enter the U.K. for prospective Roma visitors,[42] the House of Lords explained that singling out Roma for invidious treatment was unlawful, even though "there was good reason" to suspect that more Roma would be seeking asylum in the U.K. than non-Roma:

> How did the immigration officers know to treat [the Roma] more sceptically? Because they were Roma. That is acting on racial grounds. If a person acts on racial grounds, the reason why he does so is irrelevant.... The person may be acting on belief or assumptions about members of the ... racial group involved which are often true and which if true would provide a good reason for the less favourable treatment in question. But "what may be true of a group may not be true of a significant number of individuals within that group." The object of the [U.K. Race Relations Act] is to ensure that each person is treated as an individual and not assumed to be like other members of the group.[43]

While Chechen ethnicity was the sole basis for the discriminatory practices found to violate the ECHR in *Timishev*, it is not always easy to disentangle ethnicity from other possible motivations for law enforcement action. Indeed, **it** is rare that ethnicity is explicitly articulated as a reason for a stop. Police more commonly give reasons such as: the person stopped was carrying something suspicious, tried to hide something, tried to avoid the officer, appeared nervous, or seemed out of place. It is often only when a pattern of identity checks or stops and searches is examined over time that a disproportionate focus on members of a particular group clearly emerges.[44]

The European court has recently recognized that, even in the absence of an official reliance on race or ethnicity, broad patterns of differential treatment, established by statistical evidence and reports by human rights groups, may constitute proof of discrimination.[45] In *D.H. and Others v. the Czech Republic*,[46] the Grand Chamber of the European Court affirmed that patterns of discriminatory impact resulting from a policy that is not necessarily designed with discriminatory intent are a form of "indirect discrimination" prohibited by Article 14.[47]

Although *D.H* did not involve police action,[48] the concept of indirect discrimination is equally relevant to patterns of discriminatory stops stemming from ethnic profiling by police. Thus even when ethnic profiling is established through inferences derived from broad patterns of police behavior and regardless of whether it can be proven to result from intentionally racist policies, it will amount to unlawful discrimination if shown to be neither proportionate nor necessary.[49]

Policy Guidance Clearly Prohibits Ethnic Profiling

While there have been few European Court of Human Rights judgments applying the legal framework outlined above to law enforcement profiling practices, several national guidelines and nonbinding European regional standards provide clear guidance on law enforcement practices that cross the line into impermissible ethnic profiling. Notably, official policy guidance in the United Kingdom and the United States prohibits not only ethnic profiling when ethnicity is the sole or explicit basis for targeting suspects, but also when it is a significant but not exclusive factor. In the United States, federal guidance on profiling provides the following:

> In making routine or spontaneous law enforcement decisions, such as ordinary traffic stops, Federal law enforcement officers may not use race or ethnicity to any degree, except that officers may rely on race and ethnicity in a specific suspect description. This prohibition applies even where the use of race or ethnicity might otherwise be lawful.

> In conducting activities in connection with a specific investigation, Federal law enforcement officers may consider race and ethnicity only to the extent that there is trustworthy information, relevant to the locality or time frame, that links persons of a particular race or ethnicity to an identified criminal incident, scheme, or organization. This standard applies even where the use of race or ethnicity might otherwise be lawful.[50]

The United Kingdom's Police and Criminal Evidence Act (PACE) 1984 is similarly clear:

> Reasonable suspicion can never be supported on the basis of personal factors alone without reliable supporting intelligence or information or some specific behavior by the person concerned. For example, a person's age, race, appearance, or the fact that a person is known to have a previous conviction, cannot be used alone or in combination with each other as the reason for searching that person. Reasonable suspicion cannot be based on generalizations or stereotypical images of certain groups or categories of people as more likely to be involved in criminal activity. A person's religion cannot be considered as reasonable grounds for suspicion and should never be considered as a reason to stop or search an individual.[51]

In line with the approach taken by the United States and the United Kingdom, many criminal justice experts argue that ethnicity and race are such powerful markers that they will almost always predominate in law enforcement decision-making and should never be incorporated into a profile.[52] Even legitimate uses of ethnicity may have spill-over effects and, wittingly or not, generate broader patterns of ethnic profiling that depart from a basis in specific intelligence.

Similar concerns led the European Union Network of Independent Experts on Fundamental Rights, a body established by the European Commission, to conclude that ethnic profiling should "in principle" be considered unlawful in any circumstance:

> [T]he consequences of treating individuals similarly situated differently according to their supposed "race" or to their ethnicity has so far-reaching consequences in creating divisiveness and resentment, in feeding into stereotypes, and in leading to the over-criminalization of certain categories of persons in turn reinforcing such stereotypical associations between crime and ethnicity, that differential treatment on this ground should in principle be considered unlawful under any circumstances.[53]

The Legality of Ethnic Profiling in the Context of Counterterrorism

International jurisprudence has settled that non-discrimination is a customary norm of international law.[54] Non-discrimination is not one of the rights not subject to derogation during a "public emergency which threatens the life of the nation and the existence of which is officially proclaimed."[55] Nonetheless, any derogating measures must "not involve discrimination solely on the ground of race, color, sex, language, religion or social origin."[56]

The fundamental nature of the non-discrimination requirement has been reaffirmed since 9/11. The Office of the High Commissioner for Human Rights (UNHCHR) has observed:

The principle of nondiscrimination must always be respected and special effort made to safeguard the rights of vulnerable groups. Counterterrorism measures targeting specific ethnic or religious groups are contrary to human rights and would carry the additional risk of an upsurge of discrimination and racism.[57]

The UN Committee on the Elimination of All Forms of Racism has underscored the obligation of states to "ensure that measures taken in the struggle against terrorism do not discriminate in purpose or effect on grounds of race, colour, descent, or national or ethnic origin."[58]

European regional bodies have affirmed that "[a]ll measures taken by states to fight terrorism must ... exclude any form of arbitrariness, as well as any discriminatory or racist treatment...."[59] ECRI's *General Policy Recommendation 8 on Combating Racism while Fighting Terrorism* (2004) recommends that states ensure that:

- "national legislation expressly includes the right not to be subject to racial discrimination among the rights from which no derogation may be made even in time of emergency;"

- legislation and regulations "adopted in connection with the fight against terrorism are implemented at national and local levels in a manner that does not discriminate ... on grounds of actual or supposed race, color, language, religion, nationality, national or ethnic origin;"

- "no discrimination ensues from legislation and regulations—or their implementation—notably governing ... checks carried out by law-enforcement officials ... and by border control personnel."

In considering the lawfulness of counterterrorism measures prior to 9/11, the European Court of Human Rights found that terrorism increased states' "margin of appreciation,"[60] and noted that in cases of counterterrorism "'reasonableness' [...] cannot always be judged according to the same standards as are applied in dealing with conventional crime."[61] The court has recognized the need of a state to use secret surveillance of subversive elements operating within its jurisdiction[62] and the importance of confidential information in combating terrorist violence.[63]

Yet, the court has taken pains to note that "[c]ontracting States may not, in the name of the struggle against espionage and terrorism, adopt whatever measures they deem appropriate."[64] Likewise, "the exigencies of dealing with terrorist crime cannot justify stretching the notion of 'reasonableness' to the point where the essence of the safeguard secured by Article 5 para. 1 (c) ... is impaired."[65] In assessing a state's margin of appreciation, the court has applied the test of the necessity of a measure and the proportionality of the measure relative to its aim.[66] Finally, the court has clearly stated that the domestic margin of appreciation is accompanied by European supervision.[67] The court has yet to rule on these issues in the wake of post-9/11 terrorism in Europe.

European domestic courts have made clear that counterterrorist measures may not single out particular groups on the basis of ethnicity, religion or noncitizen status. The United Kingdom House of Lords has ruled that non-citizens may not be singled out for detention under counterterrorism efforts.[68] In May 2006, Germany's highest court ruled that invasions of privacy through data mining using a terrorist profile that included nationality, religion, and ethnic origin, would be warranted only in specific cases of concrete danger, and that the "general threat situation of the kind that has existed in regard to terrorist attacks continuously since Sept. 11, 2001, or foreign policy tensions, is not sufficient."[69]

UNCERD emphasized that, as the prohibition against racial discrimination is a peremptory—hence, nonderogable—norm, states must ensure that counterterrorism programs do "not discriminate in purpose or effect on grounds of race, colour, descent or national or ethnic origin and that non-citizens are not subjected to racial or ethnic profiling or stereotyping.[70] UNCERD has also urged states to "take the necessary steps to prevent questioning, arrests and searches which are in reality based solely on the physical appearance of a person, that person's colour or features or membership of a racial or ethnic group, or any profiling which exposes him or her to greater suspicion."[71]

These factors weigh heavily when judging the reasonableness and proportionality of ethnic profiling in counterterrorism efforts. Given that, as the Strasbourg organs have repeatedly underscored, "a special importance should be attached to discrimination based on race,"[72] ethnic profiling in the context of counterterrorism is not likely, if ever, to survive judicial scrutiny absent a clear demonstration that it has few negative effects, it is demonstrably effective, and no adequate alternatives exist.

Beyond Discrimination

Although this report's analysis of ethnic profiling relies principally on the discrimination framework outlined above, it is important to recognize that many of the law enforcement practices examined in this report may violate the European Convention on Human Rights (as well as other treaties) even without establishing a violation of Article 14 (nondiscrimination).[73] As noted earlier, for example, many of the police practices examined in this report implicate Article 5 of the ECHR, which ensures "the right to liberty and security of person." Among other protections, Article 5 provides for the "arrest or detention of a person affected for the purpose of bringing him before the competent legal authority on reasonable suspicion of having committed an offense"

(Article 5(1)(c)). Interpreting this provision, the European Court of Human Rights has emphasized reasonable suspicion:

> The requirement that the suspicion must be based on reasonable grounds forms an essential part of the safeguard against arbitrary arrest and detention. The fact that a suspicion is held in good faith is insufficient. The words "reasonable suspicion" mean the existence of facts or information which would satisfy an objective observer that the person concerned may have committed the offense.[74]

The court has recognized that "[w]hat may be regarded as 'reasonable' will … depend upon all the circumstances" and that, "[i]n this respect, terrorist crime falls into a special category." "Nevertheless," it has cautioned, "the exigencies of dealing with terrorist crime cannot justify stretching the notion of 'reasonableness' to the point where the essence of the safeguard … is impaired."[75] Accordingly, it has found a breach of Article 5 when the sole basis for arresting and briefly detaining three suspects was their past convictions for terrorist crimes.[76]

The succeeding chapters of this report examine police practices involving ethnic profiling that are common in many European countries. Chapter III describes various ethnic profiling practices that arise in the context of daily policing and applies the legal framework set forth in this chapter to those practices. Chapter IV turns to ethnic profiling practices used in the specific context of counterterrorism—a context that has assumed special significance since the terrorist attacks of September 11, 2001 (referred to throughout this report by the global shorthand, "9/11"). Chapter IV describes key practices of concern and sets forth a preliminary assessment of whether those practices—which by their nature involve differential treatment and pursue a legitimate aim—appear to be effective and proportionate law enforcement tools. Chapter IV also analyzes whether these practices are compatible with the ECHR, focusing on the question of whether the harm caused by their use outweighs possible law enforcement benefits.

Finally, Chapter V considers whether alternative methods of policing are more effective than the use of ethnic profiling. If so, even otherwise effective ethnic profiling practices fail the ECHR test of necessity—and are likely to violate the ECHR if used in a way that implicates a substantive violation of the convention in additon to Artcle 14.

III. Ethnic Profiling
in Ordinary Policing

Ethnic profiling existed long before the 9/11 terror attacks. Police across Europe have long targeted minorities for heightened attention and suspicion. Paris police chief Maurice Papon adopted an explicit policy of ethnic profiling in 1961, when he issued "a directive to limit the freedom of movement of these [Algerian] French Muslims, reminding officers that Muslims could be detected by their facial features."[77] Although it is difficult to document with precision, evidence summarized in this chapter indicates that police throughout Europe have made extensive use of ethnic profiling in their daily efforts to detect, investigate, and prevent common crime.

These patterns are not surprising. Public opinion across Europe tends to support ethnic profiling and has done so for many years. A 2005 national survey conducted in Hungary, for example, found high levels of public support for ethnic profiling and aggressive use of police stops. Some 60 percent of respondents agreed that Roma should be stopped and searched more often than other people and 57 percent agreed that Arabs should be stopped more often.[78]

While those polled doubtless believe that ethnic profiling enhances police efficiency, studies summarized in this chapter indicate that the opposite is true: police are more likely to identify criminals when they eschew the use of ethnic profiling and instead rely on behavior-based profiles. Equally important, throughout Europe ethnic profiling has had a deleterious effect on the lives of minorities, who are disproportionately targeted for police attention, routinely face rude and racist treatment, and are frequent victims of intrusive and violent police tactics.

A.   Existing Reporting of Ethnic Profiling in Europe

International and regional organizations as well as nongovernmental organizations (NGOs) have long raised concerns about routine ethnic profiling in Europe. The most systematic documentation appears in the regular country reports of the European Commission against Racism and Intolerance (ECRI), which in recent years has expressed concern about ethnic profiling in Austria, Germany, Greece, Hungary, Romania, Russia, Spain, Sweden, Switzerland, Ukraine, and the United Kingdom.[79] In addition, reports by a range of organizations, including the United Nations Committee on the Elimination of Racial Discrimination (CERD), Amnesty International, OSI's EU Monitoring and Advocacy Project (EUMAP), the European Roma Rights Centre, and the International Helsinki Committee, have raised similar concerns about police discrimination in these and other countries. For example:

- In 2003, Belgian antiracism NGOs reported that Muslims and immigrants were discriminated against during their interactions with police. Reports pointed to police abuse of people of foreign origin, including physical violence, xenophobic and offensive language, arbitrary identity checks, and refusal to intervene when police assistance is sought by members of certain ethnic groups.[80]

- In its 1994 concluding observations concerning France's compliance with the UN Convention on the Elimination of All Forms of Racial Discrimination, CERD observed that France should "ensure that preventive identity checks were not being carried out in a discriminatory manner by the police."[81] Five years later, ECRI noted that "[f]oreigners and people of immigrant background ... complain that they are subject to discriminatory checks" in France.[82] As discussed in detail below, minority complaints of police abuse in France, often associated with identity checks, continue to this day.

- In Germany, EUMAP raised concerns about ethnic profiling in 2002.[83] In 2003, ECRI expressed concern that members of "visible, notably black, minority groups" are "disproportionately subject to checks carried out by the police and disproportionately singled out for controls in railway stations and in airports."[84]

- In its 1999 report on Greece, ECRI noted practices of discrimination against minorities and immigrants in police checks. ECRI also found discrimination in 1998 and 1999 in deportations of Albanian immigrants.[85] More recently, the Greek ombudsman's office has also reported on arbitrary and discriminatory police identity checks, insulting language, threats of force, and public body searches.[86]

- In a 1997 report on Hungary, ECRI raised concerns about police discrimination against Roma and noncitizens, which it repeated in 2004. In both reports ECRI noted the Hungarian government's failure to abolish a law allowing police to enter noncitizens' homes without a warrant to check their identity documents.[87]

- ECRI's 2002 report on Italy expressed concern over "discriminatory checks" by Italian police directed against foreigners, Roma, and other ethnic minorities.[88] In May 2008, the Italian government adopted an open policy of ethnic profiling of Roma, by enacting a decree declaring a state of emergency with regard to "nomad community settlements" in three regions and granting state and local officials extraordinary powers to deal with the settlements.[89] Subsequent ordinances implementing the decree empowered commissioners to take a census, fingerprint and photograph inhabitants of the camps, including children—a clear singling out of an ethnic group for differential and prejudicial treatment. Leading politicians issued public statements calling for these measures, and court rulings upheld them. The Court of Cassation, Italy's highest appeals court, issued a ruling stating in part that "all the gypsies were thieves."[90]

- ECRI's 2003 report on Spain noted allegations of "misconduct among the police forces towards vulnerable groups in Spanish society,"[91] including increased and ongoing reports of discriminatory checks.[92] These checks targeted Roma, foreigners, and Spanish citizens of immigrant background. In 2002, Amnesty International reported that police discrimination against ethnic minorities is systematic in Spain, including ethnic profiling in discriminatory identity checks.[93]

The repetitive nature of this reporting indicates that ethnic profiling in Europe is and has been a persistent problem. As discussed in the next section, the quantitative data that is available tends to confirm this.

B. Quantitative Data on Ethnic Profiling in Stop-and-Search Practices

It is difficult to measure with any precision the extent of ethnic profiling in Europe. The United Kingdom, whose 43 police forces gather data on the use of stops and searches,[94] publishes information compiled by the Ministry of Justice annually.[95] But no other European country systematically gathers data on policing and ethnicity.[96]

Ministry of Justice data on stop-and-search practices in England and Wales show significant disparities in the rates at which police stop different ethnic groups. The most recent data, covering April 1, 2007 through March 31, 2008, show that black people were 7.4 times more likely to be stopped and searched than white people and that Asian people were 2.3 times more likely to be stopped and searched than white people.[97]

While these data reflect overall stops and searches nationally, there is an even greater disparity between whites and minorities when the data are disaggregated to show stops and searches under different provisions of U.K. law. Stops conducted pursuant to Section 1 of the Police and Criminal Evidence (PACE) Act 1984 must be based on a reasonable suspicion that the individual stopped is likely to be involved in criminal activity. In contrast, stops conducted under Section 60 of the Criminal Justice and Public Order Act 1994 do not have to be based on a reasonable suspicion.[98] Data for 2007–2008 show that when U.K. police exercised their authority under Section 60, black people were 10.7 times more likely to be stopped and searched than white people, while Asian people were 2.2 times more likely to be stopped and searched than whites.[99]

It is not hard to determine why stops and searches conducted under the Section 60 authority result in an even higher rate of stops of blacks and Asians relative to whites than the already high disproportionality of Section 1 stops and searches. Professor Ben Bowling has noted the relationship between discretion and discrimination:

> Wherever officers have the broadest discretion is where you find the greatest disproportionality and discrimination. Under Section 60, police have the widest discretion, using their own beliefs about who is involved in crime, using their own stereotypes about who is worth stopping—that's where the problems in police culture affect the decisions that are taken .... A power that was intended for narrow purposes is being used much more extensively against black and Asian communities.[100]

Data on arrest rates show that disproportionate stopping and searching of minorities under Section 60 is the result of ethnic profiling rather than individualized suspicion. In 2007–2008, only 4 percent of stops and searches conducted under Section 60 led to an arrest—significantly lower than the 12 percent arrest rate for stops conducted pursuant to the "reasonable suspicion" standard mandated by PACE.[101]

Beyond the United Kingdom, 2005 survey data from Bulgaria and Hungary found clear evidence of profiling. Roma pedestrians in both countries were three times more likely to be stopped by police than majority ethnic Bulgarians and Hungarians despite the fact that Roma constitute only 5 to 10 percent of Bulgaria's population and 6 percent of Hungary's population.[102]

In interviews conducted during the same study, a number of Hungarian and Bulgarian police officers (though by no means all) cited as the basis for their stops the perception that Roma are heavily involved in crime. One Bulgarian police officer said, "You can't really tell who [among the Roma] steals and who doesn't. They almost all do."[103]

Half of the Hungarian police officers interviewed stated that some of their colleagues stop members of certain ethnic groups more than members of the majority, primarily mentioning Roma in the first category. A Hungarian officer put it this way:

> One has to pay more attention to the gypsies. There is a greater chance that I catch someone off the wanted list ... I therefore assume that we should check them more closely, more frequently.[104]

Police in a number of countries have admitted to stopping people who look foreign, both for immigration enforcement and also because of their belief that people of certain ethnicities are associated with crime—even particular types of crime. The following responses to interviews with Spanish police officers reflect commonplace perceptions:

> All murders are related to immigrants (as are) 90 percent of drug crimes and gender violence.

> Foreigners are arrested more for drugs; maybe 90 percent are South Americans. The dangerous criminals are foreigners: Colombians, Poles, or Romanians are more dangerous than Bulgarians.[105]

These are personal perspectives, and not all the Spanish officers interviewed shared these views. Some officers expressed uncertainty about the effectiveness of ethnic profiling, even while describing their own certainty about the correlation between crime and particular ethnic groups. One Spanish police officer said that ethnic profiling helps people feel secure:

> The majority of arrests and immigrants are "*Gitanos*" (Roma); the majority of robberies with violence are committed by Maghrebis and South Americans. There are problems with immigrant kids in the schools, lots of violence. The majority of Muslims—no, about

100 percent—are Islamists. Since the 11 of March [bombing in the Atocha train station in Madrid in 2004] the police might stop a lot of Moroccans. I don't think this is counter-productive [because] the majority relate terrorists with Muslims and if we stop Muslims that gives more security to people. It might be counter-productive, but this is what society demands. Profiles are good.[106]

C. Disparate Treatment and Abusive Conduct during Stops of Minorities

Considerable evidence indicates that members of minority ethnic groups dispropor-tionately suffer police abuse in the course of investigations, arrests, and detention. As the reports summarized below make clear, this occurs in a broad range of European countries. Worse, it appears that the comparatively high rate of police abuse suffered by members of minority groups is related to disproportionate police targeting of minorities.

Before examining patterns of abuse in specific countries, it is important to note the limitations inherent in available data. The reports that form the basis of the analysis in this section provide only a partial picture of police abuse, because typically only the most serious incidents reach the attention of official complaints mechanisms or civil society organizations.

It is also important to recognize that the comparatively high levels of police abuse endured by members of minority groups do not necessarily mean that ethnic profil-ing is present. Even if members of minority and majority populations were stopped by police at the same rate one might see higher levels of police abuse of those minority group members who were stopped. Such a pattern might point to police propensity toward racial violence or ill-treatment but not racial profiling.

Another possible explanation for the high rates of police abuse suffered by mem-bers of minority groups is that they complain more often. One could posit that police arrest them at the same rate they arrest members of the majority group, and police treat all groups equally, but members of minority groups are more vociferous. This possibil-ity is highly unlikely, however, as organizations that work with victims of police abuse frequently find minorities are *less* likely to complain of police treatment due to fear of retaliation (and deportation in the case of illegal migrants), insufficient awareness of their rights, and inadequate access to legal assistance. In a 2002 report, ECRI noted that in Italy most acts of racism, discrimination, and violence by police officers did not result in a complaint by the victim, and investigations were inadequate and lacking transparency. Indeed, police have frequently threatened to bring or have brought coun-ter-charges against people who said that they intend to lodge a complaint.[107]

While the data on complaints of police abuse do not provide incontrovertible proof of ethnic profiling, numerous studies have concluded that the disproportionately high rate of police abuse suffered by minorities reflects more widespread targeting of minorities by the police. A 2004 Amnesty International report on Germany found that "[t]he consistency and regularity of the reports Amnesty International had received led it to the conclusion that the problem of police ill-treatment was not one of a few isolated incidents, but rather a clear pattern of police ill-treatment of foreigners and members of ethnic minorities in Germany."[108] ECRI has raised concerns that police brutality disproportionately affects minority groups in Albania, Austria, Belgium, Bulgaria, Cyprus, the Czech Republic, France, Macedonia, Germany, Greece, Hungary, Poland, Portugal, Romania, Spain, Switzerland and Ukraine.[109] Amnesty International has reported on similar dynamics in France and Spain, noting that "[t]here is a high correlation in Spain between these identity checks and ill-treatment by police."[110]

The link between police abuse and ethnic profiling has been borne out in Justice Initiative research. Surveys in Bulgaria and Hungary in 2005 found profound qualitative differences in the way Roma and non-Roma experienced police stops: in both countries, Roma were more likely to report unpleasant experiences.[111] In Hungary, 9 percent of all Roma were likely to experience a stop they described as disrespectful, compared to 3 percent of the non-Roma population.[112] In addition, Roma pedestrians in Hungary and Bulgaria were stopped in disproportionate numbers, far more than majority pedestrians were stopped.

Bulgaria

Survey data collected in Bulgaria in 2005 showed that 20 percent of Roma who were stopped by police reported experiencing insults, 14 percent reported being threatened, and 5 percent reported the use of force by police. For ethnic Bulgarians the respective rates were 3 percent, 5 percent, and 1 percent. The following experience appears all too typical for Bulgarian Roma:

> I was once stopped by the police for drugs ... I was like "Wait a minute, why don't you go and catch someone *with* drugs. Why do you check me?" I was almost about to cry, but the police said "Lift up your sleeves and don't talk too much, you dirty gypsy [otherwise] I'll put you in the trunk [of the police car]."[113]

Other Bulgarian studies have found greater frequency of police abuse of Roma compared to ethnic Bulgarians.[114] The 2002 Bulgarian Helsinki Committee annual report, which cites survey data collected in four Bulgarian prisons,[115] found similar discrepancies in abuse in detention centers where 77 percent of Roma reported being abused, compared to 27 percent of ethnic Bulgarians.[116]

Spain

Several reports on Spain have linked police abuse of minorities directly to disproportionate and discriminatory identity checks. In a 2002 report, Amnesty International noted that when members of minority groups were stopped by Spanish police, "they may be abused and assaulted and end up in the hospital, sometimes with serious injuries."[117] In 1998, the Ombudsman's Office of the Basque Autonomous Region of Spain issued a report on ethnic profiling after receiving numerous complaints about police treatment of immigrants in the San Francisco neighborhood of Bilbao.[118] The report was based on extensive interviews with police and residents (immigrants and Spaniards) and analysis of 47 police operations during 1997, with a primary focus on stop and search. It concluded as follows:

> The activity of the police towards foreign immigrants demonstrates clear violations of the rights of these persons. ... These activities demonstrate a disproportion between the reality and the objectives pursued and the results obtained. These actions have not been corrected by the legally established procedures.[119]

More recent reports suggest that these patterns have continued. In a 2005 interview, the Spanish National Ombudsman's Office stated that it was receiving regular complaints about improper police treatment and detentions of foreigners, and agreed that ethnic profiling of foreigners was probably commonplace.[120] In 2006, the Spanish antidiscrimination organization SOS Racismo reported that police officers were responsible for one in three reported incidents of racist violence.[121]

Greece

In 2004, the United Nations Committee against Torture (UNCAT) raised concerns about excessive use of force against members of racial and ethnic minorities and foreigners by Greek police.[122] Common targets included Roma, Albanians, and (other) immigrants. Roma in particular frequently have been reported to be victims of ill-treatment, verbal abuse, excessive use of force, and even lethal force.[123] Greece's 2004 report to the UN Human Rights Committee, the body that supervises compliance with the International Covenant on Civil and Political Rights, included statistics on complaints of police abuse disaggregated by citizenship status and Roma ethnicity (see box), but the government argued that "these cases reflect isolated incidents and in no way can constitute a basis for maintaining that there is a general pattern of police ill-treatment in Greece."[124] The government's submission continued: "the investigation of the relevant incidents has so far proven that [police officers] did not have a racist or xenophobic motive."[125] The UN Human Rights Committee, however, saw the figures as showing that "police and border guards continue to use excessive force in carrying out their duties, in particular when dealing with ethnic minorities and foreigners." In its view, these patterns included "the subjection of the Roma to police violence and sweeping arrests."[126]

TABLE 1.

Greece: Police Abuse Cases[127]

Year	Total	Foreigners	Roma
2001	57	19	7
2002	60	23	4
2003	47	12	0

Italy

In 2000, the European Roma Rights Center (ERRC), an NGO, reported a pattern of police verbal and physical abuse of Roma in Italy. Its report described frequent beatings by Italian police of beggars whom they believe to be Roma, and reported that male police officers subjected Roma women whom they had arrested to invasive body searches.[128] Police reportedly "single[d] out old cars in bad repair for control on the road, because it [was] assumed that such cars [were] owned by immigrants,"[129] and asked whether the occupants were "gypsies" or, in the case of dark-complexioned persons, assumed Roma ethnicity. According to ECRI's 2002 report on Italy, Roma there reported unprovoked attacks by police[130] and a greater likelihood of police use of force, including firearms, against them as compared to non-Roma.[131]

The ethnically-targeted emergency measures adopted in May 2008, which many observers compared to the ethnic registration practices of the World War II era, were accompanied by a marked increase in police abuse against Roma both in the camps and in public settings in towns.[132] In addition to official actions, private citizens attacked camps and set them on fire with gasoline bombs.[133]

Immigrants in Italy have also faced greater risk of police abuse than ethnic Italians. ECRI's 1999 country report on Italy found that police subjected foreigners, Italians of immigrant background, and ethnic minorities to "insulting and abusive speech, ill-treatment and violence"[134] and that prison guards reportedly did likewise.[135] Immigrants' associations reported, in an analysis covering 2000–2002, that the police and Carabinieri used violence during searches of immigrants in their homes or in public spaces.[136] In 2004, Amnesty International expressed concern over police ill-treatment of ethnic minorities, including "allegations of excessive force and physical assault ... in the context of police operations surrounding demonstrations."[137]

France

Various studies provide a detailed picture of police misconduct in France over a sustained period, finding consistently disproportionate abuse of immigrants and minorities, in some cases directly related to discriminatory identity checks and stop and search practices.

In 1994, Amnesty International found that a high proportion of victims of police abuse in France were of non-European ethnic origin, mostly from the Maghreb, the Middle East, and Central and West Africa.[138] In 1996, the UN Human Rights Committee, reporting on France, noted its serious concern "at the number and serious nature of the allegations it has received of ill-treatment by law enforcement officials of detainees and other persons who clash with them, including unnecessary use of firearms resulting in a number of deaths, the risk of such ill-treatment being much greater in the case of foreigners and immigrants."[139] In 1998, ECRI stated that a high proportion of cases of ill-treatment by law enforcement officers involved detainees of non-European ethnic origin.[140] While taking note of French efforts to combat discriminatory attitudes among police and other public officials, ECRI expressed concern at "allegations of persistent discriminatory behavior toward the members of certain ethnic groups."[141]

Four years later, official statistics for the Paris area showed that complaints of police ill-treatment had doubled from 216 in 1997 to 432 in 2002.[142] (This time period corresponds to the transition in ruling party from the government of President François Mitterrand to President Jacques Chirac and the abandonment of a form of community policing—the *police de proximité*—in favor of a more traditional social order approach.) In 2005, the *Commission Nationale de Déontologie de la Sécurité* (CNDS), the official national body that reviews police conduct issues, stated that it was "[s]truck by the color of the skin and the statistical frequency of foreign persons, or persons having foreign sounding names," among victims of police ill-treatment, noting the over-representation of young North African (Maghreb countries) and African males.[143] The report added that these incidents frequently arose from: "identity checks on a purely preventive basis."[144] A review of 50 individual cases of police abuse between 2002 and 2004 found that 60 percent of the victims were immigrants and the remaining 40 percent had names or physical appearance that gave the impression of immigrant origin.[145] Amnesty International's 2003 annual report noted the same dynamic of increasing complaints of abuse, the disproportionate number of minority victims, and the link to discriminatory identity checks.[146]

Amnesty International's 2003 report presented the finding of French lawyers' associations that identity checks tended to occur in urban areas with large populations of young people of non-European ethnic origin[147] and that these identity checks have led to increasing numbers of people being charged by police with "insulting behavior" or "rebellion."[148] French human rights groups and academics have also noted an increased number of stops that end with police pressing charges against the persons stopped—"insulting an officer," "rebellion," or "violence"—with disproportionate numbers of minority youths among those charged. These charges are similar to a charge of resisting arrest (sometimes termed the "contempt of cop" charge). In cities in the United States that have developed early warning systems to detect problem officers,[149] an officer pressing repeated charges of "resisting arrest" is a "red flag" indicator that triggers an investigation into the officer's conduct of stops. The high rate of these charges in combination with the persistent complaints of abuse targeting minorities raises concerns that these may reflect a pattern of counter-charges by police designed to avoid or trump citizen complaints of police abuse.[150]

A detailed academic study of court case files from 1965 to 2003 showed increasing hostility in encounters between minority youths and the French police, stemming from disproportionate policing of those groups. The study focused on specific offenses committed *against* police officers as noted above ("outrages," "rebellion," and "violence").[151] People of North African (Maghreb) origin constituted 38 percent of all those charged, a significant over-representation in relation to their percentage of the population.[152] Maghrebis were also more likely than white French people to be charged and convicted of the more severe offenses ("contempt and obstruction") and more likely than others charged with similar offenses to be incarcerated: 27 percent of people of Maghreb descent were convicted versus 11 percent of white French individuals charged with the same offense.

Ethnic profiling and the increasing hostility it engendered underlay the riots that erupted in France in November 2005. These were triggered by the death of two boys, one of Maghrebi and the other of sub-Saharan African descent, who were electrocuted while attempting to evade a police identity check by hiding in an electrical substation. Protests over the boys' deaths met with denials of police wrongdoing from then Minister of the Interior Nicolas Sarkozy. Following an incident at the boys' funeral, officers launched tear gas into a mosque, Sarkozy again defended the police action, and three weeks of riots erupted in the mostly minority suburbs of Paris and other towns across France.[153]

In the absence of any policy change to address this environment, the situation in France remains tense and, by some accounts, continues to deteriorate. In 2005, the CNDS reported that complaints of police misconduct had increased by 10 percent in 2005 over the prior year, and that many incidents were related to minors, asylum seekers, and immigrants.[154] The internal police disciplinary body reported a 14.5 percent increase in the number of officers sanctioned for abusive behavior in 2005 compared to the year before.[155] While this is a positive development, policing authorities have not examined or changed operational practices that target French minorities for disproportionate police attention and generate mistrust and hostility. The refusal to recognize ethnic profiling as a problem has costs for the police as well as for minority youths. In an alarming incident in late 2006, a group of youths ambushed two police officers and severely beat them;[156] and in November 2007, following an incident in which a police car struck and killed two minority teenagers, riots erupted, shots were fired at police, and 130 officers were injured, some seriously.[157]

D.   Police Raids Targeting Ethnic Minorities

Raids are perhaps the most intrusive police tactic. They involve a sudden invasion of a building or area, often timed to maximize the element of surprise. Unlike routine police contacts, which typically take place in public spaces such as streets or highways, raids frequently involve an intrusion into private spaces such as homes, places of worship or association, or work places.[158] They may target individual addresses or whole neighborhoods.

Raids can be a proper exercise of police power and, for certain purposes—particularly when surprise is required—an important law enforcement tactic. Legitimate objectives of raids include: apprehending wanted offenders, obtaining evidence of illegal activity, recovering property, preventing commission of a crime, or confiscating contraband.

Raids move into the category of impermissible ethnic profiling, however, when police determine targets based on stereotypes associating ethnic or religious groups with crime, or when raids target entire communities based on evidence related to the criminal activities of one or two residents. In practice, some police raids appear to stray from legitimate objectives and constitute the illegal harassment of minority communities. Such harassment is particularly clear in raids on Roma communities.

Roma camps have been the targets of police raids in many countries and Roma rights advocates view raids as an "egregious form of ethnic profiling" that subject entire communities to a form of collective guilt.[159] In some cases, raids on Roma communities have been prompted by the suspected criminal behavior of one or a few suspects; in other cases they are undertaken on the assumption that Roma as a group engage in crime. Raids have also been used to induce entire Roma communities to leave their settlements.

Several common characteristics emerge from a review of police raids on Roma settlements in Greece, Romania, Bulgaria, France, and Italy during the period 2002–2005:[160]

- Raids extend across whole Roma neighborhoods, even when police are searching for a small number of suspects or even a single suspect.

- Police often do not explain the purpose of the raid or show warrants.
- Raids often involve damage to property.
- Raids are often accompanied by verbal racist abuse.
- Raids are often characterized by excessive use of force, including lethal force.

Italy

A 2000 report of the European Roma Rights Centre (ERRC), based on an extensive investigation into life in 30 Roma camps throughout Italy, found that Italian police regularly targeted Roma settlements for raids.[161]

> Police typically enter a camp in numbers ranging from four to twenty, with exceptional large-scale actions carried out by over one hundred officers. Authorities raid most frequently late at night or early in the morning. The inhabitants of the camp receive no warning of the raid. Authorities generally proceed from dwelling to dwelling. In some instances, officers order all persons temporarily to vacate dwellings. Since many of the authorized camps have one group address, police empowered to search for one individual may effectively enter any dwelling in a camp at will. In many instances authorities have evicted Roma and destroyed their property. In raids not aimed at eviction, according to Roma victims, police do not inform camp inhabitants of why they have come. Moreover, when Roma request to know the purpose or grounds of the raid, officers usually act offended and either give no answer at all, or answer by being aggressive or using abusive or racist speech towards the individual seeking information. Although the ERRC conducted extensive interviews with eyewitnesses of police raids, not a single person recalled having been shown written authorizations by police officers.[162]

Raids on Roma camps in Italy have frequently taken place without valid judicial authorization.[163] A 2000 ERRC report included numerous cases of Italian police raiding Roma camps without warrants, forcing the Roma inhabitants to leave while they searched the camps, subjecting residents to verbal and physical abuse, and destroying their property.[164] Police have often forced Roma women to undress for searches.[165] In 2000, the International Helsinki Federation (IHF) also expressed specific concerns about Italian Carabinieri entering and searching Roma camps without producing search warrants.[166] In 2003, the UN Committee on the Rights of the Child noted that raids have produced "allegations of instances of ill-treatment by law enforcement officers against children and the prevalence of abuse, in particular against foreign and Roma children."[167]

Greece

Greek police have often raided Roma settlements to search for suspects, drugs, or weapons. Rather than target particular houses or individuals, police frequently search every house and check the identity documents of everyone in the community.[168] Furthermore, these raids have often been characterized by physical and verbal abuse of the Roma inhabitants and failure to follow legal requirements such as showing a warrant. ERRC and the Greek Helsinki Monitor have monitored numerous raids and have found a clear pattern of ethnic profiling by the Greek police directed against Roma.[169] In May 2001, a senior police officer representing Greece before the UN Committee against Torture (CAT) reflected on the use of ethnic profiling in raids:

> Roma often reside in isolated camps where drug and weapon trafficking takes place, or other crimes are committed. This fact obliges the police to intervene according to a plan—with the use of special forces, depending on the danger that police personnel face each time.[170]

A committee member responded that this appeared to be "a sweeping reference to an ethnic group." The Greek delegation stated that no discrimination was intended and the statement reflected risk-assessment considerations, but the committee member wondered "whether [the delegation's comments] might not be akin to the racial profiling that had received so much attention in the United States recently."[171]

Germany

German police have carried out raids against Roma and immigrants, especially Muslims.[172] EUMAP has reported German police raids against Roma and Sinti groups, including the following 2001 incident:

> On 11 October 2001, at six in the morning 15 police officers in full combat gear raided the house of a Sinti family in Niedererbach, Rhineland-Palatinate, on suspicion of robbery of a petrol station where the family had been seen the previous day. The fifty-two-year-old, I.L, and her forty-nine-year-old husband G.L. were pulled out of bed, ordered to the ground, and held at gunpoint while officers searched the house. The incident was later acknowledged as an "embarrassing mistake."[173]

Spain

Spanish police have conducted raids on Roma and migrant areas in operations that appear to deliberately target minorities. A 2004 raid in one such area, called Poligono Sur in Seville, involved nearly 100 local and national police, who occupied the area for over 20 hours. After conducting over 150 identity checks, one person was arrested for an outstanding warrant, and another for suspicion of driving a stolen car.[174] There is no indication that raids by Spanish police are based on solid intelligence.[175] Residents complained that the raids have no crime prevention results and are undertaken to get media attention.

Spanish police also raid bars, discos, and restaurants frequented by immigrants. On November 24, 2003, in Coslada, police entered bars and announced "Spaniards can leave without being bothered."[176] On October 26, 2003, police carried out a series of raids in the Madrid neighborhoods of Usera and Arganzuela, checking identity papers and searching hundreds of people, most of whom were South American. Forty-nine arrests resulted, but it is unclear how many arrests were for immigration violations and how many for criminal offenses. A police chief later said that the raids were necessary because a person had been murdered in the neighborhood a month earlier.[177] On November 13, 2003, in Alcorcon, police checked the identity documents of 1,050 persons, and searched many of them, in discotheques popular with immigrants; 50 people were arrested (again, there is no information on the charges and how many were for immigration offenses).

E.   Immigration Enforcement

European law stipulates that "border guards border guards shall not discriminate against persons on grounds of sex, racial or ethnic origin, religion or belief, disability, age or sexual orientation."[178] Immigration enforcement powers are established in EU member state laws and vary by country, but many states grant police broad powers to stop persons on immigration grounds within set distances of national borders and/or allow police stops on immigration grounds throughout the country. In France, for example, immigration law requires foreigners to carry documents and allows police stops to verify this proof of legal stay at any time,[179] and courts have attempted to create some guiding criteria for when police can reasonably assume that an individual is of foreign origin.[180] A 1993 French Constitutional Council judgment stated that skin color cannot be grounds for an immigration stop[181]—in contrast to the Spanish Constitutional Court which allowed the use of skin color as an indicator of probable non-Spanish nationality.[182] Other French courts have stipulated that police officers must always base their stops on the particular circumstances,[183] yet in recent years French police have been tasked with rounding up and deporting foreigners in order to meet nationally set targets.[184] Similarly, in 2008, the Spanish national police in Madrid were ordered to meet set quotas for arrests of foreigners, with an explicit preference for Moroccans due to the low cost of repatriation from Spain to Morocco.[185]

It is extremely difficult to assess the impact of immigration enforcement on ethnic minority nationals and legal residents because police in most European countries do not record and/or review their stops unless they produce a concrete outcome. In many cases, it may indeed be hard to determine if a police action is conducted for immigration or law enforcement pruposes. Immigration law and police policies, guidance, and training need to be reviewed and non-discrimination provisions strengthened in order to better reflect the challenges of policing crime, terrorism, and immigration in multi-ethnic societies.[186]

When domestic immigration enforcement is conducted by police (as opposed to immigration controls at borders), ethnic profiling often results. Indeed, immigration law may provide a façade of legality for ethnic profiling in criminal investigations unrelated to immigration. A police officer who may not have sufficient grounds for stopping someone on suspicion of committing an ordinary crime can make the stop on immigration grounds, and then conduct a search of the person leading to the discovery of evidence of a crime. Ethnic minorities are particularly susceptible to such manipulation, given that, in historically more homogenous European societies, physical appearance has traditionally been—even if it no longer is—a common indicator of noncitizen status. A French police officer explained it this way:

> If you consider different levels of trafficking it is obviously done by blacks and Arabs, and tightly linked to type of immigration....If you are on the road and see a black man or a man with Arabic features you say to yourself, he doesn't look French, and then you might stop him to see if he has papers. While he is stopped you can search him and may find drugs or guns.[187]

Several factors have contributed to heightened use of ethnic profiling in the context of immigration control practices. Political authorities can demand clampdowns and strict enforcement of national immigration laws, including proactive police efforts to seek out illegal immigrants. Under these circumstances, police are especially likely to stop people who "look foreign"—even as the number of persons of minority appearance who are in fact naturalized or native-born citizens has significantly increased.

Management tools which conflate arrests for ordinary crime with arrests for immigration violations provide a powerful incentive for police to use ethnic profiling to single out foreigners, and thus increase the number of arrests.

German studies of the use of discretionary stop-and-search powers for purposes of border control (control of transborder crime such as trafficking in drugs and stolen vehicles, illegal entry, and illegal residence) have found that these stops massively targeted migrants, rather than ordinary criminals. While German authorities have at times claimed "sensational hit rates," the actual results appear limited at best, the primary outcome being the arrest of legal asylum seekers for minor infractions of residency requirements.[188] (The "hit rate" is the percentage of stops resulting in a positive law enforcement outcome, such as an arrest.) An eight month study of discretionary police controls on trains in Bavaria under "Investigation Concept *Schiene*" carried out in 1997-98 claimed a healthy 16 percent hit rate.[189] However, about 75 percent of the arrests were for violations of travel restrictions by asylum seekers and people with temporary residence permits. Eighty-two percent of those stopped were migrants or refugees—a clear indication of ethnic profiling.[190] The operation did little to address transnational crime; barely three percent of those arrested had outstanding warrants, and the quantities of drugs seized did not exceed legal personal consumption allowances. A six month evaluation of discretionary controls in Western Munich found similar results: more than half of the 22.6 percent hit rate was made up of infringements of the Aliens Act or asylum procedure law.[191]

In 2002, the Spanish Ministry of the Interior launched a broad crime prevention initiative in Madrid called "Operation Focus." Over four months, police carried out 20,901 identity checks. The checks produced 2,382 arrests: 267 of Spaniards and 2,115 of foreigners, most of the latter for immigration violations.[192]

Some police have openly used ethnic profiling in the exercise of immigration powers, basing their judgments of nationality on appearance. A 2004 study of police internal controls of foreigners in Sweden found that both the legal framework and police practices were generating ethnic discrimination.[193] Officers acknowledged commonly using ethnic profiling and intuition—rather than more objective criteria—as the basis for discretionary searches for illegal immigrants.[194]

Despite the fact that the European Convention on Human Rights prohibits the collective expulsion of foreigners,[195] French authorities have ordered police to target specific minority groups to detect illegal migrants in order to fill chartered deportation flights to specific countries.[196] In 2006, reporters witnessed police on the Paris Metro singling out all Asian passengers and removing those without identity papers. When asked why they did this, the police responded that they "already had enough blacks."[197] A deportation flight from France to China was scheduled for departure six days later. French NGOs monitoring immigrants' rights believe that this happens routinely; according to a French Roma rights group, data from the Ministry of Interior show that 480 Romanians were expelled on eight charter flights between May and November 2006.[198]

This trend has not abated. Despite the May 2007 creation of a new French Ministry of Immigration, Integration, National Identity and Co-Development, the number of deportation orders rose from 45,500 in 2004 to nearly 70,000 in 2007 and 73,000 in 2008.[199] The French police and gendarmerie have massively increased their immigration enforcement, reporting an increase in immigration-related procedures of 72.5 percent for the gendarmerie and 21.7 percent for the national police during the first six months of 2008 compared to the same period in 2007.[200]

Such actions are facilitated by outdated immigration laws that have not kept up with a changing Europe. As Europe becomes increasingly multiethnic—with large numbers of French nationals who are of Maghrebi or black African origin, Germans of Turkish origin, and Britons of South Asian and West Indian origin—police enforcement of immigration law through identity checks and stops imposes an undue burden on minority group members, including long-standing citizens.

In an atmosphere of politically charged immigration debates, the use of immigrant profiling as a pretext for ethnic profiling is bad enough. Worse still is the tendency of some law enforcement authorities to disclose publicly statistics that fail to distinguish between immigration control and crime prevention. This is at best misleading and at worse feeds a distorted public image of widespread criminality among foreigners and migrants.

F. Negative Consequences of Ethnic Profiling in Ordinary Policing

Ethnic profiling in ordinary policing affects individuals, communities, the criminal justice system, policing institutions, and public opinion. The first casualty of ethnic profiling is the individual being profiled. Even relatively benign encounters with police can produce harmful effects when they occur repeatedly and are prompted by one's ethnic identity. Ethnic profiling has been described as a "frightening, humiliating or even traumatic" practice.[201] The American Psychological Association notes that effects on victims include "post-traumatic stress disorder and other forms of stress-related disorders, perceptions of race-related threats, and failure to use available community resources."[202] Focus groups in Spain reflected these anxieties among minority youths:

> I worry when I go on the street that they will stop me and ask me for my papers because of the color of my skin, by my tone of skin, by my way of walking.[203]

> The police always come and in the end the kids think [of themselves as] guilty. They feel bad, they feel insecure, they feel like criminals.[204]

Police controls in Lyons, France, are described by those who have experienced them as a public humiliation, arbitrary and often brutal, involving being pushed against a wall or made to lie on the ground. In 2004, a Lyons-based antidiscrimination group declared: "Police controls make life impossible for any foreigner in the country without papers, or anyone who is too black, too Arab, too tan, too stereotype, too young, too poor."[205]

To assume that criminality correlates with certain ethnicities is to stigmatize entire groups of people. This stigmatization has distinct negative impacts on minorities.

Law professor Bernard Harcourt, an expert on criminology, describes what he terms the "ratchet effect" produced by ethnic profiling in the United States:

> The ratchet effect disproportionately distributes criminal records and criminal justice contacts, with numerous secondary implications. Disproportionate criminal supervision and incarceration reduces work opportunities, breaks down families and communities, and disrupts education. It contributes to the exaggerated general perception in the public imagination and among police officers of "black criminality." ... This in turn further undermines the ability of African-Americans to obtain employment or pursue educational opportunities. It has a delegitimizing effect on the criminal justice system that may encourage disaffected youth to commit crime. It may also corrode police-community relations, hampering law enforcement efforts as minority community members become less willing to report crime, to testify, and to convict. And, to make matters worse, a feedback mechanism aggravates these tendencies. Given the paucity of reliable information on natural offending rates, the police may rely on their own prior arrest and supervision statistics in deciding how to allocate resources. This, in turn, accelerates the imbalance in the prison population and the growing correlation between race and criminality.[206]

The stigmatizing effect of ethnic profiling is exacerbated by media coverage of minorities and crime. An analysis of Flemish media published in 2004 found that 46.4 percent of newspaper coverage and 51.6 percent of television coverage of minorities focused on issues of crime and justice.[207] Earlier research showed that Flemish news coverage about ethnic minorities was not only largely focused on crime and conflicts but also cast in excessively broad terms, with many generalizations portraying minorities as perpetrators of crime.[208] A Belgian runner of Moroccan origin, Mohammed Mourhit, was described by media outlets as "Belgian" when he won many races but as "Moroccan" when he was caught with drugs some time later.[209] Insensitive media coverage functions as an echo chamber for bias, justifying and reinforcing public perceptions of immigrants as criminals.

Ethnic profiling also has a direct impact on relations between minority communities and the police, with resulting effects on both safety and police effectiveness. Research in the United States and the United Kingdom shows that unsatisfactory contacts between the police and the public can have a negative effect on public confidence in the police, not only for the individual directly involved, but also for his or her family, friends, and associates.[210] This creates profound mistrust among entire communities toward the police and reduces cooperation with law enforcement.[211] A Spanish Roma described his mistrust succinctly:

> You (the police) have accused me of everything and I have done nothing. I will no longer permit you to tell me anything. Not anything.[212]

Lack of public trust and cooperation are likely to reduce police effectiveness. Policing is profoundly dependent on the cooperation of the general public; police need the public to report crimes, and to provide suspect descriptions and witness testimony. Without public cooperation, police rarely identify or apprehend suspects, or obtain convictions. A study in the United Kingdom found that less than 15 percent of recorded crime was solved by police working alone,[213] and the number of crimes solved using only forensic evidence was less than 5 percent.[214]

Ethnic profiling has also been found to lead to increased hostility in street encounters with minorities, increasing the likelihood that these encounters will escalate into the type of conflict that presents safety concerns for officers and community members.[215] If unchecked, profiling may foster civil unrest. In the United Kingdom, the Scarman Report, which sought to explain the causes of the 1981 Brixton riots in London, criticized the policing of Brixton, particularly Operation Swamp 81, in which more than 120 officers patrolled the area with instructions to stop and search anyone who looked "suspicious."[216] Over four days, 943 people were stopped and 118 arrested, more than half of whom were black.[217] Noting the centrality of public "consent" in securing legitimacy for policing,[218] Lord Scarman saw the Brixton riots as "essentially an outburst of anger and resentment by young black people against the police" following Swamp 81.

Similar dynamics factored into the French riots of 2005.[219] There is a clear connection between the riots and heavy-handed policing that relied on constant identity checks and stops and searches targeting the minority French youths who live in impoverished suburban apartment blocks. As one young resident said, "relations with the police have become intolerable. When they come into the apartment buildings, they just grab everyone."[220]

In Denmark, abusive stops and searches conducted in areas with large minority populations have also provoked riots. In February 2008, the alleged mistreatment by Danish police of an elderly man of Palestinian origin sparked rioting in the Nørrebro district of Copenhagen.[221] Danish media reports indicate that, while triggered by this event, the riots had deeper roots in the routine use of stop-and-search tactics to single out and harass minorities. Ali Haseki of Gadepulsen, a government-supported organization that runs youth clubs, said that stop-and-search practices were an underlying cause of the unrest: "Our perception is that this has a lot to do with local youths' dissatisfaction over how the police act in the stop-and-search zones. They hassle and annoy young people, who in turn feel harassed."[222] On February 22, 2008, a Danish television station reported on an internal e-mail written by Deputy Chief of Police Claus Olsen acknowledging that stop-and-search practices were one of the principal causes of the riots. The report stated that as a result, the Copenhagen Police were planning to change these practices.[223]

G. Evaluating the Effectiveness of Ethnic Profiling in Ordinary Policing

Ethnic profiling produces substantial harm to the individuals profiled, the communities they come from, and police relations with those communities. In addition, in relying upon ethnic criteria, the use of ethnic profiling undercuts a long-standing principle of European law rooted in history. By themselves, these harms cast doubt on the existence of an "objective and reasonable" justification for ethnic profiling. In addition, the available evidence suggests that ethnic profiling does not demonstrably increase police efficiency in preventing crime and detecting criminals.

A key issue in determining whether ethnic profiling constitutes illegal discrimination is whether there is in fact a valid statistical link between ethnicity and the probability of offending.[224] Put another way, can it be objectively demonstrated that profiling is an effective tool of law enforcement? Does singling people out for police attention on the basis of ethnicity produce a larger number of legitimate arrests and more effective crime control than would result if ethnically neutral criteria were used to target suspects?

In some contexts, criminal justice statistics have shown a correlation between crime and ethnicity, although these statistics may themselves reflect biased law enforcement patterns. In the United States, there is clear evidence that offending rates for different types of crime vary with ethnicity. Both victim reports and arrest statistics show that African-Americans, who constituted roughly 13 percent of the U.S. population, committed over 40 percent of the reported robberies in the United States in 1999, and about half of the homicides committed that year.[225] U.S. studies of illegal drug use have produced mixed findings, with some showing considerably lower use of drugs among minority groups but also considerable variation among whites, blacks, and Latinos, depending upon the type of drug use surveyed.[226] U.K. studies based on self-reported drug-related offending point to comparable overall rates of offending among black and white people, though with differences in the types of drug-related crimes committed by each group, and lower rates for ethnic Asians.[227]

Proponents of ethnic profiling commonly cite figures on the number of minorities convicted for certain crimes—Roma women pickpockets, or Latin American women "drug mules," for example—as statistical evidence of a greater propensity of those groups to commit certain crimes. In the United Kingdom, the over-representation of people of African and Caribbean origin in arrest and imprisonment rates has sometimes been taken as indicative of greater criminality among these populations.[228] However, criminal justice statistics must be used with great caution. These figures reflect the activities of the criminal justice system, and are not a precise representation of the actual number of crimes being committed.[229] Figures for arrests, prosecutions, sentencing, and incarcerations reflect not just rates of offending but also the results of bias in the criminal justice system.[230]

It is quite plausible that in particular societies, ethnic groups have distinct offending profiles structured by factors such as social and economic status.[231] However, evidence suggests that police work driven by ethnic profiling responds more to stereotypes than to real differences in offending rates among ethnic groups, and that disparities in stops and searches cannot be explained by actual offending rates.[232] As the examples below indicate, disparities in police treatment of minority and majority groups are common, but disparities in rates of offending are not.

Self-report surveys in the United Kingdom show similar levels of drug use by black and white people, and lower levels for ethnic Asians.[233] Yet drug searches account for a larger proportion of stops and searches of minorities. In 2006–2007, the search for illegal drugs in the United Kingdom accounted for 40 percent of stops and searches of whites, compared with 47 percent of stops and searches of blacks and 57 percent of stop and searches of Asians.[234] Stops and searches for drugs are generally high-discretion actions, initiated by the officer on the basis if his or her perception rather than on the basis of intelligence or information from the public. As noted above, greater discretion permits the greater influence of stereotypes and the resulting increased focus on minorities even when the stereotype is clearly inaccurate, as in the case of race and drug use in the United Kingdom.[235]

Similar disproportionality has been found in U.S. police practices. In New York City, a 1999 study examined the controversial use of aggressive stop-and-search practices aimed at offenses relating to drugs and guns. The study, which examined 175,000 stops and searches by the New York City Police Department, found that although the Latino population of New York City was about 22 percent, Latinos made up about 33 percent of all of those stopped and searched. While New York City's black population was approximately 24 percent of the total, blacks constituted about 52 percent of those stopped and searched. By contrast, the city's 40 percent white population only made up about 10 percent of all of those stopped and searched.[236] Yet the productivity rate, or "hit rate," was higher for whites than minorities. The hit rate was 12.6 percent for searches of whites, 11.5 percent for Latinos, and 10.5 percent for blacks. Thus while blacks and Latinos were targeted at higher rates than whites, the hit rates do not reflect a higher propensity of these groups to commit offenses. Profiling expert David Harris goes further:

> The data do not support the profiling assumption—that using racial or ethnic appearance to target law enforcement efforts will make for more efficient, more accurate policing, or for the arrest of more criminals. In fact, the opposite is true. Using race does not cause hit rates to go up; instead, the hit rate actually drops.[237]

Very few studies of ethnicity and police efficiency have been conducted in Europe, but those that exist have found that high-discretion stops are not effective and have a disproportionate impact on minorities. A 2005 Dutch study of the efficiency of preventive searches for weapons in eight cities over a two-year period found that the searches disproportionately targeted minorities and that the hit rate was only 2.5 percent—that is for every 1,000 people searched, 25 weapons were detected—and this figure was inflated by the inclusion of items such as penknives.[238] Not only is this a low hit rate compared to U.K. or U.S. data, but the cost in terms of police man-hours was extremely high—for example, 54 operations in Amsterdam took nearly 12,000 hours of police time.[239] The Dutch example shows that stops and searches not directed by specific intelligence have a disproportionate impact on minorities while failing to enhance efficiency.[240]

A Swedish study of discrimination in the judicial system, which examined the use of stops and searches to detect drugs, similarly found that people with a non-European background were searched more often than Swedes and white Europeans.[241] The researchers concluded that police do not have good criteria for reasonable suspicion when searching minorities for drugs,[242] whereas their judgment was sound for suspicious behaviors or appearances in the case of white Swedes. With minorities, police officers had difficulties distinguishing law-abiding from disorderly immigrants. In interviews, Swedish police said that they use stereotypes to maximize efficiency—yet their use of stereotypes in fact reduced their efficiency.[243]

There is evidence that removing race or ethnicity from a criminal profile (in this case a drug courier profile) and mandating that officers look at specific nonethnic criteria can help avoid discrimination and improve efficiency. In a rare instance in which an ethnic profile was replaced by a behavioral profile, law enforcement effectiveness increased. In 1998, 43 percent of searches performed by U.S. Customs Service officers were directed at blacks and Latinos, although these groups accounted for a much lower proportion of all travelers. A particularly large number of searches—including invasive x-rays and strip searches—were carried out on Latina and black women suspected of being "drug mules." The hit rates for these searches were relatively low across all groups—5.8 percent for whites, 5.9 percent for blacks, and 1.4 percent for Latinos[244]—and were particularly low for black and Latina women, who were in fact the least likely to be carrying drugs on or in their bodies.[245] In 1999, the Customs Service changed its procedures, removing ethnicity from factors to consider in making stops; introducing observational techniques focused on behavior such as nervousness or inconsistencies in passengers' interviews; using more intelligence information; and requiring closer supervision of stop-and-search decisions.[246] As a result of this change, the racial disparities in Customs Service searches had nearly disappeared by 2000, and the hit rate improved from just under 5 percent to over 13 percent and became almost even for all ethnic groups.[247]

The experience of the U.S. Customs Service is mirrored in a recent pilot project in Spain. In 2007 and 2008, partnering with the Open Society Justice Initiative, the municipal police of Fuenlabrada, Spain, both reduced disproportionality and increased the effectiveness of police stops. The project introduced stop forms to gather data on the effectiveness and efficiency of stops and searches. When data showed certain operations disproportionately targeted members of minority groups but did not improve law enforcement productivity, police practices were changed. Using new data-driven practices, greater supervision of officers' stops, and monthly consultations with community representatives, Fuenlabrada police improved the efficiency of their stops. Over the course of six months, the use of stops declined from 958 in the first month of monitoring to 253 in the final month, while the hit rate increased from 6 percent to 17 percent. Disproportionality was also reduced for all groups, with the greatest reduction occurring in stops of Moroccans. At the start of the project Moroccans were 9.6 times more likely to be stopped than ethnic Spaniards, and six months later Moroccans were 3.4 times more likely to be stopped, largely as the result of abandoning a fruitless counterterrorism operation conducting stops at the local train station.[248]

As the Fuenlabrada example shows, there are relatively simple ways to increase the efficiency of stop-and-search practices by reducing the influence of negative stereotypes about minorities. As noted earlier, a critical factor driving ethnic profiling is the degree of officer discretion involved in deciding whom to stop and search. U.K. research indicates that "where levels of discretion are highest ... generalizations and negative stereotypes about likely offenders play a role."[249] When, instead, officers are required to justify or articulate grounds for suspicion before stopping citizens, they appear to increase their consideration of behavioral factors and consequently increase their hit rate. U.K. hit rates for stops and searches conducted under Section 1 of PACE—which requires reasonable suspicion—ranged between 10 and 13 percent for the 1997/98 to 2007/08 period.[250] This is much higher than the hit rate for Section 60 public order stops and searches or Section 44 counterterrorism stops and searches,[251] neither of which has a reasonable suspicion requirement. Many countries in Europe have no reasonable suspicion requirement, although it is recommended by the European Code of Police Ethics.[252] Indeed, the EU Network of Independent Experts on Fundamental Rights has raised concerns about the lawfulness of excessively broad police powers in many European countries.[253] The introduction of a clear standard for reasonable suspicion, accompanied by police training in how to determine suspicion, would be an important step forward.

Studies indicate that in order to be effective, police should make their stops based on factors including up-to-date intelligence on current crime patterns, observations of objectively suspicious behavior, and police-community dialogue.[254] A recent study of police practices in Bulgaria, Hungary, and Spain found no meaningful oversight or assessment of procedures used by individual officers in deciding whom to stop, and points to considerable waste of police time and resources involved in stops based on ethnic profiling. It is unclear what police performance measures are used in many European countries or whether the use of stop-and-search tactics is assessed at all.[255]

One area in which ethnic profiling may not be so inefficient is the detection of illegal migrants. Here, the use of appearance to determine who may not be of majority national origin is commonplace, and, for the time being at least, has a greater probability of effectiveness than ethnic profiling in the detection of crime. However, as the percentage of European citizens and legal residents of minority ethnic origin continues to increase, the assumption that a member of an ethnic minority group is likely to be an immigrant becomes inappropriate.[256] In an increasingly ethnically diverse Europe, the use of ethnic profiling for immigration enforcement imposes an undue burden on minority citizens, and in effect creates a dual standard in the enjoyment of basic citizenship rights that violates the principle of equal treatment.

In sum, the evidence examined in this section raises serious doubts about the effectiveness of ethnic profiling—even when there is valid data on higher rates of minority offending. Particularly in view of the substantial harm produced by it, police use of ethnic profiling generally fails the proportionality test developed by the European Court of Human Rights to determine whether differential treatment constitutes discrimination. Furthermore, there are reforms that police can and should undertake to improve their productivity and to avoid profiling, as Chapter V makes clear.

First, however, it is worth examining recent developments in law enforcement practices in response to new terror threats. In this first decade of the twenty-first century, ethnic profiling has taken on a new dimension as police and other law enforcement agencies across Europe confront new terror threats. As discussed in the next chapter, ethnic profiling appears to have increased, and Europe's diverse Muslim communities are the prime target.

IV. Ethnic Profiling
in Counterterrorism Since 9/11

The use of ethnic profiling in Europe, while long a staple of police practices, has intensified in the years since the terrorist attacks of September 11, 2001 in the United States and in response to subsequent terrorist bombings in Madrid in March 2004,[257] in London in July 2005,[258] and the attempted bombings in London and Glasgow in June 2007.[259]

Counterterrorism aims above all to prevent and detect potential terrorists or planning for acts of terrorism before they occur. Domestic and foreign intelligence services and the police conduct counterterrorism activities governed by counterterrorism legislation and criminal law. While there is some overlap in the functions of police and intelligence services, there are critical differences regarding their functions and thus in the degree of oversight to which they are generally subjected. Intelligence services are concerned with generating and maintaining a flow of information on threats to the state, and secrecy is deemed essential to enable and protect their work and, unlike police, they face no requirement to demonstrate the grounds for their suspicion. Intelligence information is generally passed to the police forces when it is sufficiently timely and precise as to support a law enforcement action (this is termed "actionable intelligence"). At that point, the police undertake the enforcement action and subsequent steps toward criminal prosecution.

In most cases, the police action—be it a raid on a premises or the arrest of a suspected terrorist—will require judicial authorization. Similarly, judicial oversight and authorization is commonly required for both police and intelligence agencies to undertake surveillance when this involves intrusive covert techniques such as wiretaps and hidden cameras. A deeply troubling tendency in the aftermath of 9/11 is the expansion of intelligence agency powers, the reduction of oversight, and an erosion in the standard of suspicion required—with religion and national origin taking on undue weight in the practices documented in this report.[260] In some cases, such as France and Spain, powerful counterterrorism legislation was introduced in response to domestic terror threats that predate 9/11 but which have been used with increasing vigor since then, as documented in this report and by other rights organizations.[261] A further trend is the use of counterterrorism powers that were originally designed to be exceptional measures on an ongoing basis for other policing objectives. This trend is discussed below in regard to the counterterrorism stop-and-search powers used on a permanent basis in London since February 2001.[262]

Governments and law enforcement authorities face tremendous public pressure to do all they can to prevent terror attacks, including using counterterrorism profiles. The principal objective of counterterrorism profiling is to use police resources as efficiently as possible to identify suspected perpetrators and prevent attacks. The aim of such profiles is to help dismantle terrorist networks, cells, and operations before they can strike, or at the very least impede terrorist groups and reduce their chances of carrying out a successful attack.[263]

Religion—and particularly, Islam—figures prominently in contemporary counterterrorism profiling.[264] Current counterterrorism profiling[265] generally targets individuals—usually men—presumed to be Muslim or originating from a country with a majority Muslim population.

The use of information about religion (or ethnicity, race, or national origin) in assembling a profile is legitimate when linked to solid, timely, and specific intelligence concerning individuals' participation in terrorist activities. However, evidence from Europe indicates that police and intelligence agencies are using generalized assumptions about certain religious or ethnic groups' involvement in terrorism, thus crossing the line from legitimate counterterrorism profiling into discriminatory ethnic profiling. When police target mosques, Muslim organizations, and businesses serving Muslim communities—based on generalized suspicion rather than specific intelligence—they are engaging in ethnic profiling.

In part because ethnic profiling is not monitored in most European countries, it is difficult to chart its use with any precision. But there are many recent examples of people being singled out for discriminatory counterterrorism related law enforcement practices solely or principally because of their religion. Stops and searches of Britons of South Asian descent increased fivefold after the July 2007 attempted bombings in London and Glasgow. Similarly, from late 2001 to early 2003, Germany undertook a massive data mining exercise that trawled through the sensitive personal data of 8.3 million people on the basis of a broad profile that relied primarily on religion and ethnic origin—without finding a single terrorist.

Other instances of ethnic profiling aimed at identifying terrorism suspects are harder to establish, because any particular police action may be driven not solely by ethnicity or religion, but also by circumstantial evidence that would seem to justify some level of suspicion. Only when cases are examined closely does it become clear that the circumstantial evidence cited is viewed as significant only *because* the person in question is Muslim or practices a certain form of Islam. As this chapter documents, ethnicity, religious practice, or national origin is often the deciding factor: circumstantial evidence that would not ordinarily lead to police action comes to be viewed as significant when that evidence is linked to individuals or groups of a specific religious or ethnic background.[266]

Reliance on generalizations about ethnicity and religion in counterterrorism profiling is especially pronounced in the context of early prevention efforts—that is, efforts to detect persons thought to be at risk of sympathizing with or turning toward terrorism, before they have actually taken steps to plan an attack. Examples of ethnic profiling described in this chapter include the abuse of France's terrorist association law, raids by "regional centers to combat radical Islam" in France, and the selection of surveillance targets in Germany, the Netherlands, and Italy.

Increasingly, these early prevention efforts are driven by theories of "radicalization," which emerged in response to the phenomenon of so-called home-grown terrorists in the Netherlands, United Kingdom, and other countries. According to these theories, certain types of Islam can be linked to the radicalization process. Police and intelligence services, therefore, target practitioners of these types of Islam, even when there is no evidence that individual practitioners are involved in terrorism.

This chapter describes a range of post-9/11 law enforcement practices involving the use of ethnic profiling in counterterrorism efforts—some influenced by radicalization theories, others not. These include stop-and-search operations and identity checks, often used in mass checks of people in public places; data mining; raids on mosques and other institutions associated with Muslims; arrest and imprisonment of presumed terrorists; and surveillance activities.

The nature of ethnic profiling in these activities varies. More overt ethnic profiling can be seen in the explicit use of ethnic profiles to conduct data mining, targeting persons perceived to be Muslim or of particular ethnic or national origin for identity checks and stop-and-search actions, and arresting Muslims on the basis of circumstantial evidence that would not lead to the detention of similarly situated non-Muslims. In some cases, people or places identified through data mining or efforts to detect radicalization are then subjected to more intrusive operations such as surveillance or raids. The common factor connecting these activities is law enforcement's reliance on ethnicity and/or religion in deciding to target individuals, institutions and, at times, whole communities for suspicion.

This chapter analyzes the effectiveness of these practices. As noted earlier, the question of effectiveness has a significant bearing on whether the profiling practices examined here can withstand legal scrutiny under European human rights standards

A. Ethnic Profiling in Mass Controls and Stop-and-Search Practices

Since 9/11, law enforcement officers in many European countries have made extensive use of their preventive powers to target persons they presume to be Muslim for identity controls—that is, spot checks of identity documents—and for stops and searches in public places. Muslims are frequently targeted for identity checks or searches in places considered to be likely terrorist targets, such as metro systems, trains and train stations, and commercial centers; or in places associated with Muslims, including predominantly Muslim neighborhoods, telephone calling centers, *halal* restaurants, and mosques.

In some cases, these are mass operations that have involved checking hundreds of people over many hours, primarily based on the targets' presumed religious affiliation. Mass controls are highly visible, which aggravates the humiliation and stigmatization felt by those targeted.

United Kingdom

Data published by the United Kingdom Ministry of Justice[267] demonstrate that U.K. stop-and-search practices have targeted persons perceived to be Muslim since 9/11, and that this pattern intensified following the London Underground bombings of July 7, 2005 and the Haymarket and Glasgow International Airport bombings of June 29–30, 2007.[268] As noted in Chapter III, discriminatory stop-and-search practices in the United Kingdom have been facilitated by a statute adopted just before the terrorist attacks of 9/11: under Sections 44(1) and (2) of the Terrorism Act 2000,[269] police officers, when given authorization by the secretary of state, can stop and search vehicles and pedestrians for articles that could be used for terrorism even without reasonable suspicion that such articles are present.[270]

In 2007–2008, police forces across England and Wales conducted a total of 117,278 Section 44 stops and searches on vehicles and pedestrians—an overall increase of 215 percent from the previous year.[271] Stops and searches increased for all ethnic groups, but the biggest rise—of 322 percent—was for black people, followed by a 185 percent increase for "Asian" people (a category that includes the United Kingdom's substantial South Asian community of persons of Bangladeshi, Indian, and Pakistani origin, and persons most likely to be Muslims), and lastly a 185 increase in stops of white people.[272]

The surge in terrorism-related stop-and-search practices during 2005–06 and 2007–2008 is doubtless largely attributable to the July 2005 and June 2007 London bombings. But an analysis of publicly available data suggests that the higher rates of stops and searches of minorities, and in particular of persons classified as "Asian," were driven largely by ethnic stereotypes rather than relevant grounds for suspicion, and that these practices were ineffective in identifying terrorist suspects.

Contemporaneous official comments acknowledged and defended the use of ethnic profiling. In March 2005, for example, U.K. Home Office Minister Hazel Blears said: "If a threat is from a particular place then our action is going to be targeted at that area.... It means that some of our counterterrorism powers will be disproportionately experienced by the Muslim community."[273] Her remarks were echoed by Ian Johnston, the chief constable of the British Transport Police, who told his officers to concentrate on particular ethnic minority groups and not "waste their time searching old white ladies."[274]

Not surprisingly, London saw a marked rise in stops and searches in the months following the July 2005 terrorist attacks, and individuals classified as Asian figured prominently in this rise.[275] According to London Metropolitan Police Service (MPS) figures, 2,405 Asian and black people were stopped while walking in the three months following the July 2005 bombings, compared with 196 the previous year.[276] Section 44 stops of vehicles rose by 86 percent for white drivers, by 108 percent for black drivers and by 193 percent for Asian drivers.

Commenting on these figures, Peter Herbert, a member of the Metropolitan Police Authority, the body that oversees the London MPS, observed:

> [I]ntelligence cannot lead to a 1,100 percent increase; this is just random stop and search. This means the police are not using their information properly, because they are too busy making random stops, which deters no one and which alienates large numbers of people and wastes time and resources.[277]

Essentially the same pattern held true for the following one-year period. From October 2005 through September 2006, the MPS conducted 22,672 Section 44 stops and searches.[278] These resulted in 27 arrests for alleged terrorism offenses and 242 arrests for other offenses. None of the arrests resulted in terrorism-related charges being filed.[279]

During public hearings convened in 2005–2006 by the Metropolitan Police Authority to examine the counterterrorism response in London, many Londoners expressed the belief that the police were exercising their authority on grounds of ethnicity and that this was unacceptable.

And yet, while police statistics clearly show rapidly expanding use of Section 44 stop-and-search powers in London and nationally during this period, to date none of these searches has resulted in an arrest or charge related to terrorism.[280] Of the 44,543 stops and searches registered by the Home Office for 2005–06, only 105 resulted in arrests. In other words, only one of every 400 people stopped and searched was arrested.[281] Similarly, of the 117,278 stops and searches registered by the Home Office for 2007–2008, only 72 people were arrested in relation to terrorism related offenses, a success rate of 0.061 percent.[282] None of these resulted in a conviction for a terrorism offense.[283]

In short, while there is abundant evidence that U.K. police powers to stop and search individuals have been misused, there is scant if any evidence that police use of these powers has been effective in detecting individuals involved in terrorist activities. Perhaps in response, the grounds cited by law enforcement authorities in support of stop-and-search powers has evolved somewhat.

Although the Terrorism Act 2000 states that the purpose of Section 44 stops is to search for articles that may be used in an act of terrorism,[284] and early remarks by Blears and other officials suggested that police stops were undertaken to identify potential bombers, security officials have increasingly argued that there is little or no expectation that police would actually be able to detect a terrorist through an identity check.[285] Instead, senior U.K. police have argued that the value of Section 44 stop-and-search powers lies in the ability to disrupt terrorists.[286] Under this argument, the arrest rate is not a relevant indicator of efficiency.[287] Hazel Blears concurred in an October 7, 2005 letter to the *Guardian* newspaper, arguing that Section 44 stops and searches help to deter terrorist activity "by creating a hostile environment for would-be terrorists to operate in."[288]

Official positions defending stop-and-search powers have increasingly emphasized their value in disrupting and deterring terrorists during the communication, planning, and reconnaissance of possible attacks.[289] It is practically impossible to determine the deterrence value of Section 44 stops, but senior police officers believe that by being open and transparent with the public and by involving the community in the review and monitoring of the ongoing use of these powers, they will negate some of the concerns about their disproportionate, inappropriate, or excessive application, and reassure the public that Section 44 is being applied appropriately.[290]

A review of the Terrorism Act 2000 conducted by Lord Carlile in 2006 concluded that Section 44 powers have not been effective in either deterring terrorism in general, or in identifying specific terrorists or thwarting specific attacks. Lord Carlile's report found that "there is little or no evidence that the use of s44 has the potential to prevent an act of terrorism as compared with other statutory powers of stop and search."[291] Carlile's report argued that these powers should be used sparingly, because misuse would be poorly regarded by the courts and could fuel demands for the repeal of Section 44. In December 2006, Metropolitan Police Assistant Commissioner Andy Hayman questioned the value of Section 44 stop-and-search powers, saying it was "very unlikely that a terrorist is going to be carrying bomb-making equipment around with them in the street."[292] Hayman went on to say that he was "not sure what purpose it serves, especially as it upsets so many people, with some sections of our community feeling unfairly targeted. It seems a big price to pay."

In his most recent report, looking at the conduct of Section 44 powers in 2007, Lord Carlile continued to express concern about the increasing use of the power. The report argues that given the dearth of evidence of the power's preventing a terrorist attack, Section 44 stops and searches should be used less.[293] In response to the latest figures released, Lord Carlile added "it [Section 44 stop and search] catches no or almost no terrorism materials, it has never caught a terrorist and therefore it should be used conservatively."[294] He draws particular attention to the wide variations in the numbers of Section 44 stops and searches being used between different police services across the United Kingdom, stating, "I find it hard to understand why Section 44 authorizations are perceived to be needed in some forces areas, and in relation to some sites, but not others with strikingly similar risk profiles."[295] It is clear that there is a growing reliance across the U.K. on the routine use of Section 44 powers, with little apparent relation to potential terror threats.

The London MPS conducted a full review of its use of Section 44 stop-and-search powers in 2007. Using a range of assessment methods,[296] the review found that, on balance, the powers are "necessary,"[297] and MPS police chiefs have again emphasized that the powers will be used to "deter, disrupt and prevent terrorist activity."[298]

In 2007, the MPS revised Standard Operating Procedures for Section 44, and now provides the following guidance for officers on how to determine whom to stop:

> The profile of people being searched should reflect the profile of the people in that area. Terrorists come from all ethnic groups and all walks of life. Actions define a terrorist, not ethnicity, race or religion.
>
> Terrorists may come from a wide variety of backgrounds and may attempt to change their behavior to disguise their criminal intentions and blend into their surroundings.
>
> Officers must never use stereotypical images of "terrorists" when deciding to use their powers of stop and search, to do so could lead to:

- Targeting of certain community;
- Disproportionality;
- Discrimination;
- Terrorists avoiding detection whilst carrying out their objective.[299]

This is a welcome caution, although it appears to have had little impact on the MPS's use of Section 44 powers. The significant increase in the number of Section 44 stops and searches made nationally in 2007–2008 largely reflects increases in the use of the power by the MPS in London. In 2007–2008 the MPS was responsible for 87 percent of all searches nationally under this power. The MPS used Section 44 stops and searches on 76,496 more occasions than the previous year, an increase of 303 percent.[300] In the United Kingdom as a whole, the latest official figures show high levels of disproportionality persist.[301]

In October 2007, Prime Minister Gordon Brown announced a review of existing guidance for police officers on Section 44 counterterrorism stop-and-search powers, in order to assure they are being used appropriately and proportionately. The review resulted in new guidelines titled "Practice Advice on Stop and Search in Relation to Terrorism," issued by the U.K. National Policing Improvement Agency (NPIA) in November 2008.[302] The document defines racial profiling as the following:

> The use of racial, ethnic, religious or other stereotypes, rather than individual behavior or specific intelligence, as a basis for making operational or investigative decisions about who may be involved in criminal activity. Officers should take great care to avoid any form of racial or religious profiling when selecting people for searching using Section 44 powers. Profiling in this way may amount to an act of unlawful discrimination as would discrimination on the grounds of age, gender, sexuality or disability.

The document notes that terrorists can come from any background and there is no profile for what a terrorist looks like. It gives these instructions:

> Great care should be taken to ensure that the selection of people is not based solely on ethnic background, perceived religion or other personal criteria. A person's appearance or ethnic background will sometimes be a factor, but an officer's decision to search them under section 44 should be made only if it is a result of evaluated intelligence. Profiling people from certain ethnicities or religious backgrounds may also lose the confidence of communities. An effective way of protecting against this is to compare the numbers of people searched in proportion to the demographic make-up of the area where searches take place.

If these guidelines are indeed heeded in practice, future statistics on stop-and-search practices should demonstrate more targeted and less disproportionate use of Section 44 powers.

As noted earlier, in most of Europe there is no data of the sort produced by the U.K. Home Office. But the data that are available reflect the same pattern found in the United Kingdom: mass identity checks identify the occasional person with an outstanding warrant for petty offenses but primarily serve to detect individuals in irregular immigration status, while generating enormous insecurity and resentment in Muslim communities. While the following sections examining the use of stops in Germany, France, and Italy cannot give as full a picture as is provided by U.K. statistics, the patterns that emerge provide no reason to believe that the dynamics are significantly different nor the results any better than in the United Kingdom.

Germany

In Germany, police intensified their reliance on identity checks targeting Muslims following the 9/11 terrorist attacks and the discovery that some of the 9/11 terrorists—a group known as the "Hamburg cell"—had planned their attack while in Germany. German police have carried out mass identity checks outside of mosques, frequently after Friday prayers when the largest number of worshippers is present. Since 9/11, police have conducted mass identity checks on numerous occasions outside 25 to 30 mosques, including those with the largest attendance in Germany.[303] The operations appeared particularly common in Germany's southern states.[304]

These checks have often been conducted in an intimidating manner: German analysts say that police—sometimes dressed in riot gear—typically surround the mosque and check the identity documents of every person leaving the building during operations that can take hours when there are thousands of people to review.[305] Individuals without valid identification have been taken to police stations and held for several hours until their status is verified.[306]

The months immediately following the July 2005 London bombings saw a surge in identity checks targeting Muslims in Germany. In early August 2005, hundreds of police officers carried out identity checks in front of mosques in the cities of Aalen, Balingen, Biberach, Esslingen, Freiburg, Friedrichshafen, Heilbronn, Karlsruhe, Lörrach, Ludwigsburg, Mannheim, Pforzheim, Ravensburg, Reutlingen, Sigmaringen, Stuttgart, Tübingen, Ulm, and Waiblingen. Approximately 900 people were checked.

In September 2005, 500 German police undertook a state-wide sweep of 20 cities in Hessen, including Frankfurt. The actions focused on shops, restaurants, and bars in the vicinity of mosques, and some streets were shut down during sweeps. Police checked 1,260 people[307] and arrested 38 men. The state's interior minister, Volker Bouffier, said 33 of those arrested lacked valid residence permits and three had been sought in connection with other offenses. Bouffier stated that the action was intended to preemptively combat "criminal Islamic structures."[308]

It is not clear what information was gathered through these exercises or what if any value they had in preventing terrorism in Germany. Whatever their intelligence value, these measures produced no significant law enforcement outcome; the only charges resulting from the checks were for minor offenses, primarily immigration violations.[309]

Baden-Wurttemberg Interior Minister Heribert Rech said that the August 2005 operations had a specific aim:

> [O]btain further information about Islamic extremists and terrorists in order to react quickly to any Islamist threat and to destroy terrorist structures. ... [P]olice need to obtain comprehensive information about Islamists. ... It must be made clear to the extremists that we will deal most forcibly with any religiously motivated claims to absolute power, intolerance and disregard for human rights.[310]

The operations described above appear designed to serve several different functions: they may be broad intelligence-gathering exercises; they may be public relations efforts to display the government's determination to combat terrorism; they may have some deterrent effect through "target hardening;" and there may be real or perceived collateral benefits, primarily in immigration enforcement outcomes. A German counterterrorism officer gave these goals:

> We do not really expect to find people who are terrorists or supporters. To reach this goal other methods are used. Preventive identity controls are instead used on top of other methods. The main goal of these controls is to find people who are living in Germany illegally or [engaged in] other related crime. We also want to show that the police are there, that we are doing something about terrorism; this increases pressure on persons involved in terrorist activities."[311]

The effectiveness of German control operations in achieving these aims is by its nature difficult to assess, but their impact on targets is clear. These highly visible and intrusive operations have directly affected thousands of people, publicly marking Muslims as suspicious solely on the grounds of their religion.

More recent developments in Germany suggest law enforcement authorities have learned that mass controls are not effective. Since mid-2006, the use of mass control operations appears to have declined. Political leaders and press reports no longer trumpet large-scale identity checks as measures to combat terrorism. Only in the state of Niedersachsen do Muslims continue to report that police regularly arrive in large numbers after prayers and check the documents of persons leaving the mosque.[312] In other areas of Germany, there has been a shift in the law enforcement approach to Muslim communities, and police have established "dialogue forums" in a number of states and at the federal level, with the goal of opening channels of communication between the police and representatives of Muslim communities.

Italy

Like Germany, Italy does not collect ethnic data. In Italy, too, law enforcement officials have used their identity-check powers in mass controls of tens of thousands of Muslims and immigrants since 9/11. These checks often occur during highly publicized raids targeting mosques and Muslim- and immigrant-owned businesses. Others take place during large-scale control operations in public places. According to individuals interviewed in 2006, Italian police single out those they presume to be Muslim for identity checks during these large-scale operations. While these are ostensibly counterterrorism operations, the primary result has been to identify illegal immigrants.

On July 9, 2005, following the London Underground bombings two days earlier, approximately 2,000 Italian police officers were deployed across the Lombardy region,[313] where they patrolled train stations, subways, commercial centers, and other sensitive sites.[314] Police reports indicate that most of the 142 persons arrested during this operation were accused of drug, petty theft, or immigration-related charges; 84 of those arrested were immigrants, 52 of whom were issued deportation orders.[315] The July 9 operation produced significant immigration control impacts, but had no discernible effect in detecting actual terrorists. Italian authorities frequently conflate immigration with the threat of terrorism, describing all Muslim immigrants as potential terrorists. This attitude drives the ethnic profiling of persons who appear to be immigrants and/or Muslims.

Identity checks outside mosques are reported to be common in Italy since 9/11. A Muslim who attends a mosque in Desio in northern Italy said during a May 2006 interview that, on two occasions in the previous few years, police had turned up at the mosque during prayer time and checked identity documents of people who had come to pray.[316] A Muslim from Turin stated that police frequently station themselves on a main road just outside the local mosque on Fridays around prayer time in order to check worshippers' identity documents.[317] In the view of the president of the Pakistani community in Italy, this is a widespread practice.[318]

Such practices continue, particularly in the north of Italy. According to Italian non-discrimination experts, authorities no longer rely explicitly on antiterrorism powers to target mosques, Muslim businesses, or Muslim individuals for controls, searches, raids, and arrests. Instead, they use general security or immigration powers as a framework for these actions.[319]

France

As in Germany and Italy, the French government does not collect data on police stops broken down by ethnicity, making it impossible to measure the existence or extent of ethnic profiling in France. Yet members of France's Muslim and North African communities are convinced that French police have increased their focus on these communities in recent years. In the aftermath of the July 2005 bombings in London and the March 2004 bombing in Madrid, French North Africans reported a noticeable increase in police check-points on trains, in the Metro, and on the streets.[320] Many Muslims and North Africans in France report that they are stopped, questioned, and searched by police, in their view solely because of their appearance.[321]

It is not clear whether these checks are conducted on the basis of antiterrorism powers[322] or whether they are a byproduct of a general climate of suspicion which leads police to use their regular discretionary powers to target people who "look Muslim."[323] Nor is it clear that such stop-and-search practices have had any effect in detecting or deterring acts of terrorism; the primary law enforcement outcome of these checks is an increase in the number of illegal immigrants detained and awaiting deportation.[324]

B. Data Mining

Explicit ethnic profiling lay at the heart of a massive—and ultimately unsuccessful—data mining effort in Germany aimed at identifying terrorists. Despite its failure, data mining based on ethnic profiling continues to attract European authorities.

In this practice, large databases of personal information,[325] such as immigration or student records, health and housing information, are subjected to computerized searches based on a specific profile.[326] Ethnicity, national origin, and religion often figure heavily in these profiles. These database searches are used to identify individuals thought to merit further investigation.

After it was discovered that several of the perpetrators of the 9/11 terrorist attacks had lived and studied in Hamburg, German officials sought to identify other potential terrorist cells. To this end, from 2001 until early 2003 the German federal government tasked the state governments to collect and process personal data in a massive data mining operation (known as *Rasterfahndung* in German).[327] German state police collected sensitive personal data[328] from approximately 8.3 million persons, who were selected using three broad criteria, including national origin.[329] Their data was then "trawled" —that is, searched using a computer program that identified pertinent information from the database, using a profile based upon common characteristics of members of the "Hamburg cell."[330] These traits included: being 18–40 years old, being male, being a current or former student, being Muslim, and being from one of 26 countries with a predominantly Muslim population.

Given the sheer number of German males between 18 and 40 who were or are students, it is clear that the key criteria in this search were religion, and national origin. Furthermore, the search was based on generalizations, not concrete intelligence concerning recent or potential terrorist attacks. The final database of potential sleeper cell members contained almost 32,000 entries.[331] In response, German authorities collected additional data from 96 different sources.[332] The supplementary data amounted to more than four million entries that the Federal Criminal Police Authotity (Bundeskriminalamt, or BKA) began to process on March 8, 2002, six months after the data trawling operation began. Computerized cross-referencing ultimately winnowed the list down—after another year's work—to 1,689 persons who were then "individually examined by regional police forces."[333]

Regional police investigated these persons through traditional methods, summoning some for interrogation; questioning relatives and employers; and, in some cases, using wiretaps and other forms of surveillance.[334] But while Germany's data mining exercise consumed enormous resources, it appears that not a single terrorist suspect was identified.[335] In 2006, Sebastien Müller of German Institute for Human Rights summarized what the police told him:

> I was just at a conference with the federal police. They said that they did not find any terrorist suspects in the Rasterfahndung operation. They only found information relating to petty crimes—one or two thefts ... also people without legal status in Germany or "immigration crimes." None were linked to any kind of terrorist activities whatsoever.[336]

Berlin Commissioner for Data Protection and Freedom of Information Alexander Dix summarized the results of the data mining operation as follows:

> Rasterfahndung was without result. No arrests or conviction resulted from this ... Two people were arrested in Hamburg soon after 9/11, but they were not caught by Rasterfahndung. They were caught using conventional methods, such as telephone tapping.... Rasterfahndung took up an enormous amount of manpower and time within the police force.... It was an exercise in wasting their time. If this had had any visible success, I am sure that politicians and the police would have published it. One can only gather that the exercise was without result.[337]

In the United States, which has also used extensive data mining, the results were much the same. Following 9/11, the Federal Bureau of Investigation (FBI) used immigration records to identify Arab and Muslim foreign nationals in the United States. On this basis, 80,000 individuals were required to register in the search for terrorists; another 8,000 were called in for FBI interviews; and more than 5,000 were locked up in preventive detention. Assessing the success of this effort, Georgetown

University law professor David Cole wrote, "In what has surely been the most aggressive national campaign of ethnic profiling since World War II, the government's record is 0 for 93,000."[338] The data mining did not produce a single conviction for a terrorist offense.

The German Rasterfahndung database was reportedly erased in June and July 2003,[339] but only after effectively branding millions of people as inherently suspicious and potential "terrorists in disguise."[340]

On May 23, 2006, by a vote of 6 to 2, the Constitutional Court of Germany ruled that data mining is illegal in the absence of a "concrete danger" to security or lives.[341] The court expressed concern that the screening focused on a particular religious community (Muslims) and was therefore likely to have a "stigmatizing impact" on those concerned and to "increase the risk of being discriminated against in working and everyday life."[342] In the court's view, a general threat situation of the kind that has existed continuously since 9/11 is not sufficient to warrant intrusions of this sort on personal data and privacy.[343] Instead, the court held, "The assumptions and conclusions which form the basis for establishing the risk must moreover be based on further concrete facts, which point to the preparation or commission of terrorist attacks."[344]

In 2008, the German Bundestag adopted new legislation authorizing the federal German police to conduct data mining operations directly instead of relying on the police and legal authority at the state level (as occurred with the 2001–2003 data mining described above). Although there is no indication that German authorities propose to undertake further data mining of this sort, the new legislation enables federal authorities to do so. By authorizing the federal authorities to carry out data mining on their own initiative, the 2008 law simultaneously concentrates all judicial scrutiny of data mining at the First Instance Court in Wiesbaden, thus depriving each state court of the power to exercise judicial review.[345]

Exploration of Data Mining by European Union Authorities and Agencies

In 2002 and again in 2004, German authorities proposed that data mining in the fight against terrorism be adopted across the European Union.[346] Counterterrorism officials from a number of other EU member states reportedly opposed the proposal based on their judgment that data mining is ineffective.[347] Nevertheless, in November 2002 the Council of the European Union—the EU's supreme law-making body—issued a draft recommendation calling for enhanced cooperation in developing profiles to assist in the identification of terrorists, although it did not specify how the profiles might be applied.[348] The recommendation stated that the terrorist profiles would be based on "a set of physical, psychological or behavioral variables, which have been identified, as typical of persons involved in terrorist activities and which may have some predictive value in that respect."[349]

The European Union Network of Independent Experts in Fundamental Rights warned that the proposed terrorist profiles presented a major risk of discrimination. According to the Network of Independent Experts, "The development of these profiles for operational purposes can only be accepted in the presence of a fair, statistically significant demonstration of the relations between these characteristics and the risk of terrorism, a demonstration that has not been made at this time."[350] In response, the European Council informed parliamentarians in July 2003 that the development of terrorist profiles would only be pursued at the EU level if there were a proven statistical link between the defined characteristics and the risk of terrorism.[351]

European civil liberties advocates are concerned about the trend of granting law enforcement authorities broad access to rapidly expanding EU databases, and worry that this is taking place without adequate protection of sensitive personal data.[352] Major EU databases include the Visa Information System (VIS),[353] the Schengen Information System (SIS I and SIS II),[354] and Eurodac, an asylum database.[355] EU authorities are proposing to create operational links between the VIS, SIS II, and Eurodac,[356] and the European Commission recently presented proposals for the development of a new entry/exit system.[357] Still pending but anticipated is a commission call for the creation of a European Union database of residence permits and passports. In June 2008, the European Council adopted a Council Decision allowing law enforcement access to VIS records for the prevention, detection, and investigation of terrorist offenses and other serious crime.[358]

The European Parliament, and its Committee on Civil Liberties (LIBE) in particular, have consistently raised concerns about privacy rights and dangers of discrimination in the use and potential abuse of European databases. As the European community presses for full availability of data for law enforcement and the fight against terrorism, the LIBE Committee has made a series of recommendations on the need for clear and consistent data protection,[359] which, among other things, would protect databases from being used in data mining exercises.

Similarly, European Data Protection Supervisor Peter Hustinx has expressed concern at the breadth of the law enforcement exemption to protections of sensitive personal data.[360] Hustinx raised serious concerns that a proposal for a Council Framework Decision on the protection of personal data "significantly weakens" protections of personal data of European citizens.[361] On November 27, 2008, the council adopted the Framework Decision, despite charges that it continues a "trend toward the lowest common data protection denominator" in law enforcement matters.[362] The activities of security services and the police in matters of national security are excluded from the decision and thus from any effective regional data protection guarantees.[363] Finally, still pending is a proposal for a Council Framework Decision on the use of Passenger Name Records (PNR) for law enforcement purposes.[364]

It is important to note that, while the systematic mining of data focused on ethnic or racial criteria amounts to ethnic profiling and is to be discouraged, this in no way undermines the need for the authorities to gather anonymous data for the purposes of documenting whether ethnic profiling is occurring. Despite widespread misunderstanding, such documentation is consistent with prevailing European data protection norms, which: a) distinguish between individual, identifiable data (which, when referring to sensitive criteria such as race or religion, are properly restricted) and collective, anonymous data; and b) do not impede the good-faith collection and dissemination of racial or religious statistics for legitimate public interest objectives such as the tracking and redress of ethnic discrimination, including ethnic profiling.[365]

C. Raids on Muslim Institutions and Harassment of Muslim Businesses

Just as raids in the context of ordinary crime prevention and detection appear to be used with fewer restrictions and greater aggression against minorities, highly publicized and aggressive counterterrorism raids targeting Muslims and immigrants are being used in many European countries. These raids single out Muslim- and immigrant-owned businesses, mosques and Muslim prayer halls, and the homes and offices of Muslims— often with the broad aim of disrupting the support base and "breeding ground" for terrorism, rather than of arresting specific perpetrators or preempting an attack.

This is not to say that raids themselves are an inappropriate tool of counterterrorism policing. When based on concrete and specific intelligence, raids are a central and important tool of counterterrorism operations. A surprise police intervention is often necessary to seize criminal suspects, evidence, contraband, or materials that may be used in an attack. Such raids are often used, appropriately, in the culmination of terror investigations. A raid based on concrete and specific information linking a particular individual to support for terrorism constitutes intelligence-based policing, not ethnic profiling. If, for example, officials have concrete evidence that weapons are being stored in a particular prayer room, raiding this site would not involve stereotypes, even though the target may be a mosque.

On the other hand, if a business is raided based on generalizations about the supposed religious beliefs, national origin, or ethnicity of those who own or frequent the business, ethnic profiling is involved. When driven by ethnic profiling, counterterrorism raids risk violating the rights of targeted communities while, correspondingly, undermining their underlying law-enforcement aims. The overwhelming majority of counterterrorism raids examined for this study appear to have been based on stereotypes linking Muslims or immigrants to terrorism. They have no apparent effect in detecting terrorists. While authorities claim these raids disrupt possible terrorist networks, it is equally if not more likely that they simply anger and alienate Muslim communities and, if anything, reduce the likelihood that they will cooperate with police in counterterrorism investigations. The high visibility of and publicity accompanying many raids has spurred criticism by Muslim communities and civil liberties advocates that they are done for political effect rather than operational necessity.

Recently, Italian and German authorities have moved away from the use of large-scale counterterrorism raids based on ethnic profiles. In Italy, law enforcement authorities appear to rely increasingly on administrative measures and immigration law rather than explicit counterterrorism measures in their preventive actions. However, these actions are harder to track, as they are less transparent and provide fewer due process guarantees than counterterrorism measures undertaken under criminal law.

France: Raids by "Regional Centers to Combat Radical Islam"

In France, Muslim-owned businesses and mosques have been subject to frequent raids, ostensibly aimed at disrupting the support base of "radical Islam" rather than at arresting actual terrorist suspects or preempting specific attacks. These have exacted a heavy toll on targeted communities while yielding no discernible law enforcement value.

The raids are coordinated by "regional centers to combat radical Islam" (*pôles régionaux de lutte contre l'Islam radical*)[366] established by the French Ministry of the Interior in 2005 in each of France's 22 metropolitan regions. Each center is headed by a representative of the Central Directorate of General Information (*Direction Centrales des Renseignements Généraux*, or RG) and works with representatives of a wide range of government agencies including police, public hygiene, public safety, revenue and taxation, and labor. The centers' mandate is broad—to monitor, disrupt, and cut off the support base of "radical Islam" in France. In addition to raids and surveillance activities,[367] the centers use administrative powers such as health or business regulations to impede and disturb businesses where "radical Islamists" are thought to meet or that are suspected of providing financial support to "radical Islamist networks."[368]

Common targets of raids include fast food restaurants, cafes, call centers, bookstores, security companies, and clothing stores. The raids typically involve officials of multiple government agencies as well as police and intelligence officials. In a typical raid, representatives of health, safety, tax, and labor agencies check a business's compliance with safety, health, and tax regulations, while police search the premises and check identity documents of everyone present. Anyone who cannot produce proof of identity is taken to the police station for verification. Individuals who cannot demonstrate legal residency face deportation. Businesses often face judicial or administrative penalties, in some cases resulting in their closure.

Raids by French authorities have adversely affected large numbers of people with no demonstrable counterterrorism results. According to official figures, in 2005 the regional centers conducted checks of 47 mosques and prayer halls, 473 businesses, and 85 cafes and call centers. These resulted in 276 judicial penalties (reportedly unrelated to terrorism) and 310 administrative penalties.[369] In 2005, in the greater Paris region alone, 88 raids were carried out involving 1,173 people, 185 of whom were taken into custody and 8 of whom were charged with judicial or administrative sanctions.[370] Activities increased in the Paris region in 2006, with 93 raids carried out between January 1 and May 15, 2006.[371]

While these raids have yielded scant discernible benefit in countering terrorism, they have had a corrosive effect on the daily lives of French Muslims. Samy Debah, president of the nongovernmental organization Collective against Islamophobia in France (CCIF), described a typical raid:

> In practice, they [French officials] arrive with numerous vehicles. They come at peak business hours. Some officials have uniforms; others wear ordinary clothes. They enter the business—health, customs, fraud, police ... They don't show their badges, they don't identify themselves. If any officials show their badges it is the health and hygiene inspectors.[372]

Debah also described a raid he witnessed at a friend's halal take-out restaurant in a town on the outskirts of Paris. According to Debah, "the owner of the restaurant is a practicing Muslim who has a beard and prays daily, but has absolutely nothing to do with any sort of 'radical movement.'"[373] Debah recalled the evening the restaurant was raided:

> The manager called me when the officials arrived and I came immediately. There were six or eight cars and at least 10 officials. It was around 8:00 p.m., a busy time. I observed the manner that they behaved and I asked them questions. I saw that there were two officials from the intelligence services. I could identify them as they did not respond when I asked where they worked. The telephone rang; the employee wanted to answer the phone. One of the intelligence officials said, "No, turn off your phone and close down the shop." I watched him [as] he went to the back of the restaurant. I asked what he was doing there. "Shut up," he responded ... The other intelligence official said, "Now, you keep quiet or we'll shut down your business permanently." I was torn between [wanting to protest] the illegal nature of their words and [my desire not to endanger] my friend. I said nothing further. The police asked everyone inside the restaurant to produce their identity documents. Those who didn't have their documents with them were handcuffed and taken to the police station.[374]

The raid concluded with an order requiring renovations to comply fully with health standards—and closing the restaurant until the renovations were completed. In this particular case, the burden was limited as the owner, having witnessed raids on dozens of local Muslim-owned businesses, had already started renovation work.

As their name suggests, the mandate of the "regional centers to combat radical Islam" is to target "radical Islam," although the term is quite vague. Any place where officials believe "radical Islam" may be supported or spread becomes a legitimate site for surveillance and "disruption," including raids. Official statements indicate that "radical Islam" is not limited to those who sympathize with the perspectives of terrorist organizations, but is defined so broadly as to include moderate Muslims.[375]

French officials argue that this is not the case. A senior French counterterrorism official said that only an extreme fringe of the Muslim population is targeted:

> It is the fringe from which the terrorists of tomorrow are recruited. ... There is a fringe of the population that can be tempted by violent radicalization. So we will show them that we are strong, that the state has the right to go everywhere. The idea is that they open halal butcher shops, call centers—and most are honest businesses—but some serve to support the cause, for instance in Algeria, or hire illegal workers. In that case, we are there.[376]

This official insisted that the "regional centers" do not base their work on stereotypes:

> The goals of these regional centers are defined one or two months in advance. They decide in advance that they will check a particular halal butcher shop, a particular mosque, a particular call center. It is the RG that takes the lead in this, but they need to justify their goals. I receive memos about these goals and I have never seen one that says simply, "We are going to check that business because the owner has a beard." It might say "the owner has contacts with other suspicious Salafists," but never just because the person is a Salafist Muslim. There is always something else.[377]

Many French Muslims are deeply skeptical of these claims and believe that their religious beliefs alone make them potential targets of the regional centers. Representatives of various Muslim organizations shared the view that the "regional centers" target not only practicing Muslims but also non-practicing Muslims. Boualam Azahoum, a spokesperson of Divercité, a human rights organization based in the Lyon area, expressed this view:

> How can they see who is "Islamist?" They cannot. So who do they check? All Muslims. How can they tell the difference? They basically spend their time checking fast food restaurants and call centers in the poor suburbs.

Muslim-run businesses make up a large portion of commercial activity in Lyon's poor suburbs, and many of them have been raided and have closed down as a result.[378] The clear perception in the community is that they are targeted solely on the basis of their religion, as the representative of one Muslim organization noted:

In reality the notion of "radical Islam" is very broad. Praying, wearing a beard or a veil suffice to define you as radical. People are discriminated against because they are Muslims; officials check their businesses because they are Muslims.[379]

This perception is widespread. At a July 2006 meeting of some twenty Islamic organizations from the Paris suburbs, representatives expressed their frustration and anger at the actions of the "regional centers." One participant voiced the opinion of the group:

People are saying that there's no point in trying to do business.... Each time there's a control—either a tax audit, or labor, or health—you feel that Muslims are being singled out.[380]

Italy

While more sporadic than in France, raids are also a key component of so-called "preventive antiterrorism" practices in Italy. Large-scale raids are typically conducted in the wake of terrorist attacks or during periods of heightened alert after bombings in other European countries. While heightened law enforcement activity is to be expected in this setting, the raids that ensue have been driven by stereotypes instead of legitimate intelligence, targeting Muslim- and immigrant-owned businesses, Muslim prayer halls, offices, and homes. These raids have resulted in the identification, round-up, and expulsion of illegal migrants. In combination with other counterterrorism tactics, such as frequent police checks and new regulations, they have also resulted in the closure of many Muslim- and immigrant-owned businesses—but there is scant if any indication that they have contributed to countering terrorism.

A nationwide series of raids on August 10, 2006 exemplifies the pattern. Immediately after British officials announced that they had thwarted a plot to detonate "liquid bombs" on trans-Atlantic flights out of British airports on August 9, 2006,[381] Italian police conducted a massive operation involving raids of mosques and informal Muslim prayer halls, Internet cafes, money-transfer offices, and call centers.[382] The Italian Interior Ministry announced that the operations targeted "Islamic gathering places" and that this was "an extraordinary operation that followed the British anti-terror operation."[383] The prime minister's office announced that in the course of the day police raided a total of 1,272 locations and checked the identification of 4,178 individuals with the following results: 114 individuals were issued deportation orders; 103 businesses were fined for administrative irregularities such as health or safety regulations; 111 people were reported for various crimes—none apparently involving terrorism; and 40 individuals were arrested—28 for immigration violations and 12 for unspecified "crimes against property."[384] Summing up the impact and results of these operations, Dacia Valent, spokeswoman of Italy's Islamic Anti-Defamation League, protested that "[m]ore than

4,000 people were stopped and humiliated to allow police to arrest 12 chicken thieves and 28 clandestine immigrants."[385]

One year earlier, on August 12–13, 2005, raids targeting similar sites were conducted across Italy a few weeks after terrorist bombing attacks on the London Underground. Targets included Muslim-associated Internet cafes, money-transfer offices, call centers, and halal butcher shops. On that occasion also, the Ministry of Interior announced that the raids were targeting "Islamic meeting places."[386] According to the Interior Ministry, over the course of the two days, police checked 7,318 locations and interrogated over 32,000 people.[387] These raids produced 701 deportation proceedings[388] and 141 arrests, two for having false documents and the rest for petty offenses.[389] None of those arrested was charged with terrorist activity.[390]

Italian officials have also carried out large-scale coordinated raids on the homes and offices of Muslims. On July 13, 2005—five days after the coordinated bombings on London subways—Italian newspaper headlines announced the detention of 174 people in a "nationwide sweep" aimed at suspected "Islamic militants."[391] The Interior Ministry announced, "The operation has been prepared for some time and confirms Italy has never lowered its guard in the face of terrorist risks."[392] Police raided 201 locations, with warrants to search for weapons and explosives. According to press reports, 423 people were detained, over half of whom were released following an identity check and questioning.[393] It is not clear what happened to the rest but a statement by Interior Minister Giuseppe Pisanu indicated that they were not charged with terrorist activity: "I'm not saying that we have seized terrorists. It is a preventive operation in high-risk environments."[394]

Italian officials have also reportedly conducted smaller-scale checks against immigrant-owned call centers and Internet cafes. These may not constitute raids per se, but represent a high degree of law enforcement attention that appears to be targeting not only Muslims, but also immigrants more broadly. The Pakistani owner of a telecommunications shop in Desio, in northern Italy, told Justice Initiative researchers that his store is checked two or three times a month by police officers. "When the police come here, they check all the Pakistani shops," he said. "Actually, they check all of the immigrant businesses," his colleague added.[395] At another Muslim-owned telecommunications shop in Milan, the owner said that every month or two the police arrive and check the identity documents of everyone in the shop. "People are afraid to come here," he commented.[396]

Italian law enforcement in the Lombardy region has also targeted Muslim-owned businesses for aggressive enforcement of new business regulations that apply specifically to small telecommunications businesses, many of which are Muslim-owned. S.M. Arshad, president of an umbrella organization representing 33 Pakistani community associations, said:

Five to six percent of the Pakistani community in Italy owns small businesses, mostly tele-communication, some grocery stores, some import-export. Officials have raided a lot of these businesses. They have also created complications for them. If you have a small telecommuni-cations shop, you need 12 square meters for people to wait. They also want these businesses to have two bathrooms ... Those who don't have the twelve square meters and a certain distance between telephone cables—they have to close.[397]

Another Muslim in Italy, identified as N.R., also expressed his frustration over these regulations:

We have to build a new bathroom. Only telephone and Internet businesses have to do this. These are for the most part immigrant-owned businesses. In Milan there must be about 850 telecommunications shops and maybe 50 are not immigrant-owned. We have a year to make the changes, and if we are unable to do so, we have to shut down. The cost of a bathroom is €5,000. I will have to sell my shop.[398]

N.R. pointed out that between these regulations and new regulations requiring businesses to ask customers for personal documents, it is very difficult to operate. "Many businesses are closing. There are about 12 shops in this neighborhood, and four or five have closed in the last few months."[399] One Muslim representative who monitors this issue estimates that as many as 80 percent of small telecommunications businesses have closed down in the last years.[400]

It appears that large-scale raids have been used less in Italy in recent years: no such raids were reported in 2007 or 2008. But large-scale identity checks targeting Muslims under general security measures and immigration law continue, and Italian authorities also continue to use administrative measures targeting immigrant-owned businesses, with an ongoing pattern of inspections of immigrant-owned call centers and Internet cafes, and the closing down of those businesses that do not comply with the regulations. However, on October 22, 2008, the Constitutional Court of Italy repealed the regulations pertaining specifically to call centers, on the grounds that the regula-tions violated a number of constitutional provisions.[401] The practical effect of this ruling on Muslim- and immigrant-owned businesses remains to be seen.

Administrative measures and new laws are also targeting mosques, closing down some existing mosques and impeding the construction of new ones.[402] In July 2008, authorities closed a large mosque in central Milan. Interior Minister Roberto Maroni reportedly stated that the decision to close the mosque was based on public order concerns, as worshippers regularly spilled out onto the street.[403] Worshippers are temporarily being allowed to pray in a local stadium, where they are charged for entry.[404]

In September 2008, the Northern League submitted a bill to parliament that would limit the construction of new mosques and Islamic cultural centers.[405] The law would require any new worship site to be authorized by the local county government, following a public consultation. In addition, any new mosque would need to be built or established at a distance of more than one kilometer from an existing church or synagogue. In December 2008, following the terrorist attacks in Mumbai, India, and the subsequent arrest in Italy of two Moroccan men on terrorism-related charges, Italian politicians from the Northern League publicly announced that they would propose legislation to freeze the building of all new mosques in an effort to curb terrorism.[406]

Germany

Since 9/11 German police have conducted regular and often massive raids of mosques, and Muslim organizations and businesses. German officials note that a judicial warrant is required before a raid can be conducted and say that that every raid has a case-specific evidentiary basis, linking it to ongoing investigations of specific persons or organizations suspected of involvement in terrorist activities or of supporting such activities.[407] Nonetheless, in some cases the weakness of the factual basis and the choice of a raid as the appropriate response raise concerns about whether stereotypes linking Islam, or certain streams of Islamic practice, to terrorism influenced the selection of targets and tactics and crossed the line from intelligence-based law enforcement into ethnic profiling.

A raid on an Islamic center in July 2004 exemplifies these ambiguities and the concerns they raise. On July 11, 2004, some 120 policemen raided the Islamic Center Mosque in Frankfurt searching for violent videos. German officials say the raid was ordered after a nine-year-old claimed that she and other children had been shown violent videos calling for "a holy war against non-believers." One of the videos, she said, showed a beheading.[408] During the raid officials seized computer hard-drives, discs, videos, and documents, and shortly afterwards told the press that they found a video showing a beheading.[409] Authorities later acknowledged, however, that the seized materials had no link to terrorism.[410]

While the nine-year-old's report merited follow-up by the police, it seems doubtful that the testimony of a single child would prompt such an intrusive response were it not for stereotypes linking Islam to terrorism. In the view of some Muslims, a simple visit and questioning by police would serve to confirm or allay suspicions without the impact on the mosque entailed in the raid. Mosque members saw the raid as highly discriminatory, and told journalists that it was an insult and an overreaction to an unconfirmed allegation. A member of the mosque's executive board said the action was too aggressive:[411]

Probably at the moment, every Muslim is under suspicion. It is the right of the police to search but not to overdo it in such an aggressive way. Somebody hears something from a child and then the police arrive with 200 men. There were other ways of finding out if something like that was shown or not.[412]

Additional raids took place during 2005. In January, 800 police officers took part in raids on 50 locations associated with Muslims, including mosques and Muslim-owned businesses. The raids resulted in the arrest of 11 people, reportedly for terrorist financing and forging documents. However, police told the press that they found no evidence of planning for an act of terrorism. It is not clear if any of these 11 individuals ultimately faced terror-related charges. In September 2005, 500 police officers conducted raids at Internet cafes and call centers in 20 cities in the state of Hesse; they questioned more than 1,000 persons and arrested 38, none on terror offenses. Of those arrested, 33 had no residence permit and three were sought in connection with other offenses.[413]

In 2005, police raided the Milaner Rami Mosque in Berlin, after the mosque was visited by a businessman believed to be involved in illegal financial transactions. Burhan Kesici, a Muslim leader in Berlin, described the raid:[414]

They searched one of our mosques. The search warrant indicated that this businessman had been to the mosque and come in with packages. We asked the police if this was really the correct reason—it's normal that a businessman comes to a mosque to sell books if he can. But it's not a reason to send police to check a mosque. They came with 20 or 30 officers. They searched the whole mosque, including the kitchen, offices, and toilets. What was interesting was that the bookshop wasn't searched very much.[415]

Officials have described the purpose of the September 2005 raids as "pre-emptively combating criminal structures."[416] Raids, being highly intrusive and sometimes frightening, are an inappropriate tactic for broad-brush efforts to prevent terrorism, particularly because they almost inevitably ensnare large numbers of innocent people. No charges or convictions for terror-related offenses are reported to have come from these actions.

The 2005 raids stand in contrast with more recent German counterterrorism raids, such as the September 5, 2007 raid that detained three persons and seized bomb-making equipment, following a six-month investigation.[417] Here, the use of a raid at the culmination of an intelligence-based investigation demonstrates a targeted and correct application of police powers. Another raid on 12 locations conducted on November 25, 2008, was based on an investigation of the Internet activities of the suspects and resulted in two arrests.[418]

German courts are also scrutinizing police actions and challenging some counter-terrorism raids. On November 22, 2007, a court in Gelsenkirchen ruled that a January 16, 2004 raid on a mosque in the town of Bochum had infringed worshippers' rights to freedom of association and religion. During the raid, police detained and interrogated 227 persons, some for over seven hours, violating the principle of proportionality required of police actions. The court also found that the police action did not adhere to judicial norms, and had not demonstrated the presence of a "concrete danger" as required by law for this type of action.[419]

Evaluating the Effectiveness of Counterterrorism Raids

If the raids described in this section were intended to apprehend terrorist suspects or to seize material evidence of terrorist activity, they did not succeed. This is hardly surprising, as raids based on ethnic profiling rarely produce positive results. On the other hand, raids based on intelligence often produce arrests and convictions on terrorism charges and seizures of evidence for trials. Police actions based on specific intelligence, such as Operation Alberich in Germany or Operation Crevice Seven in the United Kingdom (described in the next chapter),[420] often succeed. Unfortunately, many more raids have cast a wide net, targeting religious communities based on little more than generalizations. At best, such raids have produced arrests for petty offenses, immigration violations, and noncompliance with regulatory requirements.

Although raids have produced few if any measurable counterterrorism results, some officials claim they serve a broader aim. According to French officials, raids do not necessarily uncover acts of terrorism, but function instead to deter any such activity in the first place. The harm associated with these raids is recognized and accepted, as Alain Chouet, former head of France's external intelligence agency, indicated in an interview with *Le Figaro*:

> One cannot quite imagine Anglo-Saxon countries imitating our tactic of harassment, sometimes without real elements of proof. Sometimes it's a bit border-line, but it upsets the networks, prevents them from taking action.[421]

This type of claim is inherently hard to assess, as it poses the problem of how to measure something that did not happen. How can one know if in fact an act of terrorism might have been prevented by a raid on a mosque or Muslim-owned business? What is known, however, is that such raids have exacted a terrible toll on Europe's Muslims, who have been collectively branded as a threat to public safety. This has often been compounded by the high levels of publicity surrounding many raids.

Indeed, some critics and certainly many Muslims believe that—as with mass identity checks and other highly visible counterterrorism actions—political and police authorities undertake many raids primarily for their effect on public opinion. If this is the case, officials are playing on and reinforcing existing social prejudices and stereotypes. To do so is short-sighted and counter-productive, particularly when there are many alternatives to raids that do not carry the same risks of public stigmatization.

D. Arrest and Imprisonment

Important arrests of suspected terrorists have been made across Europe since 9/11[422] and the region is without doubt safer as a result. Yet there are substantial grounds for concern that vast numbers of other arrests have been based on ethnic profiling rather than reliable grounds for suspicion, and that such arrests have not contributed to greater security.

Arrests of Muslims during terror investigations, as well as extended detention during ongoing investigations, often appear to rely upon a combination of weak circumstantial evidence and suspicion based on religious practice, country of origin, or ethnicity. In effect, this form of ethnic profiling casts a *prima facie* presumption of guilt on Muslims targeted in terrorism investigations. These persons are required to prove their innocence when the case against them relies heavily not on what they did but on who they are and on generalizations about their religion.

There is cause for concern that the ethnic profiling described below is becoming more prevalent in a number of EU member states. The trend toward a decrease in some of the more overt and highly visible forms of ethnic profiling (such as mass controls outside of mosques and large-scale raids on Muslim businesses and places of worship), does not reflect a decrease in all forms of ethnic profiling. Instead, the trend reflects increased reliance on non-judicial procedures to conduct "preventive antiterrorism" measures resulting in the detention, and in some cases expulsion, of individuals. In many cases, individuals are unaware of the evidence against them and have little opportunity to challenge the reliance on stereotypes about their religious practice, ethnicity, and national origin that in effect substitute for probative evidence.

France

In recent years, particularly in the immediate aftermath of 9/11, French authorities have made extensive use of broad legal powers[423] to detain terrorist suspects based on ethnic profiling. The majority of terrorist suspects in France are arrested, detained, and sentenced based on a pre-9/11 law (known as AMT or *association de malfaiteurs en relation avec une enterprise terroriste*) that penalizes participation in a group or association formed for the purpose of preparing a terrorist act.[424] In practice, the law means individuals can be detained without proof of their involvement in the planning of a terrorist act or even a precise plan for the execution of a terrorist act.[425]

French law enforcement authorities lacking specific evidence of terrorist activity thus can fall back on their power to bring AMT charges, and data suggest they have readily done so. While the law predates 9/11,[426] its use has intensified since then. Official statistics indicate that of a total of 358 persons detained in antiterrorism operations in September 2005, for example, 300 were charged solely under the terrorist association provision of the AMT.[427]

AMT counterterrorism investigations typically begin with an extensive mapping of networks of individuals suspected on the basis of domestic or foreign intelligence information of terrorist activity. Police and intelligence officials identify a suspect's "network" based on information obtained in his or her address book and through surveillance. Anyone who has had contact with the initial suspect is a potential suspect:[428] family members, friends, colleagues, acquaintances, neighbors, those attending the same mosque, someone encountered in a bar, someone who has shaken the suspect's hand or exchanged a few words with him in the street.[429]

While law enforcement officials understandably want to interview people they believe possess information about terrorist suspects, in many cases police and investigative judges have taken law enforcement action implicating fundamental rights—including arrests and detention—on tenuous evidentiary grounds.[430] Of particular relevance to this study, many individuals targeted for law enforcement action are practicing Muslims, and the nature of their religious observance appears to play a determining role in their arrest.

Counterterrorism enforcement actions, including arrests and detention, often cast a wide net beyond the initial suspects. Evidence leading to the arrest of "related suspects" is based on associations, including praying at a mosque considered to be radical or possessing "Islamist" literature. A senior French counterterrorism official used a hypothetical example to illustrate how ethnic profiling factors into the pursuit of related suspects:

> The first [to consider] is the babysitter, the next is the baker, the next is a Muslim man —simply an ordinary religious Muslim—and the next is a Muslim who was in Afghanistan. The babysitter and baker will be easily eliminated and the Muslim that has also been to Afghanistan will be included. It is with respect to the other Muslim that things become problematic, and where a possibility of discrimination arises. The investigative judge will need to make a decision.[431]

Another high-ranking police official involved in counterterrorism described the process of selecting individuals for follow-up action among all those persons in contact with a prime suspect:

The vegetable vendor holds little interest. The chemist is more interesting; the electrician is interesting; a person who is Muslim or whose family is from Afghanistan is interesting; a person who has taken a trip to Pakistan or Syria is interesting. Imagine a ladder of "dangerousness:" people start at the bottom and then certain empirical criteria allow them to move up a rung.

In his words, criteria for suspicion might include the following:

The personal history and skills necessary to carry out a terrorist act [or] certain behaviors that differentiate a person from the rest. For example, the fact of going to the mosque every day at 5:00 p.m. This is not so common, so this behavior can differentiate a person; even within this community, everyone does not go to the mosque every day, not European Muslims. ...

Operational logic prevents us from keeping everyone under surveillance.... We look who the person knows... If they know 15 people who are good Muslims, we don't care. But if someone's sister and brother are "*Tabligh*,"[432] that is more interesting...We basically watch for criteria that differentiate a person, and these criteria include a person's skills, behavior (such as trips to certain countries or going to the mosque every day), and judicial history.[433]

While this official spoke of factors that may lead authorities to place an individual under surveillance, similar criteria have led to arrest and preventive detention, sometimes for extended periods. French defense lawyer William Bourdon described the fact pattern of an AMT case he was defending. A young Muslim man had allowed a cousin to store a bag at his house while the cousin went to Chechnya to fight. Bourdon's client was intellectually curious about armed Islam, but not a practicing Muslim. Despite the lack of any material evidence of terrorist activity, the young man was kept in provisional detention for a year before eventually being found innocent of terrorist association at trial.[434]

In another case, Q.C., a young Muslim teacher active in civil society, was surprised to find the police at his door one morning, shortly after 9/11. The counterterrorism officials who interrogated Q.C. told him that the police station of Hauts-de-Seine outside Paris had alerted them, and that they had him and three others who were arrested at the same time under surveillance.[435]

They took me to the station. On the way, when we were on the highway at a turn, they said, "You know Zorro, we can wipe you out here. We have all the rights, so if you cause us problems we'll take you down and throw you away. We have unlimited powers." When we got to the police station, they put me in the interrogation room. They took my photo and my fingerprints. They called me "Zorro." They said, "Zorro, your friends sold you, they told us everything." They asked me what I did. They brought me my old passports. They said I had been to New York. They spoke rudely. They asked questions about my life, my earnings, my rent. They said that I had been under surveillance for some time. They let me go around 6.00 p.m. the same evening.

Ultimately, Q.C. was able to find out the reasons for his arrest:

In fact, they had my cousin under surveillance. He had taken a trip to Ukraine. They had monitored him upon his return....I rarely see my cousin, but they have to find a network and a link, so they create a relationship from diverse elements that in fact are not related. There had been an armed robbery on high security vehicles. They said that this money had gone to buy arms in the Ukraine and bring them back to Paris to carry out attacks. They had no concrete elements to support this hypothesis. I think the reality is that after 9/11 they wanted to show that they were doing something; they have to carry out some arrests.[436]

French law enforcement authorities often regard religion or the nature of religious practice as a critical factor justifying arrest.[437] Jacques Debray, an experienced defense lawyer in terrorist association cases, commented:

They are asked if they are religious, how they practice their religion, how many times they pray, whether they follow Ramadan...When you see this, you wonder....There really is a stigmatization of Muslims... It is on the edge of a caricature: Muslim equals fanatic equals terrorist.[438]

Nizar Sassi was detained at the U.S. prison in Guantanamo Bay, Cuba, for two and a half years following his arrest in Afghanistan—where he had gone for his summer vacation— shortly after 9/11. French police arrested him immediately upon his release from Guantanamo and return to France. Sassi was charged with terrorist association and imprisoned for 18 months while awaiting trial. Sassi, who says that he is not at all religious, described the questions he was asked by French officials:

My departure absolutely had to have a religious connotation for them....For them, I simply had to be religious to go there [to Afghanistan]. During the investigation they asked me all sorts of questions about my religion. Everything was asked. "What stream do you belong to? What do you think about this stream, that stream?" But me, I don't have a stream, I am a Muslim by culture.[439]

Sassi was convicted on terror association (AMT) charges and sentenced to four years, but immediately released for time already served.

In another case in 2005, G.H. was arrested with her husband. She was held in police cells for the 96-hour maximum period allowed and was repeatedly interrogated, with questions focusing primarily on religion:

They asked about religion, a lot about religion. What were my impressions of certain passages in the Koran. Which verses speak about the veil? Does my god tell me to kill people? Do I agree with people who do jihad? They said that I could leave my husband, change my life. "Look how beautiful you are without your veil," they said.[440]

Religion was also the focus of the interrogations of 17 people arrested in a highly publicized raid on June 19, 2006. The raid targeted Dhaou Meskine, imam of the mosque of Clichy-sous-Bois, a well-respected figure in Muslim civil society and founder of France's first private Muslim high school. The other detainees were also connected to the school and Muslim NGOs. They all were released after four days of detention and interrogations.[441] One of the detainees described police questioning:

"Are you Muslim" they asked. The questions were about the faith of each of us. To what degree we practice the religion. They asked my wife, "Do you pray five times a day?" Questions of that sort. "What is your affinity with respect to religion?"[442]

These accounts of arrest and interrogation in France illustrate authorities' preoccupation with Islamic religion, reliance on generalizations about religious belief and use of AMT in a manner which appears to facilitate ethnic profiling.

Italy

Since 9/11, Italian police have arrested and detained and subsequently released without charge men from countries with majority Muslim populations, such as Pakistan, Afghanistan, Morocco, and Egypt, on charges of terrorist-related crimes. Authorities have often announced arrests of "terrorist suspects" with considerable fanfare, claiming that these demonstrate their success in the fight against terrorism[443]—only to release most of the suspects later for lack of evidence of criminal conduct.

During the period between 9/11 and early 2006, there were over 200 highly publicized arrests of migrants on charges of terrorism[444] but only two of these resulted in convictions for terrorism-related crimes.[445] Indeed, in the overwhelming majority of cases, those arrested on suspicion of terrorism are eventually found not to be terrorists but ordinary immigrants, and are quietly released.[446]

Italian authorities have the responsibility to control migration, including through legal detention and deportation, but this should be done on grounds of immigration law, not counterterrorism. Counterterrorism charges must be supported with probative evidence of involvement in terrorism. To imply, with no grounds for the assertion, that migrants are potential terrorists, fuels xenophobic and racist public attitudes and encourages excessive law enforcement responses.

In May 2002, Italian police arrested three Egyptian fishermen on suspicion of plotting to bomb a U.S. Army cemetery south of Rome. One of the arrests was a sensational night operation at sea using helicopters and police boats.[447] The three were charged with "subversive association aimed at international terrorism."[448] Police stated that they seized explosives and maps highlighting the cemetery in the men's apartment along with a map of Rome's Fiumicino airport and maps highlighting the location of some McDonald's restaurants. The men denied the allegations and said that they used the explosives for fishing.[449] They were detained in a maximum security jail for a year and a half before being acquitted by an Italian court.[450] According to journalist and security expert Carlo Bonini, the men were simply fishermen, and he alleges that the case against them was constructed by the Italian secret service.[451]

On August 19, 2002, four Moroccan factory workers and a retired Italian art historian were arrested in Bologna's Basilica of St. Petronius. The men, who were being watched and wiretapped, reportedly videotaped a fresco and made disparaging remarks (in Berber) about Christianity and statements to the effect that the church should be "brought down."[452] The fresco is a controversial 15th century work depicting Mohammed in hell being devoured by demons. On August 22, a judge ordered the release of all the men due to insufficient evidence.[453]

Illegal migrants trying to reach Italy by boat have been arrested and held as terrorists for extended periods in detention rather than being processed and deported as illegal migrants. In early August 2002, 15 Pakistanis traveling on false passports were arrested after the coast guard intercepted their boat off the coast of Sicily.[454] The men were first held for a month in a detention camp for illegal immigrants, before being charged with conspiracy to carry out terrorist and subversive acts and imprisoned in the city of Caltinisetta, in Sicily.[455] The chief of police of Caltanissetta told the media that the evidence indicated links to Al Qaeda.[456] Media stories also reported that key evidence included "coded notation" found on the ship. But after 10 months in jail, a magistrate ordered the men's release finding that they were simply clandestine immigrants with no links to Al Qaeda or any other terrorist organization.[457] The coded message turned out to be the name of their town of origin in Pakistan.[458]

Italian law enforcement authorities are using powers granted by antiterrorism legislation known as the Pisanu Law to preventively expel suspects.[459] Expulsion does not require a terrorism-related charge or conviction, but is permitted in cases where there are well-grounded reasons to believe that the person concerned may favor terrorist organizations and activities. Only administrative courts may hear appeals against such expulsion orders, and the lodging of an appeal does not suspend the expulsion.[460] Authorities use this procedure in cases where sufficient evidence to press criminal charges is lacking. Instead, an individual's religious practice, ethnic or national origin, and attendance at certain mosques may play an important role in assessments by officials of his support for or involvement in terrorist organizations or activities. This reliance on religion and ethnicity provides cause for concern that ethnic profiling may form the basis for many actions taken under the Pisanu Law.

United Kingdom

Muslim organizations and human rights groups have criticized the British government for the excessive use of arrest powers in a counterterrorism campaign that they argue stigmatized the entire Muslim community. From 9/11 to mid-2004, more than 600 people were arrested under antiterrorism legislation, the vast majority of them Muslims. As of August 2004, fewer than 100 of those arrested had been charged with terrorism offenses and 15 had been convicted.[461] A study of 11 of these convictions found that only 3 involved Muslims.[462] Some 200 of those arrested were charged with offenses unrelated to terrorism, while more than half were released without charge.

Based on the discrepancy between the rate of arrests and convictions under antiterrorism laws, and the discrepancy between the religious background of those arrested and those convicted, British human rights groups have raised serious concerns about excessive and discriminatory use of arrest powers against Muslims.[463] They raised additional concerns about the extensive media coverage of terrorist arrests, compared to the lack of attention when detainees are subsequently released without charge. The Islamic Human Rights Commission argued that a misleading impression was created by government figures that failed to distinguish between convictions of Muslims compared to non-Muslims, particularly those convicted for Irish terrorism.[464]

In April 2004, leaks to the media about police raids in Manchester—the leaks apparently came from senior political figures—resulted in widespread coverage of allegations that Iraqi Kurds were planning to bomb high profile targets, including the Old Trafford, the football stadium of Manchester United.[465] The Greater Manchester Police confirmed details of the leaks to reporters, and identified the 10 people detained as Iraqi Kurds. All ten detainees were later released without charge, and it emerged that they were keen Manchester United fans who kept information about the stadium among other football memorabilia in their apartments. The Greater Manchester Police later acknowledged that this had done severe damage to their relations with Kurdish and other minority communities.[466]

In May 2009, the U.K. Home Office released new figures on terrorism arrests (excluding Northern Ireland). These statistics show that from September 11, 2001 to March 31, 2008 there were 1,471 arrests for terrorism (an average of 227 a year since 2002–2003).[467] Fifty six percent (819) of those arrested were released without charge; 35 percent (521) were charged with an offense; and nine percent (131) faced alternative actions such as immigration proceedings. Of the 521 people charged, 65 percent were considered to be terror-related, though 222 were charged under terrorism legislation, while 118 faced charges under other legislation (such as conspiracy to murder).[468] These terrorism-related cases had a conviction rate of around 60 percent.[469] Both the rate of charging and of convictions has remained broadly stable over the period covered by the Home Office figures.[470] These statistics indicate a fairly targeted use of terror arrests, although the fact that one third of terrorist prisoners were on remand indicates that, in this number of cases at least, the implicated persons do not pose any immediate threat.[471]

Assessing the Effectiveness of Arrest and Imprisonment

French officials have defended the arrest and detention of innocent people as side effects of a highly effective approach, and regularly point out that despite many threats, France has not suffered a terror attack since 1996. A 2006 government white paper describes policing based on terrorist association as the cornerstone of a system that can "repress structures that support the authors of attacks or accomplices, and also prevent attacks that are in preparation."[472] According to this logic, extensive arrests for terrorist association help prevent terrorist attacks by disrupting terrorists' logistical and organizational support. This support is believed to come from family, friends, and other individuals in the community. Counterterrorism operations aim to "give a good kick to the anthill" or "dry out" the milieu in which terrorists may operate.[473] A French police officer described the reasoning:

> Above all terrorists need logistical support. Those arrested often are "good guys." For instance, someone whose sister is married to someone who is part of the Tabligh—Mustapha; if Mustapha comes to visit, he needs somewhere to stay. The goal when we want to neutralize is to create difficulties in their base of operations. We will hit the logistics. So, we will detain Mustapha and then when we release him say, "Take your suitcase and get out of here." The only goal is to get them not to seek problems with the French justice system. Ninety-seven percent of Muslims are good citizens. Perhaps he is obliged to house Mustapha, if he doesn't have good reasons to say no. But the next time Mustapha comes, he can say, "Last time I spent 6–8 hours in detention," then there will be a reason not to house him.[474]

French security authorities know that this approach results in the arrest and detention of innocent people (although they do not release any statistics), but view it as an unfortunate if inevitable consequence of preventive action.[475] This assessment fails to consider both the damage done to law enforcement relations with Muslim communities in France and the possibility of using other less intrusive measures to obtain information prior to arrest.

Arresting a person is a serious step and, in accordance with European law, it is permissible only "on reasonable suspicion of having committed an offence or when it is reasonably considered necessary to prevent his committing an offence or fleeing after having done so." (ECHR, Art. 5(1)). Many detainees are released without charge, some after only short periods of detention and interrogation. But even a short-term arrest causes enormous stress and anxiety, social embarrassment and stigma, and generates a police record. In some cases, detainees have been held in pretrial detention for as much as a year and half prior to acquittal and release. In many other cases, those detained are illegal migrants who have nothing to do with terrorism, but who are deported anyway.

Furthermore, media coverage of arrests is extensive, while releases generally warrant little attention. Too often, the publicity around arrests reinforces generalizations equating immigrants or the descendants of immigrants with potential terrorists, and frequently this appears to be a deliberate policy. In this way, public perceptions linking immigrants with terrorism are created, confirmed, or strengthened.

Given the serious harm done to those arrested and the paucity of convictions on terrorism charges, the use of arrests as an early-phase counterterrorism prevention strategy is clearly inappropriate. Arrest is a power that should be grounded in evidence. Arrests of religious or ethnic minorities for the purpose of sending a message or purportedly deterring others, and absent reasonable suspicion of involvement in crime, is improper.

However, there is some evidence that the use of arrests may be becoming more targeted and efficient over time as police and intelligence authorities in the European Union develop greater intelligence on terrorist networks. This should be accompanied by a more nuanced and cautious approach to public relations and the sharing of information with the media about arrests and releases. The more targeted use of arrests, while a welcome development, does not result from the adoption of increased accountability mechanisms or greater oversight. Thus, in the event of another serious terrorist attack, there is little guarantee that a "wide net" approach in the use of arrest powers might not be adopted again.

E.   Identifying Individuals in the Process of Radicalizing

Much of the ethnic profiling described so far in this report is based on stereotypes associated with the 9/11 attackers and those responsible for the 2004 Madrid bombings, emphasizing their status as foreign-born Muslim men. Since 2005, however, European authorities have been increasingly concerned about the phenomenon of so-called "home-grown terrorists" born in Europe. This has produced a distinctive set of ethnic profiling practices, which are the focus of this section.

In contrast to the Middle Eastern nationals who bombed the World Trade Center on 9/11 and the Moroccans who bombed Madrid's Atocha train station on March 11, 2004, the London Underground bombers of July 7, 2005 were British nationals, as were a majority of those arrested on August 9, 2006, in connection with another attempted terrorist attack in the United Kingdom. Mohammed Bouyeri, the man who murdered Dutch filmmaker Theo Van Gogh in Amsterdam on November 2, 2004 in what is perceived as the Netherlands' first jihadi terrorist attack, was a dual Dutch–Moroccan national.

Increasingly concerned about European nationals who become "radicalized," anti-terrorism officials across the EU have been keen to identify and intervene early in the process by which an individual comes to sympathize with, support, or actively engage with terrorist groups or activities. These early prevention efforts are in some circumstances driven by the theory of "radicalization."

Radicalization is now a central focus of European Union counterterrorism policy.[476] In the view of Rik Coolsaet, a Belgian member of the EU's Network of Independent Experts on Fundamental Rights, "It is nowadays a common thread within EU counterterrorism thinking and action to single out this radicalization process as the main focal point in combating terrorism."[477]

In some respects, the focus on radicalization has brought welcome attention to such root causes as discrimination and the failed integration of immigrant and minority communities into mainstream society. More problematic, however, are law enforcement efforts to identify proximate factors contributing to radicalization which have led to a form of ethnic profiling in which the nature of religious practice becomes the primary criterion in determining suspicion. Indeed, as the concept of radicalization takes hold, there is a clear risk that it will lead to increased ethnic profiling of Muslims across Europe.

While the Netherlands and Germany have led the way in articulating theories of radicalization, in November 2006 the head of the United Kingdom's MI5 intelligence service, Eliza Manningham-Buller, stated:

> We need to be alert to attempts to radicalize and indoctrinate our youth and to seek to counter it. Radicalizing elements within communities are trying to exploit grievances for terrorist purposes; it is the youth who are being actively targeted, groomed, radicalized and set on a path that frighteningly quickly could end in their involvement in mass murder of their fellow U.K. citizens, or their early death in a suicide attack or on a foreign battlefield.[478]

In a welcome note of caution, she went on to warn that a careful approach is needed based on an understanding of the "differences between non-Western and Western lifestyles" that should not confuse fundamentalism with terrorism or treat people with suspicion simply on the basis of their religion. This caution was exhibited in an internal report by MI5's behavioral science unit which, based on an analysis of hundreds of case studies, concluded that there is no single pathway to violent extremism, and that a large number of those involved in terrorism do not practice their faith regularly. In fact, the analysis is reported to state that "a well-established religious identity actually protects against violent radicalization."[479]

Fortunately, ongoing research and EU policy recommendations have focused on the need to address the root causes of violent radicalization rather than resort to ethnic profiling. An Expert Group on Violent Radicalisation has been established by the European Commission in order to provide policy advice. On May 15, 2008 this group submitted a report to the European Commission on "Radicalisation Processes Leading to Acts of Terrorism." The report makes a clear distinction between "radical" religious beliefs and a willingness to resort to violence and recommends that the European Commission's work on radicalization should limit itself to "violent radicalization" or "extremism."[480]

Theories of Radicalization and the Slippery Slope into Extremist Violence

In practice, however, radicalization theories demonstrate a dangerous tendency to conflate an individual's adoption of a conservative or "fundamentalist" practice of Islam with a willingness to resort to violence. Many radicalization theories rely on a "slippery slope" paradigm which posits a radicalization continuum along which individuals are believed to slide—gradually or rapidly—from increasing religious devotion, through conservative or "fundamentalist" streams of Islam, toward supporting terrorist activities and organizations until, in a limited number of cases, they end by directly participating in terrorist activities and organizations.[481] The implication is that all conservative Muslims are potential terrorists; this constitutes a broad generalization that stigmatizes a group of persons on the basis of their religious beliefs. When such theories are the basis for police or other law enforcement operations without reliable supporting intelligence on terrorist threats, it is ethnic profiling.

This "slippery slope" paradigm of radicalization is widespread in Europe and underpins counterterrorism practices of police and intelligence officials in many countries. A German Interior Ministry publication on "entryways into radicalization" provides the following pyramid diagram illustrating this theory:[482]

Chart 1.

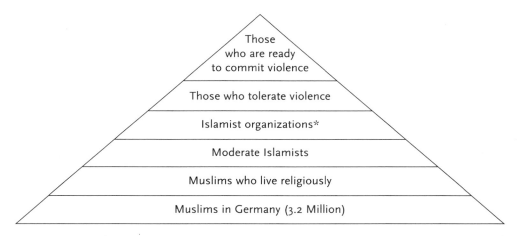

Those who are ready to commit violence

Those who tolerate violence

Islamist organizations*

Moderate Islamists

Muslims who live religiously

Muslims in Germany (3.2 Million)

* Islamist organizations have some 30,000 members

The "ring model" of the Dutch General Intelligence and Security Services (AIVD) provides a similar illustration of this paradigm. The model consists of four rings, one inside the other, representing (from the core moving out): terrorists, supporters, sympathizers, society. An AIVD official described the model:

> The innermost ring [terrorists] represents persons who are able and willing to commit attacks. The active supporters of terrorists can be put in the second ring [supporters]. These persons can and want to support terrorists, so they are aware of the connection between their activities and terrorist attacks. The third ring [sympathizers] represents the people who feel some sympathy for the cause and who are susceptible to recruitment. In general, persons in this third ring reject the Western, Dutch society. The area outside the third ring [society] encompasses the entire Muslim society. The people in this area are in no way involved in Islamist extremism, but may fall victim to its actions. In this ring model our focus should not only be on the groups to be distinguished, but also on the interaction between the rings. Centripetal movements can be designated as radicalization processes.[483]

According to this approach, observant Muslims, particularly those practicing conservative forms of Islam, are potential terrorists. Behaviors that indicate that an individual is becoming increasingly devout or adopting a more conservative form of Islam thereby become tell-tale "indicators" of radicalization. Individuals so identified may then become the focus of various antiterrorism measures.

This slippery slope paradigm is contested by experts. A French counterterrorism official with over two decades of experience recognized the differences:

> A Muslim who is not radical in his practice, but who incites to violence is dangerous, and therefore of interest to us. On the other hand, a Muslim who is radical in his faith, but who is above all very pious, is not of interest for us. ...[A]s far as Salafists, there are deeply pious Salafists who are radical but non-violent. You can compare them to Cistercian or Benedictine monks who are very pious, but not violent.[484]

Saimir Amghar, a French researcher investigating radicalization processes among Muslim youth notes that the term "radicalization" covers several different phenomena, and argues that there are really three types of radicalization: (1) nonreligious political radicalization; (2) religious radicalization involving orthodox practice of Islam but rejecting violence; and (3) political radicalization drawing from religious doctrine that manifests primarily through violent jihadism.[485] While similar factors may drive individuals toward each form of radicalization, they are distinct responses. Amghar argues that the second and third forms do not represent steps on a continuum but are in fact oppositional tendencies that are highly critical of one another. Under this view, the nonviolent forms of conservative Islam are in fact a bulwark against terrorism rather than a path toward violent jihad.

A similar perspective underlies the London Metropolitan Police Service's Muslim Contact Unit. This unit works closely with Salafist groups, based on the view that nonviolent Salafists have both the understanding and credibility to reach those most at risk of radicalization and to dissuade them from turning to violence. Under this approach, Salafist groups are treated as important allies in counterterrorism efforts, rather than targets of suspicion based on a theory that sees them as one step on the path toward violence.[486] (For more information about the work of the Muslim Contact Unit, please see the section on alternatives to ethnic profiling in the next chapter.)

The Netherlands: Operationalizing the Theory of Radicalization

The Netherlands has pioneered efforts to put into practice antiradicalization theories through a multisectoral approach that uses indicators of radicalization to identify persons who may be in the process of becoming radicalized.[487]

The development of these indicators is a component of the Netherlands' "broad-based approach" against radicalism and radicalization,[488] an approach that aims to "detect radicalization processes at an early stage and to reverse them before they lead to punishable offenses."[489] Dutch antiterrorist officials have developed a set of "indicators of radicalization" designed to help local actors, such as social workers and educators, recognize the outward signs of radicalization.[490] The objective is to enable these actors to identify persons or organizations of potential interest to the police and intelligence services.

In 2006, an official from the office of the National Coordinator on Counterterrorism, the institution responsible for developing policy and coordinating anti-terrorism measures in the Netherlands, explained their approach to profiling:

> We are also working on some initiatives in Amsterdam and Rotterdam to develop indicators—some kind of criteria of what to look for—that can also be used by people that are not specialists in using profiles in a critical way so that they can understand what kind of behavior should or would be potentially of our interest...We are refining them and refining them—trying to put in an administrative system.[491]

The city of Rotterdam took the lead with a program called "Join in or get left behind," initiated in February 2005. According to this program, indicators of radicalization include particular behavior patterns, such as frequent travel or hosting gatherings at one's home, and changes in behavior, such as a man of Arabic origin who suddenly acquires more traditionally religious Muslim approaches to hair style, dress, mosque attendance, or physical contact with women in public. Dutch officials have taken pains to avoid the inclusion of ethnicity or nationality as suspicious criteria, but the indicators developed nonetheless draw attention to individuals who are becoming more orthodox in their practice of Islam. Essentially, a Muslim who shows outward signs of more conservative practice would become suspicious. Likewise a non-Muslim who outwardly shows signs of Muslim practice, indicating that he is a convert, would also become suspicious.

Those trained to watch for these indicators are reportedly told to watch not just for one change in behavior, but several. When they believe someone is radicalizing, they are asked to report the individual to the information "switch-point,"[492] which verifies the situation and determines the most appropriate follow-up action. According to an evaluation report by the information switch-point, the Rotterdam program alerted police to 17 cases during 2005.[493] Although the numbers to date appear relatively few and the consequences of identification benign, the indicators of radicalization clearly target Muslims and are likely to stigmatize a far larger number of Muslims than those actually identified as at risk of radicalization.

The indicators of radicalization used in the Netherlands continue to conflate orthodox religious practice with a tendency to use violence.[494] A government guide for companies on detecting radicalization among their employees gives this advice:

> In determining whether there are radicalized personnel in your employment, a combination of factors must be taken into consideration. The following list provides a number of indicators which might signal the presence of radicalized personnel:

- Possession of extremist literature, pamphlets, or sound and data recording equipment, or the perusal of extremist literature by means of the internet. This can be difficult for companies to assess, as such activities are often carried out in another language, such as Arabic.

- Seeming approval of terrorist attacks.

- Travel to regions or countries in which a terrorist conflict is taking place or in which there are terrorist training camps, such as Chechnya, Kashmir, Iraq, and Pakistan.

- A sudden aversion to "Western customs" such as mixed activities (male/female), or drinking alcohol, and requesting specific Islamic meals.

- Wearing specific clothing and symbols, or a sudden change of clothing style.[495]

On a more positive note, some Dutch authorities are also distinguishing between "extremism" involving support for violence and orthodox religious practice.[496] The Amsterdam "switch-point on radicalization" has moved away from indicators focused on orthodox religious practice, and emphasizes the need to separate religious practice from political views—particularly whether an individual supports the use of violence.[497] Rotterdam is also moving away from the use of indicators of radicalization, although it remains in a process of flux. Across the Netherlands, there is a shift away from an approach that stigmatizes individuals and groups, and toward policies that address root causes of radicalization, such as discrimination, exclusion, and social polarization.[498]

The Effect and Effectiveness of Profiling People in the Process of Radicalization

Notable in discussions of radicalization is the absence of any consideration that counterterrorism strategies and operational tactics may themselves contribute to the exclusion experienced by Europe's Muslim communities and validate their grievances. Even as the U.K. government undertook a series of consultations with British Muslims, analysts following the process noted the unacknowledged consequences of counterterrorism strategies:

> It is however astonishing that neither the government, not the [Intelligence and Security Committee], acknowledged the potentially damaging effect that counterterrorism measures themselves can have in contributing to "radicalization" or in inhibiting community cooperation in identifying suspects.[499]

Terrorism scholars note that "one major component of the radical subjectivity was the feeling of humiliation,"[500] and that "joining a terrorist group ultimately revolves around a desire for revenge and that this, and the willingness to seek it in violent ways, are tied to feelings of self-worth—shame, humiliation, loss of face—retribution and deterrence."[501] While experts discuss the impact of foreign policy and the war in Iraq on radicalizing youth, they fail to examine the negative effects of aggressive law enforcement tactics on Muslim communities, even though these tactics could be changed relatively easily.

It is clear that antiterrorism measures that stigmatize Muslims may themselves be an important factor in pushing some individuals toward involvement in terrorist activities. Commenting on the German pyramid of radicalization, the International Crisis Group noted the following:

> [I]t is more accurate to visualize three independent categories: Islamists, those who tolerate violence, and those ready to commit violence. It is possible to jump from one category to the next but this requires an external shock of some kind. There is a real danger that state over-reaction could offer one such jolt.[502]

Past experience also provides a salutary warning. Paddy Hillyard, an expert on British counterterrorism operations in Northern Ireland, documented the Irish experience of being targeted under the Prevention of Terrorism Act.[503] Hillyard's extensive study examined the personal experiences of those targeted by police for stops and searches, preventive imprisonment, and other harsh tactics allowed under the act. Hillyard found that the Prevention of Terrorism Act "led to hundreds of young men ... joining the IRA and creating one of the most efficient insurgency forces in the world.[504]

F. Monitoring Mosques, Muslim Organizations, and Their Members

Monitoring and surveillance are basic tools of counterterrorism intelligence gathering. A number of covert monitoring and surveillance techniques exist, ranging from the use of informers to wiretaps and other forms of sophisticated electronic surveillance. As discussed in Chapter V, it is also possible to obtain extensive intelligence through overt means that are less adversarial and intrusive, such as contacts with community members—what is sometimes termed "community intelligence." Indeed, most intelligence is gathered this way, according to counterterrorism and law enforcement officials in several countries.

The monitoring of mosques and Muslim organizations does not necessarily constitute discriminatory ethnic profiling. When monitoring is based on specific intelligence about support for terrorism, it is entirely warranted, as was demonstrably the case in the raids on London's Finsbury Park Mosque.[505] However, in some cases, surveillance is based on the belief that certain religious views—sometimes termed "fundamentalist" or "Salafist"— pose a threat to Western democracy, and, in other cases, it reflects a theory of radicalization that views fundamentalist religious practice as the first step on a slippery slope leading to direct support for or even engagement in acts of terrorism.

When police monitor a mosque simply because it is Salafist or practices another controversial stream of Islam, rather than based on evidence of involvement in terrorism, they are engaging in ethnic profiling. While there are some Salafist leaders and mosques that advocate violence, it is a gross generalization to place all Salafist Muslims in this category, as most have no connection to terrorist organizations and activities. Indeed, some law enforcement officers (admittedly a minority) argue that effective counterterrorism requires engagement with Salafist leaders on the grounds that they are best positioned to dissuade disaffected young people from turning to violence.

Research in France, Germany, Italy, and the Netherlands indicates that law enforcement authorities in those countries rely heavily on surveillance to prevent terrorism. In some cases, specific intelligence or evidence leads officials to place a particular mosque under surveillance. But in other cases, mosques and Muslim organizations are considered suspicious and placed under surveillance due to their affiliation with certain streams of Islam rather than on the basis of specific information about support for illegal and violent activities. This has generated a widespread anxiety in the Muslim community and contributed to the perception among some Muslims, particularly observant Muslims, that they are under constant surveillance. Many Muslims are convinced that their privacy is threatened by the surveillance and, as a result, that their freedom to practice their religion is being constrained.

For two reasons, it is often difficult to determine whether particular surveillance operations are intelligence-based or involve ethnic profiling. First, surveillance practices are generally covert and information about their genesis is hard to obtain. Second, a decision to conduct surveillance may be based on both evidence and stereotyping, in which case scrutiny of the probative evidence would be needed to assure that a religious stereotype was not the determining factor. Agencies conducting surveillance need both an internal review mechanism and external oversight to prevent the use of ethnic profiling.

The difficulty in obtaining solid information on the reasons for surveillance makes it nearly impossible for civilians to draw firm conclusions on the validity of specific surveillance. But the information that does exist raises concerns about whether some countries are crossing the line in their surveillance activities, from intelligence-based monitoring into discriminatory ethnic profiling.

Germany

German authorities increased their surveillance of specific religious groups following 9/11. The German Office of the Protection of the Constitution (BfV) monitors numerous mosques and conservative Muslim organizations that it considers to be extremist and to pose a potential threat. The selection of groups for monitoring is based on the belief that certain streams of Islam present a threat to the state even when they do not advocate violence.[506]

The exact number of mosques that are monitored by the BfV is unclear. Wolfgang Wieland, a member of Germany's parliament and its national security committee, said in an interview:

> [B]efore 9/11 the Islamic community was under low surveillance pressure. This has changed completely. Today there are a lot of informants. The intelligence services either ask people who go to mosques regularly or send their own agents into mosques ... Now we have mosques, scientologists, and Islamic groups surveilled. These are the only religious groups which are monitored by the intelligence services in Germany.[507]

In July 2005, shortly after the London underground bombings, Bavaria's Interior Minister Gunther Beckstein told the newspaper *Berliner Zeitung*: "We have to know what's going on in each and every mosque. [...] We have to have an intelligence presence in places where extremist ideas are being preached."[508] Federal Interior Minister Otto Schilly echoed these remarks when he announced, on July 18, 2005, that the government was considering putting all mosques under scrutiny through closed-circuit cameras.[509] Muslim organizations, as well as a number of political parties, were very critical of these statements.

It is not clear that German authorities are in fact undertaking mosque surveillance as broadly as suggested by these remarks. A 2003 article in *der Spiegel* magazine reported that the BfV had screened all of the country's estimated 2,500 mosques. Thirty-nine of those mosques were reportedly viewed as "critical" and placed under surveillance, although only 15 of the 39 were considered "dangerous," a term used by the BfV to indicate that the mosques were used as sites for actively recruiting or radicalizing individuals for further indoctrination into violence.[510] In a July 2007 interview, representatives from the BfV and German Ministry of Interior denied the accuracy of these figures, but refused—on grounds of secrecy—to provide alternative data.

Available evidence indicates that any widespread screening of mosques was conducted largely through human sources, including discussions with contacts in the mosques and informants. This is appropriate when based on open source information or information freely volunteered as a result of outreach and building relations between Muslim religious leaders and law enforcement. More intrusive covert techniques, such as technological surveillance (including the use of hidden microphones and cameras) inside mosques, are primarily directed at a small number of mosques qualified as "critical."[511] This is a correct response if covert surveillance reflects reliable and concrete information about illegal activities in those mosques.

Muslim organizations are particularly concerned with the BfV's collection of information on individuals who attend mosques. A Berlin mosque official said, "The Office for the Protection of the Constitution has names and photos of any person going regularly to mosque."[512] The official said that he discovered he had been photographed when a police officer he knows commented on how photogenic he is. Others have discovered that they were under surveillance when applying for nationalization, as Burhan Kesici, vice president of the Islamic Federation of Berlin, explained:

> When individuals apply for German nationality, they discover that the authorities already know that they go to mosque and which mosque they go to. Authorities also know that they belong to this and this organization... for this reason many young people stopped going to mosques.[513]

The BfV has cast a particularly wide net of surveillance over Muslim organizations. The BfV makes a distinction between Islam and Islamism: "Islam" is simply a religion, while "Islamism" is categorized as a "politically extremist ideological movement" that is considered a national security threat.[514] The BfV further divides "Islamist" organizations into three subcategories. Subcategory A refers "to Islamist groups which conduct a pan-Islamist jihad (holy war) and threaten worldwide stability through terrorist acts."[515] Subcategory B is "Islamist organizations which want to change the state and society in their countries of origin by violent means [by terrorist acts or by guerrilla-warfare]. Members of these organizations have come to Germany mostly as political refugees and support armed actions in regions of crisis."[516] Organizations falling into subcategory B include Hamas, Hezbollah, and GIA,[517] among others. Subcategory C is the broadest and includes organizations "which fight for Islamist positions in the context of the social life of the Federal Republic or at least try to establish spaces for organized Islamist engagement."[518] Among these are the Islamic Community Milli Görüs (IGMG)[519] and the Muslim Brotherhood. Groups in subcategory C are said to be loyal to the German Constitution and explicitly refrain from violence as a means of political action, but create an "Islamist milieux" which poses a danger of continuing radicalization.[520]

Organizations falling under any one of the subcategories can suffer severe consequences, including denial of public funding for the organization, denial of citizenship to its members who are not yet German citizens, and even stripping German citizenship from members who already are.

Since 9/11, immigrants who otherwise met every requirement for becoming naturalized German citizens have been turned down because they belonged to an organization that is classified as working against the German Constitution. Naturalization applicants from majority Muslim countries undergo a security check against BfV files and, if they are listed as belonging to an Islamist organization, they are denied citizenship.[521]

Kenan Kolat of the Turkischer Bund (an organization representing Turks in Germany) explained that people are obliged to agree to these checks:

> Suppose I want to be a German citizen. I get a lot of paperwork and on one form there is a question: "Do you authorize us to check with the Verfassungsschutz for your personal information?" They already make an X on the box indicating "Yes, I do agree." You have no option. You cannot say, "No, I do not want this." If you say no, then they will say you cannot become a German citizen.[522]

Deutsche Welle reported a case in which a German court stripped three men of their German nationality because they had not disclosed their membership in Milli Görüs. The officials told the publication:

> The men should never have been granted German citizenship because Milli Görüs is hostile to democratic principles. Naturalization is only available to those who [...] offer allegiance to the German Constitution.[523]

The German Aliens Law permits the expulsion of persons considered a threat to the Federal Republic of Germany,[524] and German scholars have documented multiple cases of permanent residents who are members of Milli Görüs being expelled.[525] Amendments to the German Aliens Law following the 2004 Madrid bombings now allow such expulsions to be processed through an administrative procedure at state or national level, using the same fact basis.[526]

Subcategory C organizations listed as under surveillance in the BfV annual report suffer considerable public stigmatization as "anti-constitutional" and few political actors or other organizations are willing to take part in their activities, even though this subcategory is acknowledged as non-violent and not presenting a threat to the state.[527]

Most of the groups under the BfV's surveillance fall into subcategory C.[528] In such cases, surveillance is not strictly linked to counterterrorism efforts. Rather, the BfV views surveillance as a necessary response to the long-term challenges that subcategory C groups pose "to the free democratic social order."[529] With some 26,500 members in Germany, Milli Görüs is the largest of the groups in subcategory C and has been under BfV surveillance for many years. Surveillance increased significantly after 9/11, as did the negative repercussions of such surveillance for affected organizations and their members.[530]

In addition to monitoring organizations, the BfV collects extensive information on individual members of organizations. The BfV gathers this information from written sources, informants, discussions with organizations' officials and members, and in some number of cases—the exact number of which is unknown—from infiltration and technological surveillance.[531] Evidence indicates that personal data is kept on file and made available by the BfV to other German authorities for security checks and in naturalization proceedings. According to a representative of Milli Görüs:

> Personal data about thousands of Muslims is collected. I can tell you about one case of a man who worked at the airport in Munich since about 1995. This man was once a member of a Milli Görüs organization. Every few years he has to go through some kind of security check. After 9/11 there was a security check on him again. He was told that he was a danger to the security of the airport because he was a member of Milli Görüs between 1996 and 1998.[532]

Muslims in Germany continue to be deeply concerned about surveillance of places of worship and Muslim organizations. Mosque representatives are particularly concerned that surveillance of places of worship is making individuals afraid to attend the mosque. Leaders of the Muslim community say that in addition to being denied citizenship, individuals who participate in organizations classified as Islamist by the BfV are denied employment at places considered to be sensitive, such as airports or information technology firms, on these grounds.[533]

Tânia Puschnerat, head of the Islamism and Islamist Terrorism Unit of the BfV, disputes the suggestion that monitoring of subcategory C Islamist groups involves stereotypes and ethnic profiling. She highlighted the legal basis for the BfV's work, which requires "hard evidence of efforts... directed against the free democratic basic order, the existence or the security of the Federation or one of its states or aimed at unlawfully hampering constitutional bodies of the Federation or one of its states or their members in the performance of their duties."[534] She further justified the monitoring as follows:

> Practice of religion is not interesting for us. Extremist or radical efforts are, political activities and behavior are ... Subcategory C organizations are not violence prone, they do not preach hatred and violence, but all efforts have one simple and clear direction: to prepare areas of Islamic law within German society. Milli Görüs is a constant subject of discussion; but it is definitely within the mandate of the BfV, by law.[535]

Many Muslim organizations and scholars of Islam are highly critical of the distinction between Islam and Islamist organizations, particularly applying the "Islamist" label to organizations that do not advocate violence.[536] Werner Schiffauer explained the problem:

> The distinction between real Islam ("religion") and Islamism ("ideology") is drawn primarily by German politics and the German *Verfassungsschutz* [BfV]. Muslim authorities are hardly referred to when making this distinction. In fact, only Muslims supporting this distinction are accepted as partners in the debate. *Ulema* (Muslim scholars) questioning it would immediately and by this very act qualify themselves as Islamists and be deemed partisan. The self-confidence with which German politicians and intellectuals judge what is or is not Islamic is one of the debate's most striking features.[537]

Along similar lines, a 2007 International Crisis Group report on Germany noted a related problem:

> [T]he semi-annual Verfassungsschutz [BfV] reports and lawsuits against IGMG preachers and officials have sometimes included basic translation errors, defamatory material or unfair innuendo and accusations. They may also read too much into IGMG publications and selective snippets of public statements.[538]

Netherlands

According to some representatives of Dutch Muslims, Dutch intelligence services have used religion as a basis for monitoring, focusing their attention on Muslim organizations. Thus, it is alleged, monitoring has sometimes been conducted based on generalizations about the type of Islam that groups practice rather than specific information about activities in a particular mosque or organization. Such monitoring, some Muslims complain, has targeted even nonviolent streams of Islam, on the theory that they may be hotbeds of terrorist radicalization. Dutch authorities assert that surveillance has become narrowly targeted. There is wide gap between the perceptions of Dutch Muslims and Dutch law enforcement authorities of the scope and impact of surveillance practices.

Dutch Muslim organizations believe that Dutch intelligence services monitor many of the country's mosques.[539] Dutch intelligence services have argued in public reports that Salafist and other extreme streams of Islam are very active and in some cases are trying to influence or even take over less extreme mosques in the Netherlands.[540] A 2005 Dutch General Intelligence Service (AIVD) report on the links among Saudi Arabia, Salafism, radicalization processes, and terrorism in the Netherlands, was based on information gathered from monitoring mosques considered radical.[541]

In a 2007 interview, Dutch counterterrorism authorities stated that very few mosques are under surveillance as "hotbeds of radicalization." One official explained it this way:

We are not condemning the general thinking of a group... [T]his concerns less than one percent of mosques. It is really a very small number. And all of the mosques surveilled have Hofstadt group connections [and] imams who use violent rhetoric..."[542]

In a June 2007 presentation, Deputy National Coordinator for Counterterrorism Lidewijde Ongering testified before a U.S. Senate committee:

> A small number of locations in the Netherlands, such as a few Salafist centers and mosques, have been identified as potential gateways to radical milieus....Experience has shown that for some young people, non-violent Salafism is a first step towards further radicalization. The Dutch authorities keep a close watch on the imams and governing bodies of these institutions and remind them of their social responsibilities. Our message is clear: we will not allow them to cross the line and publicly preach intolerance. We also expect them to exclude jihadist recruiters and stop young people from opting for violence. If people in or around these centers prove to be promoting radicalization or spreading hatred, we do not hesitate to prosecute them or deport them as a threat to national security.[543]

Surveillance is largely conducted through direct contact with mosque authorities and individuals who attend mosques, and through established informants. However, in an unknown number of cases, intelligence services also tape record sermons, especially Friday prayers. A Muslim community leader from Rotterdam, Brahim Bursic, called attention to the taping:

> We know that all Friday prayers in mosques are taped. I told the imams not to be afraid; we are a democracy and they are not doing anything against the law. I also publicly suggested that if the intelligence officials are interested in what is being said in the mosques, the Friday prayers could be broadcast on TV.[544]

A senior Dutch police officer said that such recording only occurs in "very limited, specific cases."[545]

In addition to mosques, Dutch intelligence officials monitor Muslim organizations they believe to be spreading or supporting radical Islam. In a 2004 report, the AIVD defined "radical Islam" as "the politico-religious pursuit of establishing—if necessary by extreme means—a society which reflects the perceived values from the original sources of Islam as purely as possible."[546] The report commented on the different views within "radical Islam":

> Radical Islam consists of many movements and groups that, although related (in particular concerning faith and anti-Western sentiments), may harbor very different views on aims and means. This means that various kinds of threats can emanate from radical Islam, one of

which is terrorism. In addition to radical Islamic organizations and networks which concentrate on the jihad (in the sense of armed combat) against the West, there are other groups, which principally focus on "*Dawa*" (the propagation of the radical-Islamic ideology), while some groups and networks combine both.[547]

Both organizations classified as "jihad-focused" and those classified as "Dawa-focused" fall within what Dutch intelligence sources described as the AIVD's "professional interest,"[548] and some are kept under surveillance. While the AIVD recognizes that only "jihad-focused" groups pose an immediate threat of violence, it believes that the "Dawa-focused" groups pose a longer-term threat by feeding processes of radicalization.[549]

The AIVD's 2006 guide for local authorities explains the Dutch approach of targeting "hotbeds of radicalization":

> A hotbed of radicalism is an organization, group or place that serves as a breeding ground for activities and views that are instrumental in radicalizing individuals and can ultimately result in terrorist activities. ...
>
> Hotbeds of radicalism can also serve as an ideological breeding ground for extremists. They can function as a first step on a path that may lead to violence. This danger exists in particular in the case of organizations that advocate extreme, intolerant isolationism or promote an intolerant "us vs. them" mentality. ...
>
> The aim of the approach is to make clear through joint, coordinated government action to those in charge of the hotbed of radicalism and to its visitors that activities of a radical nature will not be tolerated and that the authorities are monitoring activities closely.[550]

It is not clear how often monitoring by intelligence services is founded on intelligence-based evidence and how often generalizations about ethnicity or religion are the determining factor. Nor is it clear how often more intrusive monitoring techniques are utilized. Certain Muslim places of worship and organizations are clearly viewed as suspicious, even without specific evidence indicating involvement in any terrorist activities or incitement to violence.[551] They are instead held to be potentially dangerous due to generalizations about the stream of Islam that they practice, albeit peacefully, and the theory that such practices represent a first step in the process of radicalization.[552] In the absence of information about support for terrorism, covert surveillance is inappropriate and law enforcement efforts should instead focus on outreach to Muslim communities and voluntary information sharing.

There is a wide gap between the way Dutch intelligence officials describe their monitoring and the way it is perceived by Muslim organizations and individuals. Dutch authorities claim their practices have become more narrowly targeted over time, but this cannot be independently verified. To this day, many Dutch Muslims believe that discriminatory and profiling-based surveillance is widespread and this perception, accurate or not, has negative consequences for policing in the Netherlands.

Italy

Since 9/11, the monitoring of Muslims in Italy has increased as the fight against terrorism moved to the top of the country's security agenda.[553] Interviews with Italian security experts indicate that Italy's security services keep many mosques under close surveillance. The use of intrusive methods such as wiretapping and infiltrating mosques and placing cameras outside mosques is reported to be widespread.

Members of immigrant associations of all sorts, including social, cultural, and athletic organizations, believe they and their members are monitored and placed under surveillance. S.M. Arshad, president of an umbrella organization representing 33 Pakistani community associations, commented on the monitoring:

> All 33 associations are monitored. The main people in them have their phones tapped and are watched physically by the intelligence services. For a period, I saw someone watching me every day—where I am going, what I am doing. Then when they saw that I have no suspicious activities, they stopped.[554]

Both Italian experts on security matters[555] and representatives of the Muslim community in Italy believe the surveillance of mosques, Muslim associations, and Muslim-owned businesses is common. These perceptions are supported by recent arrests of suspected terrorists in which the evidence relied heavily on extensive and lengthy surveillance, particularly wiretapping and monitoring mosque attendance.

In addition to its use as a basis for arrests, information gained from surveillance is reportedly used in residency and citizenship procedures. A security expert stated that reliable sources in the security services have confirmed that information about a particular individual's membership in certain mosques or Muslim organizations is used in assessing his or her immigration application.[556] However, Justice Initiative researchers were unable to confirm this practice.

France

The French Central Directorate of General Information (*Direction Centrales des Renseignements Généraux,* or RG) has long monitored Muslim associations.[557] Reflecting France's troubled history with its former North African colonies, the RG has an extensive and long-standing network that tracks activities in the country's mosques and Muslim communities.[558] Intrusive covert surveillance is generally initiated only on the basis of specific evidence indicating potentially dangerous situations—which falls well within the parameters of appropriate intelligence-based law enforcement. For example, in the case of a mosque this specific information could involve recruitment into groups supporting violence. More recently, however, some surveillance appears to have crossed the boundary into ethnic profiling, reflecting police risk assessments that conflate conservative Muslim religious practices with terrorism.

In July 2005, Central Director of the RG Pascal Mailhos told the media that 1,600 mosques were being observed, of which 80 were considered to be "sensitive," and that 40 mosques were "under constant pressure from radical Islamic structures," of which 20 were in the hands of radicals.[559] Four months later, in November 2005, Mailhos gave *Le Monde* different, though similar, numbers:

> It is a fact that there are fewer radical sermons. But surveillance of certain places is essential, less because of what is said than because of the meetings that are taking place in those locations. Of 1,700 places of worship listed a year ago, 75 were targets of takeover attempts. Half of them resisted, the other half were taken over by radicals. Since October 2003, 31 radical activists or preachers have been expelled. Some 10 imams remain under close watch.[560]

The RG monitors individuals as well as institutions and groups. Yamin Makri, who has worked with Muslim nongovernmental organizations for over 20 years, says that: "Anyone who is active in an association is in the RG files—that is, an association deemed to be "communitarian," for example, an Arab, Muslim, or Koranic association."[561]

Salafist Muslims are also singled out for surveillance, whether they are active in associations or not. In December 2005, French Senator Jean-Patrick Courtois informed the French Senate about the Salafists under surveillance:

> [T]he intelligence services have enumerated approximately 5,000 militant Salafists. Of these, 500 persons are considered to be dangerous. The fundamentalist ideology or Salafist ideology is the only strong link that unites the different terrorist groups more or less collected under the Al-Qaeda banner.[562]

As long as surveillance targets only those 500 considered dangerous for reasons other than their religious belief, and is based on reliable intelligence, this targeted monitoring also would not constitute ethnic profiling.

Despite France's already impressive domestic intelligence capacity, in January 2005 then French Minister of the Interior Dominique de Villepin announced the creation of new "regional centers to combat radical Islam," headed by the RG. As their name implies, the regional centers specifically and publicly single out Muslims for additional surveillance, in theory targeting "radical" individuals in the community. In reality, their work appears to view most practicing Muslims as suspicious and potentially dangerous. According to Christophe Chaboud, the head of France's antiterrorist coordination unit (UCLAT), the regional centers "are charged with supervising any places in which proselytizing can occur, such as Salafist prayer rooms, businesses, university courses of particular interest to these cells (for example computer science and chemistry), and sensitive businesses."[563] In a presentation to the senate during discussions of draft legislation related to the fight against terrorism, Senator Jean-Patrick Courtois similarly noted that "these regional centers are charged with monitoring certain prayer rooms and all other places where fundamentalist or Salafist proselytizing is likely to occur."[564] This remained the case at the end of 2008.

Surveillance of Muslims and Muslim organizations in France has increased since the creation of the "regional centers to combat radical Islam," which explicitly target persons and places based on religious criteria. To the extent the surveillance is based on nothing more concrete than generalizations about Islam and its practitioners, it is ethnic profiling.

Evaluating the Effectiveness of Surveillance

It is difficult to assess the effectiveness of surveillance, much of which is done covertly. Occasionally, evidence presented at a trial clearly demonstrates the value of surveillance. But this is of little use in assessing the vast majority of surveillance activities that never come to light in a courtroom. It is difficult to know how far surveillance extends, how often covert methods are applied, who is targeted and on what basis.

It is clear that, at times, suspicion is cast on selected Muslim places of worship and organizations, even without evidence of involvement in terrorist activities or incitement to violence. In many European countries, law enforcement authorities view certain types of Islam as inherently suspect. It is also clear that there is a considerable difference between Muslims' perception of the extent and basis of monitoring by intelligence services and the accounts given by intelligence officials. Whatever the reality of current surveillance practices, it is important to remember that perceptions—including inaccurate perceptions—have real effects on behavior. People who feel they are being unfairly singled out for law enforcement attention are less likely to cooperate with police.

While covert intelligence gathering is never a transparent activity, these dynamics call for increased efforts to construct dialogue with Muslim communities, to build trust and allay fears. It is critically important for EU member states to have effective democratic oversight of intelligence activities, and to ensure said oversight is not constrained or eroded in the face of political pressure that demands an aggressive stance against terrorism. Both parliamentary committees that overseee intelligence agencies and judicial oversight authorities should include explicit consideration of non-discrimination standards and assess whether measures taken and tactics used comply with the principle of proportionality. While the secret nature of intelligence gathering often precludes in-depth oversight of ongoing activities, reviews of operations following their conclusion should examine the impact these actions have on the target communities.

G. Negative Consequences of Ethnic Profiling in Counterterrorism

The use of ethnic profiling in the fight against terrorism both stems from and reinforces stereotypes that associate Muslims, foreigners, illegal immigrants, extremism, and terrorism as points along a "continuum of insecurity."[565] Ethnic profiling feeds the logic underlying public discrimination against Muslims, and impedes efforts to integrate immigrant and minority populations and address racism and xenophobia. Worse, ethnic profiling stigmatizes entire communities and makes them less likely to cooperate with police. In addition, ethnic profiling has several immediate effects on those subjected to it, ranging from deprivation of liberty and invasion of privacy to less visible but equally insidious and widespread effects such as increased fear and marginalization. Finally, as this chapter discusses, there is little evidence that ethnic profiling has in fact increased law enforcement effectiveness in combating terrorist violence.

Ethnic profiling exacts a high toll on the individuals, groups, and communities that are singled out for differential treatment. It also imposes broader social costs, aggravating tensions between different groups, legitimizing discrimination and racism, and impinging on human rights. By subjecting its targets to unjustified stops, searches, and, in some cases, intimidation and prolonged periods of detention, ethnic profiling may, in extreme cases, foster the very bitterness that may lead people to resort to violence.

Large numbers of people are directly and indirectly affected by ethnic profiling, and victims are often deeply humiliated. Moroccan immigrants in Spain report being called "*moro de mierda*" ("Arab shit") by police during identity checks, and having their trousers pulled down in public while being searched.[566] In Germany, a Muslim leader observed, "It is humiliating to have policemen with machine guns checking identification in a prayer space; even [checking] 10-year-olds. Is that the sort of image that is supposed to make children feel at home here?"[567]

Equally damaging is the sense of fear that ethnic profiling has instilled in Muslim communities. Many practicing Muslims believe that they are already subject to surveillance measures, such as wiretapping, and that they could at any time find themselves targeted for more drastic measures, such as raids, arrest, detention, and deportation. This fear was clearly evident in interviews conducted for this report with members of Muslim organizations and mosque authorities. Many individuals were very guarded about what they said on the telephone, and unwilling to be quoted for fear of repercussions.[568] In Italy, where few immigrants are Italian citizens, many members of Muslim organizations were afraid to speak at all.

Fear leads many Muslims to avoid political activities.[569] For instance, a leader of Italy's Pakistani community, S. M. Arshad, said that after the 7/7 London bombings, many in his community were afraid to attend a demonstration against terrorism and in support of the victims of the London bombings. "They were afraid that they would be photographed, that the police are watching. They are terrorized."[570] Fear has also had a chilling effect on religious observance, leading some Muslims to hide their practice of Islam and avoid mosques. A nonpracticing Muslim from Lyon, France, said, "Due to widespread suspicion, I have many friends who have shaved their beards and now pray in secret."[571] This fear is increasing the isolation of Muslims within society, and damaging interethnic relations and social cohesion.

One of the most serious effects of ethnic profiling is its contribution to stigmatizing members of targeted ethnic, religious, or national groups. When the authorities single out members of certain groups for monitoring and surveillance, and particularly when these actions are given extensive media coverage, the message is sent that the entire ethnic or religious group presents a danger to society. Negative stereotypes are fostered and reinforced, exacerbating existing social and political tendencies toward racism and xenophobia.

This issue has been extensively documented in Italy.[572] Public opinion views Muslims as "alien" to Italian society and as "potential terrorists" who undermine the security of the country.[573] A 2003 survey found that 47 percent of Italians think all Muslims are "religious fundamentalists," and 33 percent are convinced Muslims are "invading the country."[574] These intolerant attitudes appear frequently in public debate on immigration and Muslims,[575] and are often articulated by political leaders. The Northern League, a partner in Prime Minister Silvio Berlusconi's governing coalition, has used hateful language toward Muslims, encouraging intolerance.[576] In the aftermath of 9/11, Northern League leader Umberto Bossi supported a proposal to stop issuing visas to Muslim immigrants for security reasons.[577]

Most government authorities across Europe have taken pains to issue public statements emphasizing that all Muslims are *not* terrorists, and that those Muslims who support terrorism are a tiny and unrepresentative minority. But this message is directly undermined when police and intelligence officials engage in ethnic profiling that visibly singles out Muslims for extra attention and differential treatment.

When individuals are stopped on the street for identity checks, when police surround a mosque, when a business is raided or an individual arrested, the general public naturally assumes that law enforcement officials are acting because there is a reason to do so—that these persons present a real threat. The lack of any significant counterterrorism outcomes—such as detection, charges, or convictions—as a result of ethnic profiling does not serve to mitigate the damage done; the bare fact of being singled out in the context of counterterrorism measures is sufficient to create the stigma. A representative of the Dutch Association of Moroccans and Tunisians described the change in perception:

Everyone thinks that when there is smoke, there is fire. Since 9/11 and the murder of Theo van Gogh, relations between Moroccans and the broader society have deteriorated. People look at each other with suspicion. When a Moroccan man walks in the street with a beard people look at him differently than before. When the police react in that way, it creates a bigger problem. It affects people's perceptions. For instance, when a train was stopped recently and two men in Arabic dress were handcuffed and taken off the train by police, this image has a strong effect on those watching. And it makes big news in the media. Afterwards when it turns out that these men were not planning anything at all, they were just practicing Muslims, but it's too late, the damage has been done.[578]

A German academic who has researched counterterrorism raids in Germany concurred:

Many raids take place in small towns where the mosque community tried to give a representation of themselves as part of the community. They have worked hard on building relations with the community. Then the police arrive in a very visible manner and check the identity documents of individuals outside the mosque. This creates fear; the public thinks if there is a problem with these mosques, that there must be a reason. There must be something going on.[579]

For some Muslims, these practices would be more acceptable if they did in fact produce clear counterterrorism outcomes. Referring to raids and mass identity checks, a Muslim leader from Hamburg said, "We could tolerate such measures if they were actually successful."[580]

The public and sensational manner in which law enforcement officials carry out many antiterrorism operations generates profound public stigma. Whatever the effect of these operations in preventing further terrorist attacks, their impact on public perceptions is considerable. The U.K. Institute of Race Relations has raised these concerns:

[T]here is often extensive media attention when police raids result in arrests under antiterrorism laws, while there is typically only minimal coverage when those arrested subsequently are released. As a result, the public is left with the impression that the British criminal justice system is successfully prosecuting Muslim terrorists, although in reality most of those Muslims who are arrested on terrorism allegations are never charged with any terrorism offense.[581]

It appears that some operations are designed to send a message to the public that the state is doing its utmost to protect the innocent majority from the threat posed by Muslim terrorists. For example, shortly after the July 2005 London bombings, Italian authorities raided thousands of Muslim businesses and issued a press release announcing that they had conducted a large-scale nationwide operation against "Islamic meeting places." The statement went on to say that identity checks were conducted on tens of thousands of individuals, 141 had been arrested, and expulsion procedures had been initiated against thousands. But only 2 of the 141 arrests were reportedly linked to terrorism and the expulsion procedures had nothing to do with terrorism.[582] But as an Italian NGO representative noted, the authorities "achieved their purpose simply by publishing this information. These press releases are meant to calm down public opinion, to give the impression that things are under control."[583] But all too often, such messages—intended to project a government in action—are seen as suggesting that Muslims in general are a threat to the rest of the community.

Ethnic profiling directed at Muslims has the effect of stigmatizing all Muslims as potential terrorists. The imam of a Berlin mosque remarked that "before 9/11, what Muslims liked a lot was that they had certain rights, and the principle of innocent until proven guilty applied to them. From 9/11, the situation reversed. Muslims are now suspicious until they are proven innocent and we have to justify our innocence."[584]

Ethnic profiling by law enforcement authorities also lends legitimacy to broader public discrimination. If the police and government security agencies use ethnicity or religion as indicators of who is a terrorist, why should not local shopkeepers or restaurant owners do the same? If the state sets the example, why would the public hold back from harassing Muslim and immigrant businesses?[585] In fact, vandalism against Muslim places of worship and businesses, as well as harassment and violent attacks against individuals, are problems that have grown significantly across Europe since 9/11.[586] The International Helsinki Federation summarized the situation in selected EU countries as follows:

> [A]ttitudes toward Muslims have deteriorated further, and it has become increasingly commonplace in public debate to associate Islam with fanaticism and terrorism. A rise in the number of attacks on Muslims has also been documented, with the attacks ranging from slurs and insults in the street to vandalism and serious physical violence.[587]

The European Commission against Racism and Intolerance (ECRI) reported on the situation in France:

> [A] negative trend in public opinion relates to Muslims, who have been an object of manifestations of racism and intolerance, increasingly so over the last few years. [...] Mosques or Muslim graves are vandalized; Muslim religious leaders physically assaulted; and threats and insults directed against Islam and Muslims. These manifestations tend to increase as a reaction to certain international events such as the terrorist attacks in the United States and Europe and the conflict in Iraq. Sometimes elements of the public draw inaccurate parallels between terrorists, religious extremists, and the Muslim population as a whole. In some cases these prejudices are said to prompt discrimination, especially in the field of employment, with Muslims being refused jobs because of the suspicion hanging over them.[588]

Increases in verbal abuse, physical attacks, and attacks on property owned by Muslims were reported in Italy following 9/11.[589] Italian antiracism activists say that many Muslims who suffered abuse did not report it to the police because they feared they would not be taken seriously, and that, in some of the cases where Muslims did report abuse, police failed to investigate thoroughly and prosecute.[590] The UN Committee against Racial Discrimination echoed these concerns in its 2002 observations on Italy.[591] Antiracism activists have also pointed out that Muslims often find it difficult to trust the authorities because senior government officials have repeatedly expressed hostile attitudes toward Muslims.[592]

The lack of redress is raised by Muslims elsewhere as well. In France, few complaints of discrimination filed by Muslims and other minority group members ever reach the courts, and when they do, judges rarely apply discrimination provisions.[593] Reports indicate that police in some cases have refused to register complaints of discrimination made by Muslims.[594]

A final concern about ethnic profiling in the context of counterterrorism reflects the tendency for supposedly exceptional and temporary measures to become permanent and to be used for purposes beyond the original intent of the law or policy. Experience demonstrates that exceptional measures are often used for far broader purposes than originally intended and can have far-reaching negative effects.[595] In the United Kingdom, critics have already expressed concern that Section 44 counterterrorism powers are being used for situations beyond the intent of the law, such as the policing of public protests against the war in Iraq.[596] In France and Italy, observers have noted similar trends.[597]

H. Evaluating the Effectiveness of Ethnic Profiling in Counterterrorism: No Evidence of Efficacy

Even apart from the harms already identified, there is no compelling evidence that ethnic profiling has produced important gains in protecting Europe from terrorism. Ethnic profiling does appear to lead to the detection of illegal immigrants, but immigration enforcement was not an explicit objective of the operations in question, and there is little evidence to suggest that immigrant crackdowns have prevented terrorist acts. In terms of protecting European citizens from terrorism, not only is there little evidence that ethnic profiling is effective, but there is cause for concern that it is in fact counterproductive. Academic analysts and law enforcement practitioners have flagged numerous conceptual and practical problems with ethnic profiling, noting that while ethnic and religious profiles are relatively predictable, terrorists' tactics evolve in response to profiling through strategies of evasion, substitution, and adaptation.

Prediction, Evasion, Substitution, and Adaptation

In the United States, it has been argued that "those who commit acts of airplane terrorism, both before and after September 11, 2001, are disproportionately younger Muslim men of Middle Eastern background."[598] In Europe, Europol reported that half of the 706 arrests on terrorism offenses in 2006 were related to "Islamist terrorism," and that "[t]he majority of the arrested suspects were born in Algeria, Morocco, and Tunisia and had loose affiliations to North African terrorist groups."[599] Does this make it possible to predict, based on ethnicity and religion, who is likely to commit an act of terrorism? If profiling is to be a useful and legitimate tool of law enforcement, a profile including ethnicity and religion must be demonstrably efficient, achieving results that could not be produced without the use of these criteria.

The fact that a larger percentage of people who commit a certain kind of offense are members of a particular religion or ethnicity does not mean that any individual member of the group is likely to be a criminal. It can be simultaneously true that most jihadi terrorists in Europe are Muslims of North African or Pakistani origin, and that 99.99 percent of Muslims of North African or Pakistani descent are not terrorists.[600] Furthermore, even if it is true that the majority of jihadi terrorists fit this general description, there are also outliers who do not; for example, black British and white Belgian and German converts to Islam, or black Africans such as the Somalis and Ethiopians arrested in the United Kingdom for the failed bombing attempt on July 21, 2005. Some argue that the number of outliers is increasing. Ray Kelly, former chief of police of New York City, remarked on the increase:

> If you look at the London bombings, you have three British citizens of Pakistani descent. You have [the fourth London suicide bomber], who is Jamaican. You have the next crew [in London], who are East African. You have a Chechen woman in Moscow in early 2004 who blows herself up in the subway station. So whom do you profile?[601]

In short, the religious, ethnic, and nationality criteria that are relevant to post-9/11 terrorism are so broad as to offer little guidance to law enforcement. Nor have other criteria proven sufficient to provide an effective foundation for profiling.

A 2005 French parliamentary report concluded that there is no terrorist profile,[602] citing Marc Sageman's study of Al Qaeda terrorist suspects in which he found that 90 percent of persons associated with Al Qaeda had not followed religious education; 17.6 percent were upper class and 54.9 percent middle class; 70 percent were married and/or had children; and most had no criminal record.[603] The report also noted that the majority of similar studies conducted by European intelligence services reached the same conclusion, and thus efforts to profile terrorists are not useful.[604] A 2007 Dutch study examined 242 Muslim terrorists arrested in Europe since September 2001. It found the following "profile": 40 percent had been born in Europe; many were poor and had criminal records; almost all were single or divorced men; and they ranged widely in age, from their teens to near retirement.[605] None of these factors distinguished them in any significant way from the broader population of European Muslims. The most recent study by Britain's MI5 comes to a similar conclusion: there is no single pathway to violent radicalization and the nature of Muslim practice is not a consistent or reliable factor in radicalization.[606]

These studies highlight a fundamental problem of using ethnic profiles: they are both overinclusive and underinclusive. They are overinclusive in that the vast majority of the people who fall into the category are entirely innocent; and they are underinclusive in that there are other terrorists and other criminals who do not fit the profile and who would escape attention if the profile were strictly applied. While overinclusion imposes an unnecessary burden on "false positives" (persons who are innocent but match the profile), underinclusion may divert police attention from actual threats that lie beyond the prescribed profile. Thus, it was reported that, prior to the July 2005 attacks on the London public transport system, the leader of the bombers "had come to the attention of the intelligence services as an associate of other men who were suspected of involvement in a terrorist bomb plot. But he was not pursued because he did not tick enough of the boxes in the pre-July profile of the terror suspect."[607] The most authoritative report to date on the 7/7 London bombings concludes that "there is not a consistent profile to help identify who may be vulnerable to radicalization."[608]

Another fundamental problem of profiling is its failure to account for the dynamism of its target: the subjects of profiling evolve in response to policing and law enforcement tactics.[609] When a terrorist profile is known, terrorists can adapt to it through strategies of evasion and substitution. They may evade detection by recruiting individuals who do not fit the profile. In February 2006, U.S. President George W. Bush announced that a planned attack on Los Angeles had been averted. "Rather than use Arab hijackers," Bush said, "Khalid Shaikh Mohammed sought out young men from Southeast Asia whom he believed would not arouse as much suspicion."[610] New York City Police Commissioner Raymond Kelly made this observation in a magazine interview:

> You think that terrorists aren't aware of how easy it is to be characterized by ethnicity? ... Look at the 9/11 hijackers. They came here. They shaved. They went to topless bars. They wanted to blend in. They wanted to look like they were part of the American dream. These are not dumb people. Could a terrorist dress up as a Hasidic Jew and walk into the subway, and not be profiled? Yes. I think profiling is just nuts.[611]

In response to profiling, terrorist organizations "will either (i) recruit more individuals from non-profiled groups, thereby expanding the overall pool of potential terrorists, or (ii) substitute different types of terrorist attacks that are more immune to profiling."[612] Some suggest that this took place in Israel during the second intifada with the substitution of women for male suicide bombers.[613] There is some evidence that substitution is taking place in Europe, as the *Washington Post* noted in March 2007:

> [T]errorism suspects from atypical backgrounds are becoming increasingly common in Western Europe. With new plots surfacing every month, police across Europe are arresting significant numbers of women, teenagers, white-skinned suspects and people baptized as Christians.... The demographics of those being arrested are so diverse that many European counterterrorism officials and analysts say they have given up trying to predict what sorts of people are most likely to become terrorists.... Indeed, there are clear signs that al-Qaeda cells and affiliates are intentionally recruiting supporters from nontraditional backgrounds as a way to avoid detection."[614]

Tactics or modes of attack may also be changed in response to profiling, although there is little data available on the degree to which such substitution may be taking place.[615] The two reports cited above suggest that most terrorist suspects do in fact fit the stereotypical profile (though arguably the profile is so broad as to be of little practical value); but there are a number of outliers whose backgrounds suggest substitution tactics, and these may be increasing. For now, the data cannot support a firm conclusion.[616] Thus, it is not possible to say that ethnic profiling is effective. However, it is possible that profiling is counterproductive and may "actually increase rather than decrease the long-term incidence of the targeted offense."[617]

In the United Kingdom, the Islamic Human Rights Commission raised the concern that current policies may drive moderate Muslims into the arms of extremists,[618] and that measures targeting Muslims who have nothing to do with terrorism are "extremely counterproductive" because they alienate "the very community that police need to help and support the fight against terror."[619] An April 2007 telephone poll of 500 Muslim adults carried out by Britain's Channel 4 News found that 55 percent of the respondents had no confidence in the police.[620] The London Metropolitan Police Service (MPS) has itself recognized that the increase in the use of search and arrest powers against certain groups has had a "hugely negative impact" on community relations and has increased "the level of distrust" of the police.[621] In July 2004, the British government announced plans to review the use of counterterrorism stop-and-search powers and to take measures aimed at building confidence in the police among groups who believe the police treat them unfairly.[622] The MPS subsequently reviewed their use of Section 44 counterterrorism stop-and-search powers and issued new guidance to police officers about the importance of avoiding stereotypes.

Few political and security authorities in Europe have openly considered the possibility that their own tactics, including ethnic profiling, may be a significant factor in generating the sense of victimization and humiliation that can contribute to the radicalization of young Muslims, some of whom may turn to terrorist violence. Indeed, there is little evidence that European Union member states' policymakers or senior law enforcement officials are undertaking assessments of the impact and effectiveness of their counterterrorism strategies on minority communities. This lack of self-scrutiny is a serious error. Smart law enforcement requires assessments of the effects of different operational tactics in order to maximize their effectiveness and deploy scarce resources efficiently. Assessments of current operational practices should go hand in hand with consideration of the range of options that are available, with an explicit consideration of alternatives to ethnic profiling. The final section of this report examines the issues that should be considered in such policy reviews.

V. Alternatives to Ethnic Profiling

A serious effort to address ethnic profiling requires first monitoring and measuring current police practices to determine if ethnic profiling is taking place, then eliminating those practices that contribute to ethnic profiling, and finally introducing new, more effective policing practices. This requires building policing skills and capacity to operate without ethnic profiling and expanding efforts to reach out to ethnic minority communities, including increasing ethnic and religious diversity within law enforcement agencies. Institutional reforms on this scale require a clear recognition of the problem and commitment by political and police leadership to address it. But as the examples from the U.S. Customs Service and municipal police of Fuenlabrada, Spain, indicate, such reforms are possible, and when they are implemented, greater efficiency results.

Monitoring Police Practices and Identifying and Eliminating Ethnic Profiling

Police cannot identify and address ethnic profiling unless they collect data on their use of identity check and stop-and-search powers, including data on the ethnicity of the persons they stop. In December 2006, the EU Network of Independent Experts in Fundamental Rights noted that "only the monitoring of the behavior of the public authority by the use of statistics may serve to highlight [ethnic profiling] practices."[623] ECRI, the UN, and other authorities have also repeatedly called for gathering data on policing practices such as identity checks and stops and searches.[624] Despite the protestations of many EU member states that generating ethnically disaggregated data is prohibited by data protection norms,[625] it is in fact possible for police to gather ethnic data without infringing on personal data protections.

European data protection law does not ban the creation or maintenance of ethnic data, but highlights the need to protect privacy and self-identification while making provision for the good-faith collection and dissemination of ethnic data for legitimate public interest purposes. It does this, in part, by reasonably distinguishing between individual, identifiable data and collective, anonymous, data that cannot be traced to any person. The European Union Directive on the protection of individuals with regard to the processing of personal data (Directive 95/46/EC "on the protection of individuals with regard to the processing of personal data and on the free movement of such data" (October 24, 1995)) expressly exempts from its application anonymous statistical information of the kind needed to document and prove racial discrimination. The directive's "principles of protection" apply only to "personal data" and "information relating to an identified or identifiable natural person" and states that such principles "shall not apply to data rendered anonymous in such a way that the data subject is no longer identifiable." Moreover, processing even of "personal data revealing racial or ethnic origin" is permissible where, among other things, it "is necessary [to satisfy] obligations ... of the controller in the field of employment law," or it "relates to data which are ... necessary for the establishment, exercise or defense of legal claims."

The Council of Europe's counterpart norm—the Convention for the Protection of Individuals with Regard to Automatic Processing of Personal Data (1981)—similarly limits its application to "personal data" which "relat[e] to an identified or identifiable individual." The Committee of Ministers has made clear that it is "[a]ware of the needs in both the public and private sectors for reliable statistics for analysis and understanding of contemporary society, and for defining policies." To that end, Recommendation No. R(97) 18 of the Committee of Ministers distinguishes between "personal" and "anonymous" data (as to which "identification requires an unreasonable amount of time and manpower"). "Sensitive data"—including "personal data revealing racial origin"—may be processed automatically where domestic law provides for the data to be "collected in such a way that the data subject is not identifiable."

While data gathering is a necessary component of monitoring policing,[626] it is important to recognize that this is a particularly sensitive topic. The history of ethnic extermination policies during World War II has left a powerful legacy in Europe. Furthermore, ethnic data continue to be abused by politicians, and police continue to cite arrests of immigrants or overrepresentation of minorities in jail as evidence of higher minority offending rates.[627] Understandably, many ethnic groups remain uncomfortable with the gathering of ethnic data in sensitive areas such as law enforcement and offending.[628] In this regard, it is important to be clear that collecting ethnic data requires close scrutiny of data collection, storage, and access practices in order to prevent any possible misuse. This is particularly important in law enforcement, where there are evident risks that gathering ethnic data could in fact facilitate certain forms of ethnic profiling, such as the data mining discussed in this report.

Policy assessments or audits have been successful in identifying a range of institutional factors that may be driving or permitting ethnic profiling. Such audits have been effective in addressing ethnic profiling by police in the United Kingdom and Canada, particularly regarding their use of stop-and-search powers.[629] Policy audits give law enforcement institutions the opportunity to review their policies, see how policies are translated into practice, assess the effectiveness of those policies and practices, and measure their impact on different communities. Audits can identify not only problem areas, but also promising practices. A basic principle in conducting policy audits is to include the relevant communities in the audit process.[630]

Beyond monitoring, addressing police discrimination requires the development of policies and guidelines that explicitly prohibit the use of ethnicity, race, religion, and national origin in targeting persons for suspicion, and that provide clear guidance for police on how to use their powers in a fair and neutral manner. The introduction of a specific requirement that stops be based on reasonable suspicion of an actual or possible offense will constrain officer discretion and reduce the influence of stereotypes in decisions about whom to stop. As the EU Network of Independent Experts in Fundamental Rights has noted, "[i]n most EU Member States, law enforcement officers are granted broad discretionary powers in ... the performance of identity checks or 'stop-and-search' arrests."[631]

Building Police Capacity to Operate without Ethnic Profiling

As discussed earlier in this report, ethnic profiling does not work. It is particularly important to recognize this in regard to counterterrorism, which presents a special challenge, given the imperative of preventing attacks and the association of many terror movements with particular national, regional, ethnic, or religious groups. The threat of terrorism and challenge of countering it require the use of only those tactics that work, and avoidance of tactics such as ethnic profiling which are at best ineffective and possibly even damaging to counterterrorism efforts.

Common elements of successful counterterrorism strategies include: dedicating resources to identify and protect possible terrorist targets (known as target hardening), reducing the effect of a terror attack, and improving intelligence and enhancing the ability of law enforcement agencies to detect suspicious behaviors.[632] Counterterrorism officials and experts emphasize that these last two factors are key to effectively preventing terrorist attacks.

In the words of a Swiss intelligence expert, "intelligence is the sense organ of the counterterrorist organism—the faculty that takes in and processes information."[633]

The details that have emerged from trials of terrorists clearly demonstrate the painstaking intelligence and detective work that leads to successful apprehension and conviction. In the United Kingdom, Operation Crevice Seven involved intelligence-sharing among agencies in the United Kingdom, the United States, Canada, and Pakistan; around-the-clock surveillance; video surveillance and wiretaps in cars and homes; and, crucially, information provided by a member of the public who called the police to report large quantities of fertilizer in a storage unit.[634] Operation Crevice Seven resulted in the arrest and prosecution of seven men on terrorism charges, and the conviction of five of them.

Most counterterrorism intelligence comes from one of two sources: information gleaned from past terror attacks, and information from local communities.[635] One French intelligence officer estimated that "three-fifths of the information that gets to the [French intelligence services] comes from the grassroots level."[636] Police and intelligence officials must have channels into local communities to obtain reliable information. Gathering "community intelligence" is essential to all policing. As London MPS Commander Ali Dizaei noted:

> Seventy percent of crime is not solved because of Sherlock Holmes techniques, but because members of the public call my officers and say that someone is committing a crime. That is called community intelligence—without it we may as well pack our bags and go home because crime will not get solved. The intelligence doesn't come on its own; it won't come if we have no legitimacy in the communities that we police.[637]

If the confidence of Muslim communities is lost, the job of police and intelligence agencies will be much harder. London MPS Assistant Commissioner Tariq Ghaffur noted that there is a real danger of stigmatizing minority communities through ethnic profiling:

> The impact of this will be that just at the time when we need the confidence and trust of these communities, they may retreat inside themselves. We therefore need proper accountability and transparency in all policing that affects communities.[638]

Information gained from the community often provides vital leads.[639] For example, when an imam informs law enforcement officials that a group of young men are carrying out recruitment activities in the mosque, these men can be placed under surveillance. This can lead law enforcement officials to additional members of the network and also provide information on their activities.[640] Such cooperation is fundamentally based in trust and a sense of belonging to the larger society.

As with other forms of criminal activity, it is important that counterterrorism measures identify behavior that actually is suspicious, rather than be distracted by stereotypes. Specific actions—including proselytizing violence, visiting jihadi training camps, participating in jihadi chat rooms, transferring money to terrorist organizations, attending meetings of terrorist groups, and purchasing bomb-making materials, provide indications that an individual is involved in terrorist activities. Law enforcement officials and those they rely on for information need to identify such behaviors rather than falling back on generalizations based on religion, ethnicity, and national origin.

Costly mistakes have been made when tell-tale individual behaviors were overlooked. In Madrid, "just before the train bombings there, a businessman reportedly watched the terrorists making their preparations but thought it was just a petty crime in progress and never called the police."[641] In 2001, at Paris's Charles de Gaulle airport, would-be shoe-bomber Richard Reid was allowed to board an aircraft despite his strange behavior and even though, according to the final case file, "every police or security agent that was involved in this control procedure indicated being troubled by the personality and behavior of this individual who was very neglected, impassive, and who didn't seek to know why he had been controlled."[642]

Increasing Outreach to Minority Communities

Police require training about non-discrimination and how it affects their use of police powers. Police can also benefit from training to enhance understanding of and respect for minority cultures, although it is important to note that training by itself is unlikely to change police behavior. Too often, authorities respond to critiques of police practices with a new training program, while leaving other standards and practices untouched. Training is most useful when it reflects larger policy reforms that establish new laws, operational guidelines, and oversight, as well as penalties for failing to change discriminatory practices.

While strategic adjustments can reduce the negative effects of counterterrorism efforts, counterterrorism operations will continue and will likely cause anxiety and fear in Muslim communities. Even operations that try to pinpoint suspects and minimize broader impacts on the community may be perceived in some quarters as further evidence of police bias. Successfully managing perceptions is one strategy. A number of countries have developed initiatives to mitigate the negative impacts of counterterrorism operations, understanding that the best way to address misperceptions is to provide the affected communities with concrete information and opportunities for discussion about why and how operations are carried out.

Counterterrorism operations conducted in the community, such as raids and arrests, provoke high levels of anxiety and a sense of being targeted.[643] One way to alleviate these tensions is to ensure that community leaders quickly receive reliable information about the operation. In Denmark, police have sent officers to community leaders' houses even while terrorism suspects were being arrested, to tell those leaders what was transpiring and enable them to relay that information to the community, to prevent the spread of inaccurate or misleading information.[644] In London, police respond to community questions about operations through the regular meetings of the Muslim Safety Forum.[645]

Law enforcement authorities can and should use the media as a tool for providing appropriate information about police strategies and powers and soliciting public cooperation and information in return.[646] A recently concluded review by the London MPS of Section 44 counterterrorism stops found media outreach to be essential in communicating to the public how and why these powers are being used in London.[647]

As described in this report, media reports frequently reflect and reinforce public prejudices associating migrants with criminals and Muslims with terrorists. Police also need to review their press statements to assure that they avoid any discriminatory association of minority ethnic or religious identity and crime. Senior police officers also can and should criticize media reports when they make inflammatory statements of blanket association of specific groups or communities with terrorism or crime.

Policing structures and strategies vary considerably across the European Union's 27 member states, and some countries and cities already follow community policing practices that include minority outreach components. Several pan-European initiatives specifically address the policing of minority communities.[648] Nonetheless, efforts to build trust and understanding between police and minority communities in Europe continue to confront multiple challenges, particularly in ethnic minority communities with histories of tension and hostility in their relations with the police.

Improving police relations with recent immigrants can be particularly challenging given language and cultural barriers, limited integration, attitudes toward law enforcement shaped by repressive policing in the immigrants' home countries, and the presence of significant numbers of illegal migrants who fear and avoid contact with police. Immigration enforcement is a particularly delicate issue. When police aggressively enforce immigration laws, they destroy trust and directly undermine community cooperation from legal residents as well as from those persons who lack legal residency status.[649] There is no easy answer to this issue, but police must not base their use of immigration control powers on an assumption that those who "look different" are not citizens or legal residents. Police policies, guidance, and training need to reflect the challenges of policing crime, terrorism, and immigration in multiethnic societies.[650]

There are many strategies for reaching out to minority communities and Box 1, below, provides some concrete examples from the United Kingdom. Building trust and cooperation is not easy and requires dedication and ongoing effort. An example of good intentions gone awry is the 2005 Preventing Extremism Together (PET) initiative in the United Kingdom, which had at best limited results. Indeed, some argue that it worsened rather than improved government relations with the Muslim community due to a series of flaws including a rushed timetable, scheduling meetings on Muslim holidays, the perception that government predetermined the agenda, and a lack of follow through.[651]

BOX 1

Police Outreach to Muslim Communities in the United Kingdom

The London Metropolitan Police Service (MPS) launched multiple initiatives to improve relations with Muslim communities in response to the new strains created by counterterrorism efforts. These initiatives included the following:

- Creating some 300 third-party reporting centers that allow people who are reluctant to go to a police station to report crimes or other concerns at schools, places of worship, community centers, and other locations in their local communities.

- Working with the Muslim Safety Forum (MSF), a body created in 2000 by a coalition of Muslim organizations concerned with police focus on Muslim communities. Police officials say that the MSF has been an important arena for police and Muslim community representatives to exchange information and discuss problems, including terrorism, Islamophobia, police sensitivity, and similar issues.

- Developing a Cultural and Community Resources Unit (CCRU) that runs a confidential database of police officers with expertise in particular areas. Officers possessing relevant ethnic or religious backgrounds and language skills can volunteer to participate in CCRU. (Of 30,000 police in London, 300 are Muslim.) The database has proven useful in several situations, including negotiating the police relationship with the Finsbury Park Mosque and the Algerian community in that neighborhood.

- Beyond London, the British police developed a "Community impact assessment document and guidance" that has been circulated to all U.K. police services for use in terrorist operations, and another guide on policing religiously sensitive premises.

Sources: Ali Dizaei, remarks made at a May 31, 2007 meeting co-hosted by the European Policy Center, the King Badouin Foundation and the Open Society Justice Initiative, Brussels; http://muslimsafetyforum. org/history.html; Sixth Report, Select Committee on Home Affairs, House of Commons, session 2004–2005, at http://www.publications.parliament.uk/pa/cm200405/cmselect/cmhaff/165/16509.htm#n169; Briggs, Fieschi, and Lownsbrough, *Bringing It Home*, (London: DEMOS, December 2006), at 33–34.

Community outreach efforts almost always confront the question of who represents the community and which voices are accepted as legitimate partners or interlocutors. In ordinary policing, there are typically certain groups, such as young people, that are notoriously difficult to include in dialogues with the police. Current police efforts to build bridges to Muslims are challenged by the existence of many Muslim communities, of varied national origin, ethnicity, and religious belief and practice. The challenge is magnified by the lack of police officers in Europe who are Muslim, and the lack of non-Muslim police officers who are well-versed in Islam.

A 2006 British study of efforts to build police relations with Muslim communities emphasized that such initiatives be locally based, transparent, and rooted in an understanding of the faith.[652] If possible, police outreach efforts should be inclusive of the diverse voices in different communities and avoid generating or aggravating divisions in the Muslim community. Some experts argue that a strategy of encouraging moderate Muslim voices to create a bulwark against more radical forms of Islam is based in lack of understanding of different streams of Islam and is as likely to create divisions and problems as it is to advance a solution.[653] This perspective notes that moderate Islamic voices have little relation with the communities or individuals who are attracted to radical forms of Islam, and that Salafist groups are not monolithic and many are highly critical of violent jihad. Radical streams of Islam that reject violence are those with the most authentic voice and greatest ability to counter violent jihadists and therefore, though the process is extremely difficult, these communities should be included in community outreach initiatives. This is the approach of the work of the London MPS's Muslim Contact Unit, which works with Salafist and Islamist groups.

The London Metropolitan Police Service (MPS) created the Muslim Contact Unit (MCU) in 2002 to reach out to Salafist and Islamist groups and work with them to reduce the pool of recruits for Al Qaeda-inspired terrorism. The MCU's work reflects the understanding that most Salafist and Islamist groups are non-violent and can reduce terrorism rather than contribute to it. The MCU includes Muslim officers who have been central to the MPS's ability to develop a dialogue with Muslim communities. The head of the MCU notes that the unit does not develop indicators of radicalization, but instead looks to the leaders of Salafist organizations for insights and information:

> "They tell us. They lived with Abbu Qattada and the Finsbury Park Mosque and they know better than we do what is happening....The community and religious leaders would be the ones with the skills to deal with that situation and dissuade people from violence."

The former head of the MCU says that the partnership approach led Muslim community groups to assist terrorist investigations in important operational matters over the 2002 to 2007 period.

The "Street" project is another model of outreach to young Muslims in South London. It is run by the former chairman of the Brixton Mosque, a trusted figure in those communities. Street offers leisure activities—computer games, TV, sports, and outdoor camping trips—as well as counselling and advice services that provide "legitimate accounts of Islam that challenge the jihadis." Street also offers services to recently released prisoners, and has informal relationships with both local police and special police units.

Sources: Justice Initiative Interview, Robert Lambert, head of the MPS Muslim Contact Unit, Washington, DC, June 14, 2007; Briggs, Fieschi, and Lownsbrough, *Bringing It Home*, at 75–6.

Media Strategies

While counterterrorism may be the catalyst for initiatives to build trust and cooperation in Muslim communities, it cannot be the sole focus of community outreach efforts. To build real trust and cooperation, police must also address the communities' security concerns regarding ordinary crime, hate crime, and the negative effects of discriminatory policing practices. A proactive stance on hate crimes may be especially important in demonstrating that police take community safety seriously and are sensitive to the plight of vulnerable groups. While certain European Union member states have clear legal standards and mechanisms in place to encourage the reporting of hate crimes, the European Union Monitoring Center (EUMC) concluded in 2005 that police forces in the majority of member states required "further development" in responding to hate crimes effectively.[654]

Any genuine effort to improve police relations with minority communities must also take seriously concerns about discriminatory policing practices. Results of an EUMC survey of ethnic minorities in 12 member states found that a quarter of the respondents felt they had been subject to discrimination by the police in the past year, but that few of them reported this discrimination.[655] Police must treat all reports of police abuse with utmost seriousness and, if necessary, strengthen complaints mechanisms to ensure they are accessible, known, and trusted. Where independent civilian review of police does not exist, it may be advisable to create such an entity, given the often poor track record of internal police disciplinary mechanisms.

Police efforts to reach out to and build better relations with Europe's diverse and extensive ethnic and religious minority communities will foster greater accountability of the police to the communities they serve. This in turn will foster community trust and increased collaboration. These are not simply cosmetic measures: studies in various countries show unambiguously that regular community consultation contributes directly to reducing crime and improving the public's sense of security.[656]

Police training and recruitment must also reflect a commitment to non-discrimination and the challenges of policing multiethnic societies. Police, like other institutions in democratic societies, should represent all segments of the society itself.[657] It is easier to develop a dialogue and build trust with minority communities when the police look like the community that they serve. Community engagement may well be necessary in efforts to recruit police officers from minority groups.

Given the evidence indicating that ethnic profiling is not only ineffective, but counterproductive in fighting crime and terrorism, the onus is on law enforcement authorities to explore and implement better alternatives. These alternatives include reducing officer discretion in the use of stops and searches, improving intelligence through improved relations with minority communities, and enhancing police capacity to identify suspicous behaviors. By adopting these ethnically neutral strategies, police can reduce discrimination and become more effective in reducing crime and preventing terrorism.

VI. Conclusion

Ethnic profiling—a longstanding practice that has increased since 9/11—is pervasive in the European Union. As documented in this report, it is also inefficient, ineffective, and discriminatory. Evidence gathered from multiple countries with highly varied ethnic minority communities consistently indicates that police officers across the European Union routinely use generalizations about race, ethnicity, religion, or national origin in targeting suspicion and deciding whom to pursue for an identity check, a search, a raid, or surveillance. Whether in counterterrorism efforts or in ordinary policing practices, the harms associated with ethnic profiling are many, and they are felt by all sectors of society.

As this report has argued, ethnic profiling is a form of discrimination that focuses disproportionate law enforcement attention on particular individuals and communities, based on generalizations about religion or ethnicity. In light of European law's historical aversion to distinctions based on ethnic origin, and in light of the considerable harms caused by ethnic profiling and the absence of any evidence to support claims that it actually prevents crime or terrorism, there can be little doubt that ethnic profiling violates international human rights standards. The practice clearly falls afoul of the principle of nondiscrimination, which must be respected even in times of terrorist threat.

In addition, specific law enforcement measures based on ethnic profiling violate other human rights, such as the right to liberty and security, including freedom from arbitrary detention and imprisonment; a fair trial; respect for private and family life; home and correspondence; freedom of thought; conscience and religion; freedom of expression; and freedom of assembly and association. Any interference with liberty must be in accordance with a clear legal process and for specific reasons that are defined in the law. A proportionality test is applied with the right to respect for private and family life, home and correspondence; freedom of thought, conscience and religion; freedom of expression; and freedom of assembly and association. In general, no derogation is permitted from fundamental rights during times of emergency. If governments seek to opt-out of some human rights guarantees, then they must do so clearly and unambiguously, and any emergency responses must also be proportionate to the threat that is claimed. As this report makes clear, these practices fail that test. Ethnic profiling practices violate not only the right of individuals to be free from discrimination, but also other fundamental rights.[658] The UN Special Rapporteur on the promotion and protection of human rights and fundamental freedoms while countering terrorism has concluded that:

> Terrorist profiling practices that are based on "race" are incompatible with human rights. Profiling based on ethnicity, national origin and/or religion involves differential treatment of comparable groups of people. Such differential treatment is only compatible with the principle of non-discrimination if it is a proportional means of countering terrorism. Profiling practices based on ethnicity, national origin and/or religion regularly fail to meet this demanding proportionality requirement: not only are they unsuitable means of identifying potential terrorists, but they also entail considerable negative consequences that may render these measures counterproductive in the fight against terrorism.[659]

Ethnic profiling affects thousands of people every day. It harms the Roma pedestrian who is stopped and searched just because a police officer subscribes to anti-Roma stereotypes. It harms the Muslim owner of a call center whose shop is raided just because he prays at a particular mosque. More broadly, ethnic profiling harms entire communities, which are traumatized by raids and mass controls and stigmatized by generalizations linking certain ethnic or religious groups to crime and terrorism. As a pervasive practice that does not work and that wastes law enforcement resources, ethnic profiling ultimately leaves millions of people in the EU—even if they are never profiled themselves—less safe.

Ethnic profiling leads to the misuse of police resources. In an environment marked by a plethora of crime and terrorism threats and a paucity of law enforcement resources, such misuse is not just profligate, it is dangerous.

Ethnic profiling does not work. Many factors render ethnic profiling ineffective, regardless of the law enforcement method being used: stops and searches, identity checks, data mining, antiradicalization efforts, raids, arrests and detention, or surveillance. When they rely on ethnic profiling, these law enforcement methods are impeded by problems of over- and underinclusion, evasion, substitution, and distortion. They also produce worrisome counter-effects. Ethnic profiling may hinder the ability of law enforcement officials to gather necessary intelligence by alienating the very communities that could help police identify potential terrorists and ordinary criminals. Furthermore, ethnic profiling may actually increase the pool of potential terrorists by humiliating those who are profiled, creating the possibility of a greater terrorist threat in the future.

Fortunately, a number of the practices described in this report are less prevalent in mid-2009 than they were immediately following the March 11, 2004 Madrid and July 7, 2005 London bombings. In particular, highly visible forms of ethnic profiling, such as large-scale raids, broad data mining, and mass identity checks outside places of worship, are now less common. This is both because ethnic profiling is ineffective and because counterterrorism authorities are targeting their investigations somewhat more narrowly.

The decline in ethnic profiling also reflects a political reality that is subject to change: in the absence to date of further major terrorist attacks in Europe, elected authorities do not currently face public pressures to be seen to be tackling terrorism. The apparent decline in the more egregious forms of ethnic profiling does not however reflect an increased awareness of and concern with ethnic profiling as a form of discrimination, nor the creation of greater oversight or accountability. Another terrorist attack would likely put ethnic profiling back at the center of law enforcement practices.

Better, more effective alternatives to ethnic profiling exist. Examples taken from a federal law enforcement agency in the United States and a municipal police force in Spain indicate that police are more efficient and effective when they abandon ethnic profiling. Policing based on intelligence, data, and community consultation has proven to work better than policing based on stereotypes and generalizations.

It is incumbent on European authorities, national governments, law enforcement authorities, and civil society groups to take concrete steps that will reduce the use of tactics based on ethnic profiling and replace them with more rational law enforcement measures. An important first step would be to define ethnic profiling and outlaw it at the European level and in national legislation. Many other steps must be taken as well, from gathering data on law enforcement and ethnicity, to funding police collaboration with minority communities, to implementing new police practices.

As this report has shown, the damage from ethnic profiling—to the rule of law, to effective law enforcement, to police-community relations, and especially to those targeted by the practice—is considerable. Until ethnic profiling is recognized as a problem, expressly outlawed, and replaced by better law enforcement measures, the damage it does will only increase. In a Europe threatened by ordinary crime and terrorist attacks, the stakes are too high to allow this ineffective, inefficient, and discriminatory practice to continue.

Notes

1.   Arun Kundnani, *Analysis: The War on Terror Leads to Racial Profiling*, (London: Institute for Race Relations, IRR News, July 7, 2004). Vickram Dodd, "Surge in Stop and Search of Asian People After July 7," *The Guardian*, December 24, 2005.

2.   Islamic Institute for Human Rights, "Country Profile: The Conditions of Muslims in France," *Monitoring Minority Protection in EU Member States: Overview*, (New York: Open Society Institute, 2004), at 53, available at: http://www.eumap.org/.

3.   European Commission Against Racism and Intolerance, *General Policy Recommendation No. 8 on Combating Racism while Fighting Terrorism*, (Strasbourg: ECRI, March 17, 2004), at 11, available at: http://www.coe.int/t/e/legal_affairs/legal_co-operation/fight_against_terrorism/3_codexter/ working_documents/2004/ECRI%20(2004)%2026%20recommendation_N%25B0_8_eng.pdf.

4.   For example the EU arrest warrant, and data exchange under Treaty of Prüm (Schengen III) 2002/584/JHA: Council Framework Decision of June 13, 2002 on the European arrest warrant and the surrender procedures between Member States. See also the Convention between the Kingdom of Belgium, the Federal Republic of Germany, the Kingdom of Spain, the French Republic, the Grand Duchy of Luxembourg, the Kingdom of the Netherlands and the Republic of Austria on the stepping up of cross-border cooperation particularly in combating terrorism, cross-border crime, and illegal migration, Prüm (Germany), May 27, 2005, Council Secretariat, Brussels, July 7, 2005, 10900/05. The principle of availability of information for law enforcement cooperation under the 2004 to 2009 Hague Programme for the area of Freedom, Security and Justice also moves along this path, particularly in advocating a "principle of availability" of information for law enforcement cooperation. This trend is continued under the successor 2009 to 2014 Stockholm Programme.

5.   Discussed in detail in Chapter IV of this report.

6. David Harris, "Confronting Ethnic Profiling in the United States," in *Justice Initiatives: Ethnic Profiling by Police In Europe*, (New York: Open Society Justice Initiative, June 2005). Bernard Harcourt, "Rethinking Racial Profiling: A Critique of the Economics, Civil Liberties, and Constitutional Literature, and of Criminal Profiling More Generally," *The University of Chicago Law Review*, Vol 71, No. 4, Fall 2004. E.J. van der Torre and H.B. Ferwerda, *Preventive Searching, an Analysis of the Process and the External Effects in Ten Municipalities*, (The Hague: Beke, Arnhem, Politie & Wetenschap, Zeist 2005). Claes Lernestedt, Christian Diesen, Tove Pettersson and Toren Lindholm, "Equal before the Law: Nature or Culture," in *The Blue and Yellow Glasshouse: Structural Discrimination in Sweden*, (Stockholm: Swedish Government Official Reports 2005:56). Paul Quinton, Nick Bland, et al., *Police Stops, Decision-Making and Practice*, (London: Home Office, 2000).

7. London Metropolitan Police Service Assistant Commissioner Tariq Ghaffur, quoted in Andrew Blick, Toufyal Choudhury, and Stuart Weir, *The Rules of the Game: Terrorism, Community and Human Rights, Democratic Audit*, (Human Rights Center, University of Essex, Joseph Rowntree Reform Trust, 2006), at 34.

8. "Detectives draw up new brief in hunt for radicals," *The Times*, December 28, 2005. The Intelligence and Security Committee of the U.K. Parliament's *Report into the London Terrorist Attacks on 7 July 2005*, presented to parliament May 2006, while making no mention of the use of a specific profile, makes clear that two of the attackers, Mohammad Sidique Khan and Shehzad Tanweer, were known to the security services through another investigation, but were not considered a high investigative priority.

9. U.S. Customs Service, *Personal Searches of Air Passengers Results: Positive and Negative, Fiscal Year 1998*, (Washington: U.S. Customs Service, 1998). Commissioner of U.S. Customs Service Raymond Kelly: Speech to the National Press Club (March 17, 2000), available at: http://www.cbp.gov/xp/cgov/newsroom/commissioner/speeches_statements/archives/2000/mar172000.xml.

10. Open Society Justice Initiative, *Addressing Ethnic Profiling in the European Union: A Report on the Strategies for Effective Stop and Search (STEPSS) Project*, (New York: Open Society Institute, 2009), at 30–31.

11. Bruce Hoffman, *Inside Terrorism*, (New York: Columbia University Press, 2006 edition), at 169.

12. Grounded in Articles 29, 30, 31, and 34(2)(b) of the Treaty on the European Union.

13. Principle 2.4, Basic Principles, Appendix to Recommendation (87) 15 addressed by the Committee of Ministers to the Member States of the Council of Europe, regulating the use of personal data in the police sector, adopted by the Committee of Ministers 17 September 1987. The European Union's most recent legislative action in this field would, at least in one interpretation, fall short of the Council of Europe's requirements. Thus, Framework Decision 2008/977/JHA of November 27, 2008, on the protection of personal data processed in the framework of police and judicial cooperation in criminal matters, arguably allows authorities more latitude in the processing of sensitive data, including data relating to the race, ethnic origin, or religion of individuals, for the prevention of criminal offenses in general, without this having to relate to a specific inquiry. Article 6 of the Framework Decision provides as follows: "The processing of personal data revealing racial or ethnic origin, political opinions, religious or philosophical beliefs or trade-union membership and the processing of data concerning health or sex life shall be permitted only when this is strictly necessary and when the national law provides adequate safeguards."

14. See Olivier de Schutter and Julie Ringelheim, "Ethnic Profiling: A Rising Challenge for European Human Rights Law," *71 Modern Law Review*, 2008; 358–384, at 6.

15. This might be due to its relatively limited use, which has generally been confined to certain crimes such as serial rape and murder, and the comparatively small role of ethnicity in this type of profile. Janet Jackson, Paul van den Eshof, and Esther De Kleuver, "A research approach to offender profiling," in Janet L. Jackson and Debra-Anne Bekerian (Eds.), *Offender Profiling: Theory, Research and Practice*, (Chichester: Wiley, 1997) at 107–132.

16. One impact study found that criminal profiling leads directly to the identification of subjects in less than 10 percent of cases. Robert Hazelwoord, Robert Ressler, Roger Depue, and John Douglas, "Criminal investigative analysis: An overview," in Robert Hazelwood and Ann Wolbert Burgess (Eds.), *Practical Aspects of Rape Investigation* (2nd Edition), (London: CRC Press, 1995), at 115–126. See also Malcolm Gladwell, "Dangerous Minds: Criminal Profiling Made Easy," the *New Yorker*, November 12, 2007, available at http://www.newyorker.com/reporting/2007/11/12/071112fa_fact_gladwell. Gladwell cites a U.K. Home Office study that found that profiles only led to the arrest of the suspect in 2.7 percent of cases.

17. European Union Network of Independent Experts on Fundamental Rights, "Ethnic Profiling," December 2006, Ref. CFR–CDF, Opinion 4, 2006.

18. These limits have not been well-defined by the courts, however. A U.S. case is the only one of which we are aware in which this matter has been addressed judicially. In September 1992, in the town of Oneonta, New York, with some 450 black residents in a population of about 17,500, the police stopped and questioned over 200 young black men on the basis of a limited suspect description (the victim had only seen her assailant's arm, not his face). No suspect was apprehended. The court upheld the actions of the police, while recognizing the negative impact of their actions. It limited its findings to the circumstances of the case, stating that another case would be more appropriate for determining what would be the threshold beyond which police questioning of persons whose race matched the physical description of the suspect might violate the Equal Protection Clause of the U.S. Constitution. *Brown v. City of Oneanta*, 221 F.3d 329, 334 (2d Cir.2000) (amending 195 F.3d 111 (2d Cir. 1999)), rehearing denied 235 F.3d 769 (2d Cir. 2000), cert. denied 534 U.S. 816 (2001).

19. Ramirez, Deborah, Jennifer Hoopes, and Tara Lai Quinlan, "Defining Racial Profiling in a Post-September 11 World," *American Criminal Law Review*, 2003, Vol. 40:1195–1233, at 1206.

20. David Harris, *Profiles in Injustice: Why Racial Profiling Cannot Work*, (New York: The New Press, 2002), at 16–23. As the U.S. Customs Service discovered, however, their ethically-based "drug mule" profile resulted in systematic profiling of black Caribbean and Latin American women while failing to enhance efficiency in terms of arrests and seizures of drugs. See further discussion at p. 53 in this report.

21. U.S. Customs Service, *Personal Searches of Air Passengers Results: Positive and Negative, Fiscal Year 1998*, (See detailed discussion of this case at p. 53).

22. Police officers conduct several different types of stops: a distinction can be made between officers stopping people to ask them to account for their actions or to check their identity, and encounters where officers frisk (pat down) or search a member of the public on the suspicion that that person may have illegal items in his or her possession. Stops and searches can also take place

as part of large-scale operations and raids in which police have been authorized to stop and search people in a designated area for a limited period. There is considerable variation in legal powers of European police to conduct identity checks and stops.

23. Laurence Lustgarten, "The Future of Stop and Search," *Criminal Law Review*, 2002, at 603–618.

24. "As with other systemic practices, racial profiling can be conscious or unconscious, intentional or unintentional. Racial profiling by police officers may be unconscious." *The Queen v. Campbell*, Court of Quebec (Criminal Division) (no. 500-01-004657-042-001), Judgment of January 27, 2006, quoted in European Union Network of Independent Experts on Fundamental Rights, "Ethnic Profiling," CFR–CDF, Opinion 4, 2006, at 7.

25. Although our analysis focuses on ECHR law, the anti-discrimination norm is fundamental in international law. International human rights treaties routinely prohibit discrimination in the enjoyment of protected rights, some of which are directly implicated by police action. Article 2(1) of the International Covenant on Civil and Political Rights, 999 U.N.T.S. 171, entered into force March 23, 1976 (ICCPR), provides: "Each State Party to the present Covenant undertakes to respect and to ensure to all individuals within its territory and subject to its jurisdiction the rights recognized in the present Covenant, without distinction of any kind, such as race, colour, sex, language, religion, political or other opinion, national or social origin, property, birth or other status." "Rights recognized in the present Covenant" that are especially relevant to police practices examined in this report include "the right to liberty and security of the person," which includes freedom from "arbitrary arrest or detention" (Article 9(1)) and the right to "be equal before the courts and tribunals") (Article 14(1)). Article 1 of the International Convention on the Elimination of All Forms of Racial Discrimination, 660 UNTS 195, entered into force January 4, 1969 ("Race Convention"), provides: "In this Convention, the term 'racial discrimination' shall mean any distinction, exclusion, restriction or preference based on race, colour, descent, or national or ethnic origin which has the purpose or effect of nullifying or impairing the recognition, enjoyment or exercise, on an equal footing, of human rights and fundamental freedoms in the political, economic, social, cultural or any other field of public life." The Race Convention requires States parties to ensure non-discrimination in the enjoyment of enumerated rights, including two that are often implicated by the police practices addressed in this report—"freedom of movement" (Article 5(d)(i)) and the "right to equal treatment before the tribunals and all other organs administering justice" (Article 5(a)).

26. Article 14 of the ECHR provides:

> The enjoyment of the rights and freedoms set forth in [the] Convention shall be secured without discrimination on any ground such as sex, race, colour, language, religion, political or other opinion, national or social origin, association with a national minority, property, birth or other status.

European Convention for the Protection of Human Rights and Fundamental Freedoms, art. 14, E.T.S. 5, entered into force September 3, 1953, as amended by Protocols Nos. 3, 5, 8, and 11.

27. Protocol No. 12 entered into force on April 1, 2005. As of January 18, 2008, 15 States were parties to the protocol. See http://conventions.coe.int/Treaty/Commun/ChercheSig.asp?NT=177&CM=&DF=&CL=ENG.

28. Protocol No. 12 to the Convention for the Protection of Human Rights and Fundamental Freedoms, Explanatory Report, 22(iii).

29. *Timishev v. Russia*, App. Nos. 55762/00, 55974/00, Eur. Ct. Hum. Rts., Judgment of December 13, 2005, at 56.

30. *Belgian Linguistics Case* (No. 2), 1 EHRR 252, 10 (1968); see also *Abdulaziz and Others v. United Kingdom*, Eur. Ct. Hum. Rts., Judgment of May 28, 1985, at 72.

31. See *Abdulaziz and Others v. United Kingdom*, Eur. Ct. Hum. Rts., Judgment of May 28, 1985, at 81.

32. *Belgian Linguistics Case* (No. 2), 1 EHRR 252, at 10 (1968).

33. In the *Inze* case, for example, the court found that proposed legislative amendments "show that the aim of the legislation in question could also have been achieved by applying criteria other than that based on [birth in or out of wedlock]," which it found to violate the ECHR. Case of *Inze v. Austria*, No. 8695/79, Eur. Ct. Hum. Rts., Judgment of October 28, 1987, at 44.

34. *Timishev v. Russia*, App. Nos. 55762/00, 55974/00, Eur. Ct. Hum. Rts., Judgment of December 13, 2005.

35. Ibid., at 39–44.

36. Ibid., at 40–41.

37. In *Nachova v. Bulgaria*, the Grand Chamber held that the failure to investigate vigorously the racially motivated shooting of two Roma by Bulgarian military police violated the nondiscrimination guarantee of Article 14 taken in conjunction with Article 2 (right to life). Pertinent to ethnic profiling, the court affirmed that, "[i]n order to maintain public confidence in their law enforcement machinery, Contracting States must ensure that in the investigation of incidents involving the use of force a distinction is made both in their legal systems and in practice between cases of excessive use of force and of racist killing." *Nachova and Others v. Bulgaria*, Eur. Ct. Hum. Rts., Judgment of July 6, 2005, at 160.

38. *Timishev v. Russia*, App. Nos. 55762/00, 55974/00, Eur. Ct. Hum. Rts., Judgment of December 13, 2005, at 59.

39. Ibid., at 58–59.

40. *Hoffmann v. Austria*, Eur. Ct. Hum. Rts., Judgment of June 23, 1993, at 36 (religion); *Gaygusuz v. Austria*, Eur. Ct. Hum. Rts., Judgment of September 16, 1996, at 42 (nationality).

41. Direct discrimination shall be taken to occur where one person is treated less favourably than another is, has been or would be treated in a comparable situation on grounds of racial or ethnic origin. EU Race Directive, Council Directive 2000/43/EC of 29 June 2000 implementing the principle of equal treatment between persons irrespective of racial or ethnic origin, para. 2(a).

42. *Regina v. Immigration Officer at Prague Airport*, December 9, 2004, [2004] UKHL 55. For countries within the Schengen remit (the U.K. is not), such contact would be clearly unlawful under the Article 6 of the Schengen Borders Code on the conduct of border checks, which states that: (1.) Border guards shall, in the performance of their duties, fully respect human dignity. Any measures taken in the performance of their duties shall be proportionate to the objectives pursued by such measures. (2.) While carrying out border checks, border guards shall not discriminate against persons on grounds of sex, racial or ethnic origin, religion or belief, disability, age or sexual orientation. Regulation (EC) No 562/2006 of the European Parliament and of the Council of 15 March 2006

establishing a Community Code on the rules governing the movement of persons across borders (Schengen Borders Code).

43. Ibid., para. 82 (Baroness Hale) (internal citations omitted).

44. To undertake this kind of analysis, researchers need data on police stops including the ethnicity of the person stopped. These data sets are generally lacking in Europe; many police forces do not record their stops or do not make this information publicly available and, almost no countries record ethnic data. The United Kingdom is the only EU Member State that collects and, since 1992, regularly publishes statistics on ethnicity and police stop and search practices.

45. For example in *Cobzaru v. Romania*, a case involving police violence against a Roma victim, the court observed

> that the numerous anti-Roma incidents which often involved State agents following the fall of the communist regime in 1990, and other documented evidence of repeated failure by the authorities to remedy instances of such violence were known to the public at large, as they were regularly covered by the media. .... [U]ndoubtedly, such incidents, as well as the policies adopted by the highest Romanian authorities in order to fight discrimination against Roma were known to the investigating authorities in the present case, or should have been known, and therefore special care should have been taken in investigating possible racist motives behind the violence.

Cobzaru v. Romania, App. No. 48254/99, Eur. Ct. Hum. Rts. Judgment of July 27, 2007, at 97. Far from taking "special care" to investigate possible racist motives behind the violence, Romanian prosecutors had "made tendentious remarks in relation to the applicant's Roma origin throughout the investigation." Id., at 98. The court found that these comments disclosed "a general discriminatory attitude of the authorities," Id., at 100, and that this, together with "the failure of the law enforcement agents to investigate possible racial motives in the applicant's ill-treatment," constituted discrimination in violation of the ECHR. Id., at 101.

46. *D.H. and Others v. the Czech Republic*, App. No. 57325/00. Eur. Ct. Hum. Rts., Grand Chamber, judgment of November 13, 2007.

47. The court has already accepted in previous cases that a difference in treatment may take the form of disproportionately prejudicial effects of a general policy or measure which, though couched in neutral terms, discriminates against a group. Such a situation may amount to "indirect discrimination," which does not necessarily require a discriminatory intent. Id., at 184.

48. This case involved a challenge to discriminatory practices in public education.

49. European courts have yet conclusively to resolve whether there may be greater scope for the use of ethnic profiling in the context of immigration enforcement. In *Cissé v. France*, App No. 51346/99, Eur. Ct. Hum. Rts., January 16, 2001, the court declared inadmissible the portions of an application alleging a violation of Article 14 in conjunction with Article 5 in relation to a police evacuation of a Paris church that had been occupied by "a group of aliens from various African countries who had settled in France without residence permits" and who "in 1996 decided to take collective action to draw attention to the difficulties they were having in obtaining a review of their immigration status in France." The Article 14/5 allegations related to the following facts: When evacuating the church, the police stopped and questioned all of the occupants. "Whites were immediately released while the police assembled all the dark-skinned occupants, apart from those on hunger strike, and sent them by coach to an aliens' detention center." Noting that a majority of the occupants of the church, including the applicant, belonged to the group of aliens from Africa

who did not possess residence permits, the court noted that "the system set up at the church exit for checking identities was intended to ascertain the identity of persons suspect[ed] of being illegal immigrants. In these circumstances," the court "[could not] conclude that the applicant was subjected to discrimination based on race or colour."

National courts have taken divergent approaches to the question of whether there is greater scope for ethnic profiling in an immigration enforcement context. In a 2001 ruling, the Spanish Constitutional Court accorded the police broad latitude, ruling that it is permissible for the police to "use the racial criterion as merely indicative of a greater probability that the interested party was not Spanish." (*Rosalind Williams*, Spanish Constitutional Court Decision No. 13/2001, January 29, 2001 (STC 13/2001)). The court reasoned that when police controls serve the purpose of "requiring that foreigners in Spanish territory are obliged to have documentation which proves their identity and their legal status in Spain...specific physical or ethnic characteristics can be taken into consideration as reasonably indicative of the national origin of the person who has them." A dissenting judge noted that using race as a proxy for nationality makes little sense in what is "already a multi-racial society." The Spanish decision is currently being challenged before the United Nations Committee on Human Rights. The Spanish court's reasoning is at odds with that set forth more recently by the United Kingdom House of Lords in the *Roma Rights Case*, discussed *infra*.

50.   U.S. Department of Justice, Civil Rights Division, *Guidance Regarding the Use of Race by Federal Law Enforcement Agencies* (Washington DC: Department of Justice, June 2003), available at http://www.usdoj.gov/crt/split/documents/guidance_on_race.htm (emphasis added).

51.   Home Office, Police and Criminal Evidence Act 1984, Code of Practice A, revised December 31st 2005, para. 2.2, available at http://police.homeoffice.gov.uk/news-and-publications/publication/operational-policing/PACE_Chapter_A.pdf?view=Binary.

52.   Center for Human Rights and Global Justice, *Irreversible Consequences: Racial Profiling and Lethal Force in the "War on Terror,"* (New York: New York University School of Law, May 2006). See also Randall Kennedy, "Racial Profiling Usually Isn't Racist," *The New Republic*, September 13, 1999.

53.   European Union network of independent experts on fundamental rights, "Ethnic Profiling," at 6.

54.   In *Barcelona Traction*, the International Court of Justice observed that "racial discrimination" is among the "principles and rules concerning the basic rights of the human person" which are obligations *erga omnes* as a matter of customary international law. ICJ Reports (1970), 3 at 32.

55.   International Covenant on Civil and Political Rights, Art. 4. See also European Convention on Human Rights, Art. 15 (authorizing derogation for most rights, including Aritcle 14, "in time of war or other public emergency threatening the life of the nation").

56.   ICCPR, Art. 4(1). See also General Comment No. 29, para. 8 ("Even though article 26 or the other Covenant provisions related to non-discrimination (Articles 2, 3, 14, paragraph 1, 23, paragraph 4, 24, paragraph 1, and 25) have not been listed among the non-derogable provisions in article 4, paragraph 2, there are elements or dimensions of the right to non-discrimination that cannot be derogated from in any circumstances. In particular, this provision of Article 4, paragraph 1, must be complied with if any distinctions between persons are made when resorting to measures that derogate from the Covenant").

57.   United Nations Office of High Commissioner for Human Rights, Digest of Jurisprudence of the UN And Regional Organizations On the Protection Of Human Rights While Countering Terrorism, at 5, available at http://www.ohchr.org/english/about/publications/docs/digest.doc.

58.   UNCERD statement of March 8, 2002, (A/57/18, chap. XI, sect. C, para. 5).

59.   "Guidelines on human rights and the fight against terrorism," Article II, adopted by the Council of Europe Committee of Ministers, Adopted July 11, 2002.

60.   "The Court has pointed out in several judgments that the Contracting States enjoy a certain 'margin of appreciation' in assessing whether and to what extent differences in otherwise similar situations justify a different treatment in law ... The scope of the margin of appreciation will vary according to the circumstances, the subject matter and its background." *Rasmussen v. Denmark* (1984) 7 E.H.R.R. 371 at [40]. Cited in Daniel Moeckli, "Discriminatory Profiles; Law Enforcement After 9/11 and 7/7," *European Human Rights Law Review*, 2005, 5, 517–532.

61.   Para. 32, *Fox, Cambell and Hartley v. the United Kingdom*, Eur. Ct. Hum. Rts., August 30, 1990, addressing the right to be informed of reason for arrest. Cited in Council of Europe Committee of Ministers, Guidelines on human rights and the fight against terrorism, adopted by the Committee of Ministers on 11 July 2002 at the 804th meeting of the Minister's deputies.

62.   *Klass and others v. Germany*, 6 September 1978, Series A, no. 28, para. 48. "The Court has therefore to accept that the existence of some legislation granting powers of secret surveillance over the mail, post and telecommunications is, under exceptional circumstances, necessary in a democratic society in the interests of national security and/or for the prevention of disorder or crime." Tapping must be done in accordance with law. Council of Europe Committee of Ministers, "Guidelines on human rights and the fight against terrorism," adopted by the Committee of Ministers on 11 July 2002 at the 804th meeting of the Minister's deputies.

63.   *Murray v. the United Kingdom*, October 28, 1994, para. 58.

64.   *Klass and Others v. Germany*, September 6, 1978, Series A no. 28, para. 49.

65.   *Fox, Cambell and Hartley v. the United Kingdom*, at 32.

66.   *The Sunday Times v. the United Kingdom* (No. 2) November 26, 1991, Series A, No. 217, at 28–29.

67.   *Brannigan and McBride v. the United Kingdom*, May 26, 1993, para. 43.

68.   *A v. Secretary of State for the Home Department*, UKHL 56 (2004) (finding anti-terrorism legislation may not single out non-citizens for preventive detention consistent with the non-discrimination principle). In any event, as this report notes, a substantial number of persons involved in terrorist incidents have been native-born citizens. Robert S. Leiken, "Europe's Angry Muslims." *Foreign Affairs*, 2005. Targeting only nationals of certain countries may permit the argument that a government practice is not *driven by* ethnicity or religion, but it may nonetheless amount to unlawful racial/ethnic discrimination, if—as is often the case—the countries at issue are overwhelmingly Muslim.

69.   Geir Moulson, "German high court curbs database-mining," Associated Press, Tuesday, May 23, 2006. Bundesverfassungsgericht—Pressestelle, Pressemitteilung Nr. 40/2006 vom 23. Mai 2006. Zum Beschluss 4. April 2006—1 BvR 518/02—Rasterfahndung nur bei konkreter Gefahr für hochrangige Rechtsgüter zulässig.

70. CERD, General Recommendation No. 30 (Non-Citizens), para. 6, January 10, 2004.

71. CERD, General Recommendation No. 31 (Administration of the Criminal Justice System), para. 20. (2005).

72. *East African Asians*, 3 EHRR 76 (1973), para. 207.

73. As noted earlier, violations of Article 14 can be committed only in conjunction with a violation of another right protected by the ECHR. The point emphasized here is that the reverse is not true.

74. *Gusinskiy v. Russia*, App. No. 70276/01, Eur. Ct. Hum. Rts, Judgment of May 29, 2004 (Final November 11, 2004), at 53 (citation omitted).

75. *Fox, Campbell and Hartley v. United Kingdom*, at 32.

76. Ibid., at 35–36.

77. John R. Bowen, *Why the French Don't Like Headscarves*, (Princeton: Princeton University Press, 2007), at 36.

78. Open Society Justice Initiative, *I Can Stop and Search Whoever I Want*, (New York Open Society Institute, 2006). Interestingly, even interviewees who had been stopped, about third of whom were Roma, were predominantly in favor of stop tactics, considered the tactic to be right and justified, and would not want to change it.

79. European Commission against Racism and Intolerance, *Second Report on Austria*, (Strasbourg: ECRI, 2000), para. 39; *Second Report on Romania*, (Strasbourg: ECRI, 2001), para. 46; *Second Report on the Russian Federation*, (Strasbourg: ECRI, 2001), para. 62; *Second Report on Spain*, (Strasbourg: ECRI, 2002), para. 38; *Third Report on Switzerland*, (Strasbourg: ECRI, 2003), at 29; *Second Report on Ukraine*, (Strasbourg: ECRI, 2003), para. 42; *Second Report on the United Kingdom*, (Strasbourg: ECRI, 2000), para. 45. For a summary of this reporting, see Misti Duvall, "Ethnic Profiling by Police in Europe," *Justice Initiatives*, (New York: Open Society Institute, June 2005), at 14–25.

80. Marianne Gratia and Siham Nouar, *ENAR Rapport Alternatif 2003: Belgique*, (Brussels: European Network Against Racism, 2003).

81. Committee on the Elimination of Racial Discrimination, *Concluding Observations of the Committttee, France, 1994*, para. 125.

82. ECRI, *Second Report on France*, (Strasbourg: ECRI, 1999).

83. EUMAP (Budapest: Open Society Institute, EUMap, 2002), at 189–190.

84. European Commission against Racism and Intolerance, *Third Report on Germany*, (Strasbourg: ECRI, 2003), para. 69.

85. European Commission against Racism and Intolerance, *Second Report on Greece*, (Strasbourg: ECRI, 1999) at 13 and 17.

86. U.S. Department of State, *Country Reports on Human Rights Practices: Greece*, (Washington, D.C.: U.S. Government Printing Office, 2003).

87. European Commission against Racism and Intolerance, *Report on Hungary* (Strasbourg: ECRI, 1997): *Second Report on Hungary* (Strasbourg: ECRI, 2000), at 8; and *Third Report on Hungary* (Strasbourg: ECRI, 2004).

88. European Commission against Racism and Intolerance, *Second Report on Italy*, (Strasbourg: ECRI, 2002), para. 51.

89. European Roma Rights Centre (ERRC), Open Society Institute, Roma Criss, Roma Civic Alliance in Romania and Centre on Housing Rights and Evictions (CORHE), *Security a la Italiana; Fingerprinting, Extreme Violence and Harrassment of Roma in Italy*, July 8, 2008, at 7, available at http://www.errc.org/db/03/21/m00000321.pdf. See also: Memorandum by Thomas Hammarberg, Commission for Human Rights of the Council of Europe following his visit to Italy June 19–20, 2008, (Strasbourg, July 28, 2008); and Fundamental Rights Agency, *Incident Report: Violent attacks against Roma in the Ponticelli district of Naples, Italy* (Vienna: FRA, 2008).

90. Ibid. ERRC et al, *Security Italian Style,* at 10. See also, European Roma Rights Center (ERRC), Associazione Studi Giuridici sull'Immigrazione (ASGI), Centre on Housing Rights and Evictions (CORHE), Centro di Ricera Azione Contro la Discriminazione di Roma e Sinti (observAzione), National Roma Centrum (NRC), Romani CRISS, *Memorandum: Request for Expedited Engagement of Follow-Up Procedure and/or Urgent Action/Early Warning Procedure Concerning Italy ICERD Compliance*, July 2, 2008, available at http://www.errc.org/cikk.php?cikk=2966&archiv=1.

91. European Commission against Racism and Intolerance, *Second Report on Spain*, at 11 and 16.

92. Ibid., at 16.

93. Amnesty International, Spain*: Crisis of Identity: Race-related Torture and Ill-treatment by State Agents*, (London: Amnesty International, April 2002).

94. The data collected include both stops and stop/searches and measures among other factors the ethnicity of the person stopped, the reason for the stop and the outcome of the stop.

95. Since 1992, the United Kingdom's Home Office and Ministry of Justice have published statistical information as required under Section 95 of the 1991 Criminal Justice Act. The aim of these publications is to help those in the administration of justice to avoid discrimination on the grounds of race.

96. Some information is available on policing practices as they pertain to non-citizens, as many countries distinguish between foreigners and nationals in their criminal justice statistics.

97. Ministry of Justice, *Statistics on Race and the Criminal Justice System—2007/8*. (London: Ministry of Justice, 2009), at 28, available at: http://www.justice.gov.uk/publications/docs/stats-race-criminal-justice-system-07-08-full.pdf   Ministry of Justice statistics compare the numbers of stops and searches performed to the resident population and have consistently shown considerable differences between different ethnic groups. On April 1, 2003, a standard system of recording was introduced into all criminal justice system agencies based on self-classification into one of 16 categories used in the 2001 census. Classification is based around five main groups: white, mixed, black, Asian, and "other." Disproportionality figures are calculated by dividing the number of stops and searches per 1,000 people in an ethnic group by the equivalent rate for white people. It is a measure of how many times a member of an ethnic group is likely to be stopped under the various stop and search legislation.

98. Section 60 of the Criminal Justice and Public Order Act 1994 as amended by Section 8 of the Knives Act 1997allows an Inspector or higher ranked officer who reasonably fears serious violence or the carrying of weapons in a particular locality to authorize uniformed officers to search any person or vehicle in that locality for weapons for a period of 24 hours. Subsection 3 allows a super-

intendent to extend this authorization for a further 24 hours. Section 60 limits stops and searches to a specific time and place but do not require police to have any basis of reasonable suspicion.

99. Ministry of Justice, *Statistics on Race and the Criminal Justice System—2007/8*, at 29, 49, 205.

100. Vikram Dodd, "Black People 27 times more likely to be stopped," *The Guardian*, April 21, 2003, citing Professor Ben Bowling, of King's College, London.

101. Home Office, *Police Powers and Procedures England and Wales 2007/08*. (London: Home Office Statistics, 2009) at 34.

102. It is worth noting that when all police stops—both vehicle and pedestrian—are considered, there was no overall measurable difference in the frequency of stops between Roma and non-Roma. These differences can be reasonably assumed to reflect higher rates of vehicle ownership among non-Roma in both countries, but shows that it is necessary to disaggregate vehicle stops from pedestrian stops in order to detect bias. In Bulgaria, 51 percent of ethnic Bulgarians own cars compared with 20 percent of Roma, and in Hungary 58 percent of ethnic Hungarians own cars compared with 35 percent of the Roma. Open Society Justice Initiative, *I Can Stop and Search Whoever I Want*, (New York: Open Society Institute, 2006), at 31. Research includes survey data in Bulgaria and Hungary and interviews of police officers in the three countries. Another Justice Initiative study of policing in the Moscow metro system found that non-Slavs are stopped more than 20 times more often than Slavs—the highest rate of disproportion ever detected in a study of police profiling. Open Society Justice Initiative, *Ethnic Profiling in the Moscow Metro*, (New York: Open Society Institute, 2006). Rates of disproportion measured in the U.S. and U.K. tend to range between 3:1 to 8:1. John Lamberth, a preeminent U.S. expert on documenting profiling, says that any odds ratio above 2:1 represents ethnic profiling, and that police should be concerned when the odds ratio is at or above 1.5:1. See www.lamberthconsulting.com.

103. Open Society Justice Initiative, *I Can Stop and Search Whoever I Want*, at 43.

104. Ibid., at 44.

105. All quotes from interviews conducted by GEA21 during research on ethnic profiling; pre-editing interview records on file with Open Society Justice Initiative. See also Daniel Wagman and Begonia Perñas, *Ethnic Profiling in Spain; Investigations and Recommendations* (Madrid: GEA21, July 2006), and Open Society Justice Initiative, *I Can Stop and Search Whoever I Want*.

106. Ibid.

107. European Commission against Racism and Intolerance, *Second Report on Italy*, at 52.

108. Amnesty International, *Back in the Spotlight; Allegations of Police Ill-Treatment and Excessive Use of Force in Germany* (London: Amnesty International, January 14, 2004).

109. European Commission against Racism and Intolerance, *Second Report on Albania,* (Strasbourg: ECRI, 2000), para. 31; *Third Report on Austria,* (Strasbourg: ECRI, 2004), paras. 78 and 82; *Second Report on Belgium,* (Strasbourg: ECRI, 2003), para. 64; *Third Report on Bulgaria,* (Strasbourg: ECRI, 2003), paras. 76–77; *Second Report on Cyprus,* (Strasbourg: ECRI, 2000), para. 41; *Third Report on the Czech Republic,* (Strasbourg: ECRI, 2003) para. 75; *Third Report on France,* (Strasbourg: ECRI, 2005), para. 109; *Second Report on "the Former Yugoslav Republic of Macedonia,"* (Strasbourg: ECRI, 2000), para. 32; *Third Report on Germany,* (Strasbourg: ECRI, 2003), para. 79; *Third Report on Greece,* (Strasbourg: ECRI, 2003), para. 105; *Fourth Report on Hungary,* (Strasbourg: ECRI, 2009),

para. 175; *Third Report on Poland,* (Strasbourg: ECRI, 2004), para. 82; *Third Report on Portugal,* (Strasbourg: ECRI, 2006), para. 94; *Third Report on Romania,* (Strasbourg: ECRI, 2005), para. 102; *Third Report on Spain,* (Strasbourg: ECRI, 2005), para. 87; *Third Report on Switzerland,* (Strasbourg: ECRI, 2004).

110. Amnesty International, *Spain: Crisis of Identity.*

111. Open Society Justice Initiative, *I Can Stop and Search Whoever I Want,* at 34–37.

112. Ibid., at 36.

113. Roma interviewee, Bulgaria, cited in Center for the Study of Democracy, *Police Stops and Ethnic Profiling in Bulgaria* (Sofia: Center for the Study of Democracy, 2006).

114. See Bulgarian Helsinki Committee, *Alternative Report to the Report Submitted by Bulgaria Pursuant to Article 25, Paragraph 1 of the Framework Convention for the Protection of National Minorities* (Sofia: Bulgarian Helsinki Committee, 2003), at 6–7.

115. Bulgarian Helsinki Committee, *Annual Report of the Bulgarian Helsinki Committee,* (Sofia: Bulgarian Helsinki Committee, 2002), at 4.

116. Ibid. The 2002 figures represent a high point in a long-term trend of different treatment based on ethnicity.

117. Amnesty International, *Crisis of Identity.*

118. Report to the Basque parliament. Informe al Parlamento Vasco del Ararteko 1998. "Intervention on police actions against persons of foreign origin in the area of San Francisco," available at www.ararteko.net/webs/ioridnarios/ord1998.pdf.

119. Ibid.

120. Daniel Wagman interview with Bartolomé Martínez, Madrid, January 10, 2005.

121. Cited in Amnesty International, *2007 Annual Report: Spain* (London: Amnesty International, 2007), available at http://www.amnesty.org/en/region/europe-and-central-asia/western-europe/spain.

122. *See* Committee Against Torture, *Concluding Observations of the Committee Against Torture: Greece,* (CAT/C/CR/33/2, 2004), para. 5. Committee Against Torture, *Concluding Observations of the Committee Against Torture: Greece,* (A/56/44, 2001), para. 87.

123. European Commission against Racism and Intolerance, *Second Report on Greece,* (Strasbourg: ECRI, 1999).

124. Ibid., at 56.

125. Ibid., "In light of the above, it is clear that complaints about racist prejudice of police officers against aliens and Roma are ill-founded. This is also corroborated by the fact that from the 164 complaints in the period 2001–2003, only 54 concerned aliens and only 11 Roma, while from the 66 cases of use of firearms by police officers in the period 2000–2003, only 27 concerned aliens and 5 Roma."

126. Ibid., para. 5.

127. Human Rights Committee, *Initial Report: Greece,* (CCPR/C/GRC/2004/1, 2004), available at: http://www.unhchr.ch/tbs/doc.nsf/(Symbol)/CCPR.C.GRC.2004.1.En?Opendocument. Official

estimates of the Roma population in Greece range from 70,000 to 300,000 out of a total population of 11 million.

128. European Roma Rights Centre, *Campland: Racial Segregation of Roma in Italy,* (Budapest: European Roma Rights Centre, November 2000), at 43.

129. Ibid., at 43.

130. Ibid., at 41–42.

131. Ibid., at 34–36.

132. ERRC et al., *Security a la Italiana,* at 12–18.

133. Ibid.

134. ECRI, *Second Report on Italy.*

135. Committee on the Elimination of Racial Discrimination, *Concluding Observations of the Committee,* (1999), para. 13.

136. A. Rivera and P. Andrisani, *Analytical Study on Discrimination and Racist Violence in Italy: 2000–2002,* (EUMC, Raxen National Focal Point Italy, September 2002), at 34.

137. Amnesty International, *Europe and Central Asia, Summary of Concerns in the Region,* (January–June 2004), at 45, available at: http://web.amnesty.org/library/Index/ENGEUR010052004?op en&of=NEG-ITA.

138. Amnesty International, *France: Shootings, Killings, and Alleged Ill-Treatment by Law Enforcement Officers,* (London: Amnesty International, 1994).

139. Human Rights Committee, *Concluding Observations of the Human Rights Committee: France (1997),* (CCPR/C/79/Add.80), para. 16, available at: http://www.unhchr.ch/tbs/doc.nsf/(Symbol)/ CCPR.C.79.Add.80.En?Opendocument.

140. ECRI, *Report on France,* (Strasbourg: ECRI, 1998), at 9.

141. Committee on the Elimination of Racial Discrimination, *Concluding Observations of the Committee,* (France, 2004) *supra,* para. 19.

142. Amnesty International, *Annual Report: France,* (2003), reporting statistics released by the General Inspection Services (IGS), available at: http://web.amnesty.org/web/web.nsf/print/2004-fra-summary-eng.

143. The Commission Nationale de Déontologie de la Sécurité (CNDS) is the national body charged with the review of police conduct. CNDS, "Etude sur la part des discriminations dans les manquements à la déontologie," in *Rapport 2004,* (Paris: April 18, 2005), available at: http://www. cnds.fr/ra_pdf/ra_2004/CNDS_rapport_2004.pdf.

144. Jacky Durand, "Bavures au faciès," *Libération,* April 18, 2005.

145. Commission nationale sur les rapports entre les citoyens et les forces de sécurité, sur le contrôle et le traitement de ces rapports par l'institution judiciaire (comprised of Ligue des droits de l'Homme (LDH), Mouvement contre le Racisme et pour l'Amitié entre les Peuples (MRAP), Syndicat des Avocats de France (SAF), Syndicat de la Magistrature (SM)), "Citizens—Justice—Police," in *Activity Report for July 2002 through June 2004,* (Paris: LDH/MRAP/SAF, 2004), at 8.

146. "The number of complaints of ill-treatment [by police] has increased in recent years. A rise in such incidents, especially in the context of police identity checks or in police custody, has also been detected. Identity checks often degenerate into violence and, in many cases, this is the result of aggressive or insulting conduct of law enforcement." Amnesty International, "Public statement on France," November 10, 2005. Amnesty International, *2003 Annual Report: France*, at: http://web.amnesty.org/report2003/Fra-summary-eng.

147. Ibid. See also, Ligue des droits de l'Homme, Syndicat des avocats de France and Syndicat de la Magistrature, *A report of the commission of inquiry into police behavior in Châtenet-Malbry, Poissy et Paris 20ème*, (Paris, July 2002).

148. Amnesty International, *2004 Annual Report: France*, at: http://web.amnesty.org/web/web.nsf/print/2004-fra-summary-eng. In particular, the report cites a study of a human rights committee in the Department of Seine-Saint-Denis which asserts that many incidents continue to arise out of identity checks and to be race-related.

149. Pittsburgh is one example. See Robert C. Davis, Christopher W. Ortiz, Nicole J. Henderson, Joel Miller, and Michelle K. Massie, *Turning Necessity into Virtue: Pittsburgh's Experience with a Federal Consent Decree*, (New York: Vera Institute of Justice, September 2002), at 27.

150. This tactic is common across many settings. As noted above, ECRI has noted the use of counter-charges in Italy, *Second Report on Italy*, 2002. In Germany, Amnesty International reported in 2004 that: "long-standing concerns about the incidence of police counter-charges persist. A sizeable number of the individuals featured in this report who lodged complaints about their ill-treatment also faced police counter-charges, such as resistance to state authority or insulting behavior." *Back in the Spotlight; Allegations of Police Ill-Treatment and Excessive Use of Force in Germany*. See also, Police Foundation, *Police Use of Force: Official Reports, Citizen Complaints and Legal Consequences*, (Washington, D.C.: Police Foundation, 1993), and Mary O'Rawe and Linda Moore, *Human Rights on Duty*, (Belfast: Committee for the Administration of Justice, 1997).

151. Fabien Jobard and M. Zimolag, "When the police go to court: Analysis of a sample of judgments in cases of offenses against public authorities in a local court in Paris (1965–2003)," in *Questions pénales*, no. 97, March 2005, available at: www.cesdip.org/IMG/pdf/EDP_no_97.pdf. The study used names and place of birth as proxies for ethnicity to examine differential treatment of persons charged with the same offenses. The *"descent and consonance groups"* used birthplaces and name consonance to break the study population into seven relevant groups: "South Europeans," "East Europeans," "North Africans," "Africans," "Born Africans," "Born in DOM–TOM" (French overseas departments and territories), "Other." The offenses studies are "outrages," "rebellion," and "violence" which are roughly equivalent to contempt, resisting arrest, and assaulting an officer. In France, private individuals can initiate cases for crimes that have directly harmed them, Criminal Procedure Code, Art 1. It is worth noting that in the U.S., police forces that have created "early warning systems" to flag potential problem officers use an excessive number of charges by an officer of "resisting arrest" as a "red flag" indicator of potentially poor conduct of stops.

152. The absence of any official ethnic statistics makes it extremely difficult to calculate the number of French citizens and residents of Maghreb origin. However, in 2003 the French Ministry of the Interior estimated the total number of Muslims in France to be five to six million, many but not all of whom would originate from the Maghreb. The population of France is just under 65 million. Jonathan Laurence and Justin Vaïsse, *Integrating Islam*, (Paris: Odile Jacob, 2007).

153. Cathy Schneider, "Police Power and Race Riots in Paris," *Policing and Society* Vol. 35, No. 4, December 2007.

154. *Amnesty International 2007 Annual Report: France*, available at http://thereport.amnesty.org/eng/Regions/Europe-and-Central-Asia/France.

155. Cited in *Amnesty International 2007 Annual Report: France*, available at http://thereport.amnesty.org/eng/Regions/Europe-and-Central-Asia/France.

156. "Violence Overshadows Upcoming French Elections," *Morning Edition, National Public Radio*, October 4, 2006. Audio available at: http://www.npr.org/templates/story/story.php?storyId=6193891.

157. "Paris Burns," *The Economist*, December 1–7, 2007, at 64.

158. Accordingly, raids potentially implicate Article 8 of the European Convention on Human Rights, which protects the right to respect for private and family life.

159. Iulius Costas, "ID checks and police raids: Ethnic profiling in Central Europe" in "Ethnic Profiling by Police in Europe," *Justice Initiatives*, June 2005, at 27.

160. Iulius Costas, "ID checks and police raids: Ethnic profiling in Central Europe." European Roma Rights Centre and Greek Helsinki Monitor, *Cleaning Operations: Excluding Roma in Greece*, (2003); See also the following reports by the European Roma Rights Centre: *Always somewhere else: Anti-Gypsyism in France* (Budapest: ERRC, Country Report Series No. 15, 2005); *The Non-Constituents: Rights deprivation of Roma in post-genocide Bosnia-Herzegovina*, (Budapest: ERRC, Country Report Series 13, 2004); *In Search of Happy Gypsies: Persecution of pariah minorities in Russia*, (Budapest: ERRC, 2005); *The Limits of Solidarity: Roma in Poland after 1989*, (Budapest: ERRC, 2002). OSCE Human Dimension Implementation Meeting, *Statements by the International Helsinki Federation for Human Rights (IHF)* (Warsaw, September 9–19 2002).

161. European Roma Rights Centre, *Campland: Racial Segregation of Roma in Italy*, at 23.

162. Ibid., at 23–4.

163. European Network Against Racism, *Shadow Report: Italy, 2003*, (Brussels: ENAR, 2003), at 29.

164. European Roma Rights Centre, *Campland: Racial Segregation of Roma in Italy*, at 23–34.

165. Rivera and Andrisani, *Analytical Study on Discrimination and Racist Violence in Italy: 2000–2002*, at 13.

166. With reference to a 2002 raid against the Roma camp Arco di Travertino in Roma. OSCE Human Dimension Implementation Meeting, *Statements by the International Helsinki Federation for Human Rights (IHF)*, Warsaw, September 9–18, 2002 18. See also International Helsinki Federation, *Annual Report Italy 2002*, at 181–182.

167. Committee on the Rights of the Child, *Concluding Observations: Italy*, 2003, (CRD/15/Add.198), para. 31, available at www.unhchr.ch/tbs/doc.nsf. See also Amnesty International, *Annual Report 2004: Italy*, available at http://web.amnesty.org/report2004/ita-summary-eng.

168. In January 28, 2002, the Roma settlement of Nea Zoe in Aspropyrgos, near Athens, was raided by police ostensibly searching for drugs: "[O]nce officers had searched all the homes and everyone was outside, the officers herded all the residents together. According to residents, the police did not produce any search warrants. Greek law requires the presence of a judicial officer

during house searches, but none of the witnesses [...] had actually seen one." European Roma Rights Centre and Greek Helsinki Monitor, *Cleaning Operations: Excluding Roma in Greece*, April 2003, (Budapest and Athens: ERRC and GHM, Country Report Series No. 12), at 104, available at http://www.errc.org/db/00/09/m00000009.pdf.

169. Ibid., at 104.

170. Ibid., Quoting *Summary Record of the First Part of the 463rd Meeting*, (Greece, May 9, 2001), (CAT/C/SR.463 (Summary Record)), 47, para. 7.

171. Ibid.

172. Busch Heiner, "Foreigners and Police: An Unholy Allaince," in *Bürgerrechte und Polizei/ CILIP* 65, (January 2000), at 42–43. Antirassismusbüro Bremen, "They Treat Us Like Animals: Police and Judicial Racism in Germany," 1997.

173. EUMAP, 2002, at 192.

174. *ABC Sevilla.* November 4, 2004

175. "Granda, free to integrate," *Nueva España*, November 7, 2004. Residents of Granda, a Roma neighborhood, denounce constant Spanish Civil Guard surveillance and control, affirming that there is no criminal activity there.

176. "New immigration law comes into force," *Molotov Magazine*, No. 41, December 2003.

177. Statement made at the seminar "Police and Ethnic and Cultural Diversity in Spain." Organized in Madrid by the Fundación Secretariado General Gitano and Ministerio de Trabajo y Asuntos Sociales, June, 3, 2004.

178. Regulation (EC) No. 562/2006 of the European Parliament and of the Council of March 15, 2006 establishing a Community Code on the rules governing the movement of persons across borders (Schengen Borders Code), Article 6 (2).

179. Article L611-1 of the Code of Entry and Stay of Foreigners and of the Right to Asylum, in effect since 1945, requires all foreigners in France to carry with them at all times proof of their legal stay or right to transit through the country.

180. Court de Cassation, Cass. Crim 25 April 1985, cited in Jeremy Buisson, "Identity Checks and Verifications of Identity: Article. 78-1 to 78-5," *Jurisclasseur of Criminal Procedure* 10 (1998).

181. See Groupe d'Information et de Soutien des Immigrés (GISTI), *Le contrôle d'identité des étrangers* (Paris : GISTI, May 2003), at 5.

182. *Rosalind Williams Lecraft*, Spanish Constitutional Court Decision No. 13/2001.

183. One court asserted that police could stop people participating in a demonstration against deportations of undocumented migrants, even as it prohibited the exclusive singling out of all dark-skinned people. Other courts found that reading a foreign-language newspaper or book, driving or riding in a car with foreign license plates, and/or playing "folk" instruments in a public place could be considered objective indications of foreign origin. Group Information and Support for Immigrants, *Identity Checks of Foreigners*, (Paris: *Groupe d'Information et de Soutien des Immigrés*, or GISTI, 2003) at 5, available at http://www.gisti.org/IMG/pdf/np_controle_identite.pdf.

184. For train stations and other rail areas, a specific regulation was passed in January 2006 that charged those police forces responsible for rail security (including the National Police and

the SNPF) to combat illegal migration. Ministry of Immigration, *Guidelines for Immigration Policy: Ministerial report on Immigration (art. L. 111-10 CESEDA)* (2008), at 79.

185. Victor Mallet, "Madrid police told to target illegal migrants," *The Financial Times*, February 16, 2009.

186. Two U.S. studies examined police relations with Arab-American communities in the wake of 9/11. The issue of immigration enforcement was particularly prominent in the U.S. because the Federal Bureau of Investigation (FBI) made extensive use of immigration enforcement as a counter-terrorism tool after 9/11. The studies found that Arab–American communities were more concerned about being targeted by government policies than they were about hate crime, and that immigration enforcement was the most troubling. Both studies also found that these communities want better relations with the police. The studies' recommendations emphasized the importance of good communication, and commitment to work together, as well as the need for both police and communities to dedicate resources to the effort. Deborah A. Ramirez, Sasha Cohen O'Connell and Rabia Zafar, *A Promising Practices Guide, Developing Partnerships between Law Enforcement and American Muslim, Arab and Sikh Communities*, (New York and Boston: Northeastern University, Open Society Institute and The Whiting Foundation, 2004), and Nicole J. Henderson, Christopher W. Ortiz, Naomi F. Sugie, and Joel Miller, *Law Enforcement and Arab American Community Relations sfter September 11, 2001: Engagement in a Time of Uncertainty*, (New York: Vera Institute of Justice, June 2006).

187. Cathy Schneider, "Police Power and Race Riots in Paris," *Politics and Society*, Vol. 35, No. 4, December 2007.

188. Martina Kant, "Evaluation of the 'Railbased Police Search': Train inspections under Schleierfahndung" (Schleierfahndung are special stop powers for use on trains), in *Civilians and Police* (CILIP 77, January 2004), at 53.

189. Dieter Richter and Udo Dreher, "Controls without suspicion: Migrants in the web of Schleierfahndung," in *DiePolizei 1998*, No. 10.

190. Martina Kant, "Stops and Suspicion: Migrants caught in the center of the investigation," in *Civil Rights and Police*, (CILIP 65, January 2000), at 30. The primary infraction was violation of internal travel restrictions which require people going through the asylum process to remain in a restricted area within Germany.

191. *Süddeutsche Zeitung*, March 18, 1998, cited in Martina Kant, "Stops and Suspicion," at 34.

192. Senate briefing by Interior Minister Acebedes, BOCG, Senado, Serie 1, Num. 571, (January 9, 2003).

193. Sophie Hydén and Anna Lundberg, *Internal alien control in police work: the rule of law ideal and efficiency in the Schengen area Sweden*, (Malmö: IMER, Malmö högskola; Linköping universitet: Tema Etnicitet, 2004).

194. The author, Sophie Hydén, noted in an interview with Justice Initiative staff that Swedish police officers were aware of this and saw it as a problem, repeatedly stating their need for improved guidance on domestic immigration control as an urgent need given the increased diversity of Sweden's population.

195. In 2002, Belgium was convicted of violating this principle when it rounded up and expelled 74 Slovakian Roma. *Čonka v. Belgium*, App. No. 51564/99, Eur. Ct. Hum. Rits., Judgment of May 2, 2002.

196. Agence France-Presse, *Human Rights Groups Slam France over Grouped Deportations,* September 17, 2006.

197. Ibid.

198. Ibid., citing La Voix des Roms.

199. *Les orientations de la politique d'immigration.* Rapport du ministère de l'immigration au Parlement (art L. 111-10 Ceseda), 2008, at 77.

200. National Police Circular of September 28, 2006, at 79.

201. R.T. Shuford, "Civil Rights in the Next Millennium: Any Way You Slice It: Why Racial Profiling Is Wrong," *St. Louis University Public Law Review* 18 (1999): 371–385, at 373.

202. American Psychological Association, August 9, 2001, letter to the U.S. House of Representatives in support of the End Racial Profiling Act, available at http://www.apa.org/ppo/issues/pracial-prof.html.

203. Minority youth in focus group, Spain, 2005. GEA21 research on file with Justice Initiative.

204. Ibid., focus group with adult minority-group members.

205. From the email text "Police profiling, that's enough! March 23 at Part-dieu," a protest rally called by Témoins Lyon, March 23, 2007.

206. Bernard Harcourt, "Rethinking Racial Profiling: A Critique of the Economics, Civil Liberties, and Constitutional Literature, and of Criminal Profiling More Generally," *The University of Chicago Law Review,* Vol. 71, No. 4, Fall 2004, at 1329–1330.

207. Ilse Devroe, '*The White News Show': An Analysis of the Depiction of Ethnic Minorities in the News,* paper presented at the IAMCR conference on Communication and Democracy, July 25–30, 2004, Porto Alegre, Brazil, at 12.

208. Ilse Devroe and F. Sayes, "Stories about immigrants in the Flemish media," *Tijdschrift voor Comminicatiewetenscap,* 30 (2): 56–76. Cited in Ilse Devroe, *The White News Show.*

209. Ilse Devroe, University of Ghent, '*Minority Report': Ethnic Miniroties' Diasporic News Consumption and News Reading,* mimeo, copy on file with authors, at 15.

210. Joel Miller, Nick Bland and Paul Quinton, *The Impact of Stops and Searches on Crime and the Community,* Police Research Series Paper 127, (London: Home Office, 2000); Ronald Weitzer and Steven A. Tuch, "Determinants of Public Satisfaction with the Police," in *Police Quarterly* No. 8 (3) 2005: 279–297; Joel Miller, Robert C. Davis, Nicole J. Henderson, John Markovic, and Christopher W. Ortiz, *Public Opinions of the Police: The influence of Friends, Family, and Media,* (Washington, D.C.: National Institute of Justice technical report, 2004, 2001-IJ-CX-0038); Dennis P. Rosenbaum, Amie M. Schuck, Sandra K. Costello, Darnell F. Hawkins, and Marianne K. Ring, "Attitudes toward the Police: The Effects of Direct and Vicarious Experience" *Police Quarterly,* No. 8 (3) 2005: 343–365.

211. McCluskey, John D., Stephen D. Mastrofski, and Roger B. Parks, "To Acquiesce or Rebel: Predicting Citizen Compliance with Police Requests," *Police Quarterly* No. 2: 389–416.

212. Focus group with Roma conducted by GEA21 in Spain in 2005, summary on file with Open Society Justice Initiative.

213. Rod Morgan and Tim Newburn, *The Future of Policing,* (Oxford: Clarendon Press/Oxford University Press, 1997).

214. Ibid.

215. Ontario Human Rights Commission, Inquiry Report: *Paying the Price: The Human Cost of Racial Profiling*, (Toronto: Ontario Human Rights Commission, undated document; the inquiry started in February 2003).

216. Lord Scarman, *The Brixton Disorders, 10–12 April 1981, Report of an Inquiry*, (London: Home Office, 2001).

217. B. Bowling and C. Phillips, *Racism, Crime and Justice*, (Harlow: Pearson Education Limited, 2002), at 139–40.

218. Scarman, *The Brixton Disorders*, at 45.

219. In the United States, riots in Los Angeles in 1992 followed the failure to convict police officers involved in the beating of a black motorist that was captured on video.

220. Yvelines Matin, "Young people march against the police," *Le Parisien*, Poissy local edition, December 24, 2001. Cited in Ligue des droits de l'homme, *Commission d'enquete Poissy*, July 2002. "[L]e rapport des forces avec les police est devenue insupportable. Lorsqu'ils font une descente dans les immeubles, ils embarquent tout le monde, deplore un jeune." ["Relations with the police had become intolerable. When they come into the apartment buildings, they just grab everyone, complained one youth." Translation by the Justice Initiative.]

221. The victim reportedly was trying to prevent police from stopping and searching another person at the time he was assaulted by police. "The public prosecutor investigating Police Director over possible case of police violence to be linked to unrest in Nørrebro," *Politiken*, February 19, 2008, available at http://politiken.dk/indland/article473454.ece.

222. "Young people demonstrate: A group of young people will demonstrate against Nørrebro stop-and-search zones, which they see as the direct cause of the last days of unrest," *Politiken*, February 15, 2008, available at http://politiken.dk/indland/article471982.ece.

223. At http://nyhederne.tv2.dk/krimi/article.php/id-10544900.html.

224. See Chapter II. B. This issue illuminates the question whether ethnic profiling is effective or, in the terms used above, whether it increases police efficiency.

225. Samuel R. Gross and Debra Livingston, "Racial Profiling Under Attack," *102 Columbia Law Review*, 2002, at 1413, 1415.

226. Bernard Harcourt, "Rethinking Racial Profiling: A Critique of the Economics, Civil Liberties, and Constitutional Literature, and of Criminal Profiling More Generally," *The University of Chicago Law Review*, Vol. 71, No. 4, Fall 2004, at 1329–1330.

227. Bowling and Phillips, *Racism, Crime and Justice*, at 106.

228. D.J. Smith, "Ethnic Origins, Crime and Criminal Justice in England and Wales," in Michael Tonry (ed.), *Ethnicity, Crime and Immigration: Comparative and Cross-National Perspectives. Crime and Justice: A Review of Research*, Vol. XXI, (Chicago: University of Chicago Press, 1997).

229. As shown by victim surveys, as much as fifty percent of crimes are never reported to the police, although rates vary significantly by the type of crime, its seriousness, whether property was insured, and other factors.

230. See United Nations Commission on Human Rights, Final Working Paper prepared by Leila Zerrougi, on Discrimination in the Criminal Justice System, E/CN.4/Sub.2/2002/5 May 23, 2002; Michael Tonry (ed), *Ethnicity, Crime and Immigration*

231. T. Modood, R. Berthoud, J. Lakey, J. Nazroo, P. Smith, S. Virdee and S. Beishon, *Ethnic Minorities in Britain*, (London: Police Studies Institute, 1997).

232. C. Phillips, B. Bowling, "Racism, ethnicity, crime and criminal justice," in M. Maguire, B. Morgan and R. Reiner (eds.) *The Oxford Handbook of Criminology*, 3rd edition, (Oxford: Oxford University Press, 2002); Rebekah Delsol and Michael Shiner, "Regulating Stop and Search: A Challenge for Police and Community Relations in England and Wales," *Critical Criminology* Vol. 14:4, 2006, 241–263.

233. J. Graham and B. Bowling, *Young People and Crime*, (London: Home Office, 1995); M. Ramsay and S. Partridge, *Drug Misuse Declared in 1998: Results From the British Crime Survey*, (London: Home Office, 1999).

234. Ministry of Justice, *Statistics on Race and the Criminal Justice System—2006/7*, at 31.

235. In the United Kingdom, the majority of arrests resulting from high-discretion drugs searches are for the possession of cannabis, and this is driving concerns that young men from minority groups are being disproportionately criminalized under cannabis warnings and arrests, and raising questions about police priorities and resource use. Marian FitzGerald, *Searches in London under s1 of the Police and Criminal Evidence Act 1984*, (London: Metropolitan Police Service, 1999); P.A.J. Waddington, K. Stenson, et al., "In Proportion: Race, and Police Stop and Search," *British Journal of Criminology* 44, 2004, 889–914.

236. Eliot Spitzer, Attorney General of the State of New York, "The New York City Police Department's 'Stop and Frisk' Practices: A Report to the People of the State of New York," December 1, 1999, 94–95.

237. David Harris, "Confronting Ethnic Profiling in the United States," in *Justice Initiatives*, (New York: Open Society Justice Initiative, June 2005), at 69.

238. E.J. van der Torre and H.B. Ferwerda, *Preventive searching: An analysis of the process and the external effects in ten municipalities*, (The Hague: Beke: Arnhem, Politie & Wetenschap, Zeist 2005). Data are available from 187 preventive search operations conducted from 2002 to 2004 in the cities of Amsterdam, Maastricht, Haarlemmermeer, Den Helder, Rotterdam, Heerlen, Utrecht, and Tilburg. Data include information on the cost of the policy in terms of man-hours and police conduct. During these operations, 79,499 persons were searched and 2,010 weapons (as defined by the Weapons and Ammunition Act) were found: 68 percent were stabbing weapons; 16.8 percent were striking weapons, and 2.6 percent were firearms (52 units); 12.6 percent fell into the category of "other." The study involving all 10 cities suggests that creative counting took place on a modest scale to increase the apparent effectiveness of the results. Thus hobby knives (fishing knives), for example, were also counted.

239. Ibid. During 54 preventive search operations in Amsterdam from November 2002 to March 2004, police searched 32,332 individuals and detected 702 weapons, only 15 of which were firearms. The operation cost 11,687 officer hours. Results in Rotterdam were similar: in 50 operations totalling 9,124 officer hours, 18,687 searches were carried out that detected 578 weapons, 23 of which were firearms.

240. The evaluation also looked at the impact on public opinion, finding overall approval of the operations, with only four percent of respondents having a negative reaction while almost half said their sense of security had improved. The responses of ethnic minorities, however, differed strikingly, with 24 percent disagreeing or strongly disagreeing that the searches improved safety. Police conduct was respectful and only three complaints were lodged related to these searches. There was considerable debate in the Netherlands about the use of preventive searches. In addition to the high cost of these extensive police deployments and their limited returns, there were concerns in larger urban areas that the searches would have negative impacts on police relations with the groups most frequently stopped. In response, politicians and authorities tended to prefer random searches, and also undertook a series of other steps including searching all citizens in the area. This resulted in the searching of many tourists or elderly people in operations that were ineffective but also often an embarrassment to the police. The study called into question the value of preventive searches, noting that weapons detection was higher in more limited "hit-and-run" operations. The city of Groningen decided to end preventive searches after studying their impact.

241. This is an ongoing study being conducted by University of Stockholm criminologist Tove Pettersson. The study covers reports from Stockholm city in the year 2000. Initial findings reported in Lernestedt, Diesen, Pettersson and Lindholm, "Equal before the Law: Nature or Culture".

242. Ibid. The study disaggregated drug searches by age and nationality and found that while elderly white Swedes and white Europeans were less subject to searches, elderly people of non-European background were just as likely to be stopped as young people of non-European origin. Of non-Europeans, 48 percent of youth up to the age of twenty were searched; 52 percent of the 22 to 29 year old age bracket, and 45 percent of the age group 30 and over were searched. Among Swedes and white Europeans the search rates were 40 percent of the 20 and under group and of the 22 to 29 year old group, but only 25 percent of the over-30 group. The hit rate was highest for searches of the ethnic Swedes and white Europeans in the 30 and over age group, and the lowest success rate when searching non-Europeans in the same age group.

243. Rolf Granér, *The Occupational Culture of Patrol Police,* (Lunds: University, 2004: 229ff).

244. In the U.S., hit rates for searches have been as high as 30 percent on state highways. MD State Police, see comparative chart in *Justice Initiatives*, (New York: Open Society Justice Initiative, June 2005). In the U.K., for example, PACE stops that require reasonable suspicion produce hit rates between 11 and 13 percent; see discussion above.

245. U.S. Customs Service, *Personal Searches of Air Passengers Results: Positive and Negative, Fiscal Year 1998*, (Washington, D.C.: U.S. Customs Service, 1998).

246. Customs officers had to get supervisor approval for any search, including a pat down (frisk). Harris, *Profiles in Injustice*, at 219.

247. Ibid., at 220–222.

248. Open Society Justice Initiative, *Addressing Ethnic Profiling by Police: A Report on the Strategies for Effective Stop and Search Project*, (New York Open Society Institute, 2009).

249. Paul Quinton, Nick Bland, et al., *Police Stops, Decision-making and Practice*. (London: Home Office, 2000) at 16–17.

250. Home Office, *Police Powers and Procedures England and Wales 2007/08*. (London: Home Office Statistics, 2009) at 31.

251. Sections 44 (1) and 44(2) of the Terrorism Act 2000 allow officers to "stop and search vehicles, people in vehicles and pedestrians for articles that could be used for terrorism whether or not there are grounds for suspecting that such articles are present." Section 60 of the Criminal Justice and Public Order Act 1994 as amended by s.8 of the Knives Act 1997 allows an Inspector or higher ranked officer who reasonably fears serious violence or the carrying of weapons in a particular locality to authorize uniformed officers to search any person or vehicle in that locality for weapons for a period of 24 hours.

252. Council of Europe, Code of Police Ethics, adopted by the Council of Ministers on September 19, 2001. http://cm.coe.int/ta/rec/2001/2001r10.htm.

253. European Commission, EU Network of Independent experts in fundamental rights, December 2006, CFR–CDF.Opinion 4, 2006. (In 2007, the network was incorporated into the new EU Fundamental Rights Agency.)

254. Paul Quinton, Nick Bland, et al., *Police Stops, Decision-Making and Practice.*

255. It should be noted that this is not unusual, and that policing is notoriously challenging to assess. However, the trend in modern policing is toward greater emphasis on efforts to monitor and measure the use of police resources and their impact.

256. It is extremely difficult to provide figures on the number of citizens of immigrant origin in the European Union. Figures can be obtained country-by-country but, as each country categorizes immigrants, foreign-born residents, and citizens in a different manner, comparable statistics do not exist. Countries such as France and the United Kingdom have long-standing populations of citizens of immigrant origin dating to the 1960s and before. Germany changed its laws on naturalization and citizenship in 2000. In addition, in 2005, the Spanish government announced a nationalization policy that will grant legal residency and citizenship to some 700,000 migrants. Useful overviews are provided in Andrew Geddes (ed.), *The Politics of Migration and Immigration in Europe*, (London: Sage Publications, 2003). See also Craig Parsons and Timothy Smeeding (eds.), *Immigration and the Transformation of Europe*, (Cambridge: Cambridge University Press, 2006). See also Christina Boswell, *Migration in Europe: A Paper Presented for the Policy Analysis and Research Programme of the Global Commission on International Migration*, September 2005, available at http://www.gcim.org/attachements/RS4.pdf.

257. On March 11, 2004, bombs exploded on four commuter trains in Madrid within minutes of each other, killing 191 and injuring 1,841 people. On April 3, 2004, four suspects detonated explosives during a police raid, killing themselves and one officer. Spanish authorities believe that a further five to eight suspects escaped. The perpetrators were Spanish residents of Moroccan, Syrian, and Algerian origin. See "11-M Massacre in Madrid," *El Mundo* special report, available at http://www.elmundo.es/documentos/2004/03/espana/atentados11m/. See also http://news.bbc.co.uk/2/shared/spl/hi/guides/457000/457031/html/default.stm.

258. On July 7, 2007, coordinated attacks by suicide bombers at four sites in London—three Underground train locations and one bus—killed 52 people and injured hundreds. See *Report of the Official Account of the Bombings in London on 7th July 2005*. Ordered by the House of Commons to be printed on 11th May 2006. (London: The Stationers Office, HC 1087).

259. On June 30, 2007, two men drove a car loaded with propane canisters into Glasgow airport, but security barriers prevented the car from reaching its target and causing deaths; five people were

injured. The perpetrators were Indian and Iraqi, both doctors working in the United Kingdom; one later died of his injuries in hospital. See http://news.bbc.co.uk/2/hi/uk_news/scotland/6257194. stm and http://news.bbc.co.uk/2/hi/uk_news/6264230.stm.

260. In 2008, Sweden introduced a new law permitting surveillance and intelligence gathering with judicial authorization.Law on Signals Intelligence in Defense Operations (2008:717) approved by parliament on June 18, 2008. The U.K.'s introduction of "control orders" and extended periods of pretrial detention similarly erode basic due process guarantees. The U.K. Prevention of Terrorism Act of 2005 creates "control orders" which, while falling short of house arrest, impose serious restrictions on freedom of movement, association, and expression, and the right to privacy and family life on persons suspected of involvement in terrorism. The restrictions may be imposed for an indefinite period of time on the basis of a low standard of proof and even secret evidence. Violation of the control order is a criminal offense. The person subject to a control order is not allowed to know about the evidence discussed in closed hearings or to give directions to the special advocate appointed by the court to defend his interests. Human Rights Watch letter to the British parliament, "U.K.: 'Control Orders' for Terrorism Suspects Violate Rights; Improve Safeguards to Ensure Rights to Liberty and Fair Hearings," (New York: Human Rights Watch, March 2, 2009).

261. Human Rights Watch, *Preempting Justice: Counterterrorism Laws and Procedures in France*, (New York: Human Rights Watch, July 1, 2008); Human Rights Watch, *Setting an Example? Counter-Terrorism Measures in Spain*, (New York: January 2005, Vol. 17, No. 1(D).

262. See opinion of the Lords of Appeal, *Gillan v. Commissioner of Police for the Metropolis*, House of Lords, March 8, 2006, at para. 16. Section 44 was used throughout London until 2005, and since then has been used in selected but changing London boroughs on an ongoing basis to the present time.

263. As one scholar has noted, ethnic profiling is used across a range of counterterrorism practices: "Profiling can be used as part of both defensive and proactive counter-terrorist measures. The profiling of young Muslim men in the New York City subways exemplifies the former. But profiling can also be used in pre-emptive strategies, as when, for example, the FBI targeted interviews of Muslim and Arab–Americans in order to gather intelligence." Bernard E. Harcourt, "Muslim Profiles Post-9/11: Is Racial Profiling an Effective Counter-terrorist Measure and Does It Violate the Right to be Free from Discrimination?" in Goold and Lazarus (eds.), *Security and Human Rights*, (New York: Hart Publishing, 2007), at 73–98.

264. As noted in Chapter II, throughout this report the terms "ethnic profiling" or "ethnic and religious profiling" are used to encompass profiling based on racial or ethnic origin, national origin, or religion.

265. Terrorist profiles are not always instances of ethnic profiling. A terrorist profile is an ethnic profile when ethnic origin, race, national origin, and/or religion are among the criteria used to construct the profile. In practice, there are grounds for concern that many if not most terrorist profiles are based in significant measure on ethnicity, religion, and/or national origin, and that these criteria figure heavily in shaping law enforcement perceptions and actions even when other factors drawn from intelligence reports are also present in the profile.

266. As noted in Chapter II, ethnic profiling encompasses situations where ethnicity, race, national origin or religion is a significant, even if not the exclusive, basis for making law enforce-

ment and/or investigative decisions about persons who are believed to be or to have been involved in criminal activity.

267. Since 1992 the United Kingdom's Home Office and Ministry of Justice have published statistical information as required under Section 95 of the Criminal Justice Act 1991. These publications aim to help law enforcement and judicial authorities avoid discrimination on the grounds of race or ethnicity. Ministry of Justice figures are calculated on an annual basis for year periods running from April 1 through March 31. On April 1, 2003, a standard system of recording was introduced into all criminal justice system agencies based on self-classification into one of 16 categories or a "not-stated" category used in the 2001 census. Classification is based around four main groups: white, black, Asian, and "other."

268. On June, 29 2007 two car bombs were discovered in the Haymarket area of London. Both devises were recovered intact and no one was injured. The attempted bombing was directly linked to the suicide attack on Glasgow International Airport the following day. During this attack a car bomb was driven into the glass doors of the terminal. The driver died, the passenger and five others in the vicinity were injured.

269. The U.K. Terrorism Act 2000 came into force in response to the changing threat from international terrorism, and replaced the previous temporary antiterrorism legislation that dealt primarily with Northern Ireland. The act changed the definition of terrorism, and established a more unified counterterrorism regime, including the introduction of new powers (such as increased stop and search powers and longer periods of pre-charge detention) and offenses (such as incitement to terrorism and providing or seeking terrorist training) as well as some additional safeguards (including publishing statistics). Further amendments have since been passed in 2001, 2005 and 2006. The terrorism act is available at http://www.opsi.gov.uk/acts/acts2000/ukpga_20000011_en_5#pt5-pb1-l1g43.

270. The U.K. Terrorism Act perversely provides greater powers of stop and search under Section 44 where there is no requirement of reasonable suspicion than it does under Section 43 which authorizes stops and searches of a person whom a constable "*reasonably suspects* to be a terrorist to discover whether he has in his possession anything which may constitute evidence that he is a terrorist." (Italics added.) Yet unlike searches authorized under Section 44, the removal of headgear and footwear in public cannot be required and the removal of more than an outer coat and jacket or gloves can only be required if the search takes place out of the public view and near to where the person was stopped. *Terrorism Act 2000, Chapter 11, Part V, Section 44, power to stop and search.*

271. Ministry of Justice, *Statistics on Race and the Criminal Justice System—2007/8.* (London: Ministry of Justice, 2009), at 29–30.

272. Ministry of Justice, *Statistics on Race and the Criminal Justice System—2007/8.* (London: Ministry of Justice, 2009), at 29–30. The Home Office does not publish figures broken down by ethnicity for those arrested who are subsequently charged with an terrorism offense, those dealt with under mental health or extradition legislation, those convicted or those who are acquitted. It is the author's understanding that none of the 72 arrests as a result of Section 44 stops and searches led to a conviction.

273. Ms. Blears was speaking before the Commons Home Affairs Committee Inquiry into the impact of anti-terrorist measures on community relations. Vikram Dodd and Alan Travis, "Mus-

lims face increased stop and search," *The Guardian*, March 2, 2005. See also discussion in Andrew Blick, Toufyal Choudhury and Stuart Weir, *The Rules of the Game, Terrorism, Community and Human Rights, Democratic Audit*, (Human Rights Center, University of Essex, Joseph Rowntree Reform Trust, 2006), at 43.

274. A. Travis and R. Cowan, "Call for 'intelligence-led' approach," *The Guardian*, August 3, 2005.

275. The four perpetrators of the July 7, 2005 bombings were all U.K. citizens, three of South Asian origin and the fourth of Afro-Caribbean origin. House of Commons, *Report of the Official Account of the Bombings in London on 7th July 2005.*

276. London Metropolitan Police Service figures, cited in Vickram Dodd, "Surge in stop and search of Asian people after July 7," *The Guardian*, December 24, 2005.

277. Ibid.

278. Metropolitan Police Authority, *Counter-Terrorism: The London Debate*, (London: Metropolitan Police Authority, 2007), at 47.

279. The self-defined ethnicity of those stopped was: 52 percent white, 16 percent Asian, 9 percent black, 3 percent mixed, 4 percent other and 16 percent not stated. Asians make up 12 percent of London's population and blacks account for 11 percent; thus the figures represent limited disproportionality in terms of ethnicity: Asians are slightly over-represented and blacks under-represented. The figures also reveal significant levels of the stopped person's self-defined ethnicity being recorded as "not stated," potentially masking higher levels of disproportionality. Ibid., at 44–49.

280. Lord Carlile, *Report on the Operation in 2007 of the Terrorism Act 2000 and of Part 1 of the Terrorism Sct 2006,* June 2008. Available at: http://www.statewatch.org/news/2008/jun/uk-carlile-report-2007.pdf.

281. Vikram Dodd, "Only 1 in 400 anti-terror stop and searches leads to arrest," *The Guardian*, October 31, 2007.

282. Ministry of Justice, *Statistics on Race and the Criminal Justice System—2007/8.* (London: Ministry of Justice, 2009), at 29, 57, 63.

283. Lord Carlile, *Report on the Operation in 2007 of the Terrorism Act 2000 and of Part 1 of the Terrorism Sct 2006,* (London: Home Office, June 2008). At http://www.statewatch.org/news/2008/jun/uk-carlile-report-2007.pdf. Ministry of Justice, *Statistics on Race and the Criminal Justice System—2007/8.* (London: Ministry of Justice, 2009).

284. As noted below, when Section 44 powers were debated in the English Parliament, they were justified as a focused and intelligence-based tool.

285. There are at least two instances in the United States in which police stops have led to apprehension of terrorists: the so-called "millennium bomber" Ahmed Rassam was stopped by a U.S. Customs official who then searched Rassam's car because "his story just didn't add up," and found explosives. Oklahoma City bomber Timothy McVeigh was arrested as a result of a routine traffic check prompted by the fact that his car had no rear license plate.

286. M. John-Baptiste and M. Dale, *Stop and Search in London: The Disproportionality Issue*, (London: Greater London Authority, 2007), at 32. Also, Blick, Choudhury and Weir, *The Rules of the*

Game, Terrorism, Community and Human Rights, Democratic Audit (Human Rights Center, University of Essex, Joseph Rowntree Reform Trust, 2006), at 49. When Section 44 powers were debated in the English parliament: "The intention was that their use would be tied to specific intelligence and used with a view to disrupting and arresting terrorists. Furthermore, any plausible deterrent effect would require a reasonable likelihood that any terrorist would be stopped and searched in the midst of carrying out a terrorist operation. That would require such a massive use of stop and search powers as to severely disrupt the daily lives of millions of people in London, especially if, as the MPS argue, there is a permanent London-wide threat of a terrorist attack. To swamp the capital with such a large degree of arbitrary stops and searches that terrorists are likely to be deterred from attacking London is not only a huge waste of police resources, which could be used more efficiently in preventing terrorism; it is also a hugely disproportionate price to pay in terms of particular communities' civil rights." Arun Kundnani, *Racial Profiling and Anti-Terror Stop and Search*, (London: Institute of Race Relations, 2006).

287. Andrew Blick, Toufyal Choudhury and Stuart Weir, *The Rules of the Game, Terrorism, Community and Human Rights, Democratic Audit*, (University of Essex: Human Rights Center, Joseph Rowntree Reform Trust, 2006), at 49.

288. See at http://www.guardian.co.uk/politics/2005/oct/07/terrorism.terrorism.

289. Deterrence is one form of prevention, which may be achieved through "target hardening" among other tactics. "Target hardening" is the dedication of resources to the protection potential targets of terror attacks; this may be achieved through the use of guards or electronic surveillance at those places, and in the use of stop and search in specific localities.

290. In order to reassure the public about the use of the power, from September 2007 Section 44 stop and search data broken down geographically by borough are available on the MPS website. This allows members of the public in the Stop and Search Community Monitoring Network and members of the Metropolitan Police Authority's Stop and Search Review board to critically assess the use of the powers at a community level. Justice Initiative interview with Commander Rod Jarman, London, August 2007.

291. Lord Carlile, *Report on the Operation in 2005 of the Terrorism Act 2000*. (London: Home Office, 2006), at 28.

292. Mayorwatch, "Hayman Questions Stop and Search Effectiveness," December 12, 2006, available at http://www.mayorwatch.co.uk/article.php?article_id=517.

293. Lord Carlile, *Report on the Operation in 2007 of the Terrorism Act 2000 and of Part 1 of the Terrorism Act 2006*, (London: Home Office, June 2008), at 28.

294. Anna Cavell "Capital sees rise in terror stops," BBC London News, May 6, 2009, available at http://news.bbc.co.uk/1/hi/england/london/8034315.stm.

295. Ibid., at 29. This is supported by independent analyses that have also questioned whether Section 44 stop powers are being properly used in view of research showing wide variations in numbers of Section 44 stops among different police services across the United Kingdom. An October 2005 BBC survey highlighted great variation among police forces' use of Section 44 powers and calls into the question the high numbers of stops and searches made by some forces. The survey of 18 U.K. police forces found that half of these had stopped more people during the three months following the July 7, 2005 bombing than they had during the entire previous year. The Hampshire

police, for example, carried out 4,438 stops and searches between July and October 2005, compared to a total of 696 for the 2003–2004 year. Kent police, on the other hand, conducted just 56 stops and searches in the same period despite the fact that their region houses the Channel Tunnel and channel ports that would seem to be potential terror targets. The survey also found that the number of Asians and black people stopped and searched in London increased twelve-fold in the three months after the bombings. Christian Fraser, "Are police misusing stop and search?," BBC News Online, October 23, 2005, available at http://news.bbc.co.uk/1/hi/uk/435572.stm.

296. Assessment methods included: comparing the use of Section 44 in different locations, review of complaints, and extensive public discussion of the power and the way in which it is used by police through both existing and specially created community consultation groups. The review by location revealed that officers in certain areas appeared to be making broad use of Section 44 instead of ordinary policing powers requiring reasonable suspicion. Those areas remain under monitoring as a result. Justice Initiative interview with Commander Rod Jarman, London Metropolitan Police Service, London, August 7, 2007.

297. BBC News Online, "Stop and search powers 'damaging,'" May 31, 2007, available at http://news.bbc.co.uk/go/pr/fr/-/1/hi/england/london/6706885.stm.

298. BBC News Online, "Anti-terror stops surge in London," June 8, 2007, avaialble at http://news.bbc.co.uk/go/pr/fr/-/1/hi/uk/6933034.stm.

299. Metropolitan Police Authority, Section 44 Terrorism Act 2000 standard Operating Procedures, Issue 1, at 16, January 8, 2007, available at: http://www.met.police.uk/foi/pdfs/policies/stop_and_search_s44_tact_2000_sop.pdf.

300. Ministry of Justice, *Statistics on Race and the Criminal Justice System—2007/8*, at 30.

301. Ministry of Justice, *Statistics on Race and the Criminal Justice System—2007/8*, at 30, 53, 205. It should also be noted that these figures do not include stops made by the British Transport Police who operate in many stations throughout London's extensive Underground and rail transport system.

302. National Police Improvement Agency, *Advice on Stop and Search in Relation to Terrorism*, November 2008, available at http://www.npia.police.uk/en/docs/Stop_and_Search_in_Relation_to_Terrorism_-_2008.pdf.

303. Justice Initiative interview with Burhan Kesici, Vice President, Islamic Federation in Berlin, Berlin, March 2006. The total number of mosques that have been checked may well be far higher. As there is no official record, these numbers include only those controls that have been brought to the attention of non-governmental organizations.

304. Ibid.

305. Justice Initiative interview with Werner Schiffauer, Professor of Cultural and Social Anthropology, Europa Universität Viadrina in Frankfurt/Oder, Berlin, March 2006.

306. Justice Initiative interview with Dr. Rolf Gössner, President, International League for Human Rights Germany, Berlin, March 2006. While anyone subject to an identity check, including German citizens, would have to produce valid identification, there is particular attention to immigration status during these checks.

307. Justice Initiative interview with representative of Milli Görüs, Berlin, March 2006. IGMG Press Release, " Muslims return to religious practice following disruption," September 29, 2005, available at http://www.igmg.de/index.php?module=ContentExpress&func=display&ceid=1863&meid=&itmid=1.

308. Sarah Plass, "World Briefing: Europe: Germany: Raids Aim At Islamic Radicals," *The New York Times*, September 29, 2005.

309. Justice Initiative interview with Dr. Rolf Gössner, Berlin, March 2006. Justice Initiative interview with Professor Werner Schiffauer, Berlin, March 2006. German regulations place restrictions on the freedom of movement of asylum seekers. In its third report on Germany, the European Commission against Racism and Intolerance commented on these regulations as follows: "ECRI notes that the freedom of movement of asylum seekers in Germany is seriously restricted. Asylum seekers cannot leave the district (*Kreis*) they have been registered in without the authorization of the Office for Foreigners. However, ECRI has received numerous reports indicating that authorizations are often delayed or denied without valid reasons. ECRI has been informed that the Immigration Bill contains provisions aimed at regulating the discretion of the Office for Foreigners in granting authorizations to leave the district." European Commission against Racism and Intolerance, *Third Report on Germany*, (Strasbourg, December 5, 2003), at 23.

310. "Germany: Arbitrary control of persons in front of mosques continue," *Muslim Affairs*, August 8, 2005, available at http://www.muslim-lawyers.net/news/index.php3?aktion=show&number=289.

311. Justice Initiative telephone interview with G.X., Counterterrorism Unit, Rheinland-Pfalz, July 2006. This source stated that those who bring individuals to Germany illegally are sometimes connected with terrorist organizations.

312. Justice Initiative telephone interview with Professor Werner Schiffauer, November 2008, and telephone interview with Reim Spielhaus (member of the Board of the Muslim Academy in Germany and lecturer at Humboldt University of Berlin), November 2008.

313. Lombardy is in the north of Italy where the conservative Northern League is powerful and runs on explicitly anti-immigrant platforms. The Northern League is a member of President Berlusconi's current (April 2008 on) and past governing coalition (1994–5 and 2001–2006), and doubled its voter base in the April 2008 elections.

314. "Italy arrests 142 in anti-terrorism sweep," *Associated Press*, July 9, 2005; and Holly Manges Jones, "Italian police arrest 142 in post-London anti-terror sweep," *Jurist*, July 9, 2005.

315. Ibid., citing Gen. Antonio Girone, Lombardy regional commander of the paramilitary police.

316. Justice Initiative interview with Mr. S.S., Milan, May 2006.

317. Justice Initiative interview with Mr. I.H., Torino, May 2006.

318. Justice Initiative interview with Mr. S.A., Milan, May 2006.

319. Justice Initiative telephone interview with Lucianno Scagliotti, Coordinator of the European Network Against Racism in Italy, November 2008.

320. In researching a book on the *Goutte d'Or*, a northern Paris neighborhood with a high immigrant population, Professor Maurice Goldring observed that all of the North African men that he

spoke with who were less than 50 years old mentioned that they believe that they are targeted after terrorist attacks. He spoke to between ten and twenty individuals. Justice Initiative interview with Professor Maurice Goldring, Paris, May 2006.

321. Islamic Institute for Human Rights, "Country Profile: The Conditions of Muslims in France," in Open Society Institute (OSI), *Monitoring Minority Protection in EU Member States: Overview* (New York and Budapest: OSI–EUMap, 2004), at 53.

322. In 2001, France amended the *Loi de Sécurité Quotidienne* (Law on Everyday Security or Code on Criminal Procedure) to empower judicial police officers to conduct stops and searches of both vehicles and individuals for the purpose of detecting "terrorist acts," provided that a prosecutor has first issued a formal request detailing the criminal acts the police are seeking to deter, the specific geographic location where the stops and searches will take place, and the duration of activities (not to exceed 24 hours). Subsequent modifications to the Code on Criminal Procedure have extended this authority to international trains traveling through French territory. An additional element is the permanent enforcement of the VIGIPIRATE plan, France's national security alert system created in 1978, which allows law enforcement and military officers to check individuals' identities and belongings in large public spaces such as airports and train stations without having to adhere to any suspicion standard. This system was previously activated in 1995 (after Paris Metro bombings). See Article 23 of the *Loi N° 2001-1062 du 15 novembre 2001 relative à la sécurité quotidienne*, available at http://www.legifrance.gouv.fr/WAspad/UnTexteDeJorf?numjo=INTX0100032L) modified Article 78.2.2 of the *Code de procédure pénale; also LOI N° 2006-64 du 23 janvier 2006 relative à la lutte contre le terrorisme et portant dispositions diverses relatives à la sécurité et aux contrôles frontaliers*, Article 3; and http://www.cdef.terre.defense.gouv.fr/publications/doctrine/doctrine06/us/retex/art_23.pdf.

323. "According to British and French Muslim leaders there is a growing perception in Muslim communities that they are being stopped, questioned, and searched not on the basis of evidence and reasonable suspicion but on the basis of "looking Muslim." Islamic Institute for Human Rights, "Country Profile: The Conditions of Muslims in France," at 53. See also: International Helsinki Federation for Human Rights, *Intolerance and Discrimination against Muslims in Selected EU Member States; Report to the OSCE Conference on Tolerance and the Fight against Racism, Xenophobia and Discrimination*, (Brussels: September 13–14, 2004), at 15. Article 78.2 of the Penal Code of Procedure authorizes law enforcement officials to ask any person to justify his or her identity by any means where one or more plausible reasons exist to suspect that: (a) the person has committed or attempted to commit an offense; (b) the person is preparing to commit a crime or misdemeanor; (c) that person is able to five information useful for an inquiry into a crime or misdemeanor; or (d) that person is the subject of inquiries ordered by a judicial authority.

324. Justice Initiative interview with Mr. Michel Tubiana, Honorary President, French League for Human Rights (LDH), Paris, November 2005. At the end of September 2001, the nongovernmental organization Cimade, which monitors 13 administrative detention centers for foreigners, observed a near 30 percent increase in the number of foreigners without legal residency papers being held in detention centers in major urban areas, including Paris, Marseille, Lyon, Strasbourg, and Toulouse. The majority were of North African origin. Cimade noted that the increase correlated with an increase of the terror alert program—"VIGIPIRATE plan"—to a high level. Cimade also noted that the primary outcome of "VIGIPIRATE" appears to be the detention of illegal immigrants due to an increase in the number of identity checks conducted by the police. Jean Martinez, *Vigipirate fills up detention centers*, (Paris: Cimade, September 25, 2001).

325. Personal information is defined, and its use regulated by, the European Union Directive 95/46/EC on the protection of individuals with regard to the processing of personal data and on the free movement of such data. Personal data are defined as "any information relating to an identified or identifiable natural person" (Art. 2, a). Within the category of personal data, there are aspects that constitute sensitive personal data including: religious beliefs, political opinions, health, sexual orientation, race, membership of past organizations. The directive stipulates that personal data should not be processed unless conditions are met that require that the processing be transparent, for a legitimate purpose and proportional. When sensitive personal data are processed, additional restrictions apply (Art. 8). See EU data protection page available at http://ec.europa.eu/justice_home/fsj/privacy/.

326. See Wilhelm Achelpöhler and Dr. Holger Niehaus, "Data Screening as a Means of Preventing Islamist Terrorist Attacks on Germany," *German Law Journal*, Vol. 5, No. 5, May 1, 2005.

327. According to one writer, "This method had been previously used—without much success—in the late 1970s and 1980s to track down members of the Red Army Faction who had changed their identity and gone underground. At that time, the police searched for 'conspiratorial flats' by screening the data of electricity providers and other agencies for clients who apparently tried to avoid contact with the authorities, were using only little electricity and water, or who paid their utility bills in cash to avoid opening a bank account, and similar criteria." Daniel Moeckli, "Discriminatory Profiles: Law Enforcement after 9/11 and 7/7," *European Human Rights Law Review*, No. 5, 517–532, 2005. According to Berlin Commissioner for Data Protection and Freedom of Information Alexander Dix, the *Rasterfahndung* operation carried out in the 1970s turned up one terrorist. But there is disagreement over whether this person was identified due to the computerized search or other methods. Justice Initiative interview with Alexander Dix, Berlin, March 2006.

328. A wide range of institutions were asked to provide police with personal data of individuals who fit the established profile: registration offices (*Einwohnermeldeämter*/EMÄ), universities/polytechnics, the German database on foreigners, and the Central Foreigners Register (*Ausländerzentralregister*/AZR); health and social insurance agencies, private security companies, builders and utility companies. Each state transferred the resulting data sets to the Federal Criminal Police Authority (*Bundeskriminalamt*/BKA), where it was stored in a specially created sleeper cell database (*Verbunddatei Schläfer*). Due to variations among the profiles used by different states, in some cases the BKA had to eliminate data that clearly did not correspond to the profile. Martina Kant, "Nothing doing? Taking stock of data trawling operations in Germany after 11 September 2001," Statewatch Bulletin, Vol. 15, Nos. 3–4, August 2005; Daniel Moeckli, "Discriminatory Profiles: Law Enforcement after 9/11 and 7/7," in *European Human Rights Law Review*, 2005; Ian Johnson and David Crawford, "Germany's Terrorist Hunt Spurs Corporate Defiance," *Wall Street Journal*, August 9, 2002; Dietmar Henning, "Arab students witch-hunted," *World Socialist Website*, October 6, 2001. A senior German police official said that in Berlin, they felt that it was important to include private security companies amongst the source providers as these companies might have access to sensitive areas, such as the Hahn-Meitner Institute that works with nuclear materials. Justice Initiative interview, Berlin, March 2006.

329. Data based on the "Hamburg cell profile" was collected by state (*länder*) police authorities based on their respective police regulations. In practice, profiles varied slightly from one German state to another. Martina Kant, "Nothing doing? Taking stock of data trawling operations in Ger-

many after 11 September 2001," *Statewatch Bulletin*, Vol. 15, Nos. 3–4, August 2005. According to an official working on the *Rasterfahndung* operation in the Berlin region, the criteria used there evolved over time and with each change, state officials went before a judge to ensure the legality of their search. Initially, Berlin authorities established the following criteria: male, Muslim, legal residence in Germany, aviation training, and technical studies. Authorities discovered that the fact that someone is Muslim does not necessarily appear on files and that their data providers, especially universities, could not know whether an individual had a legal residence in Germany. They therefore changed the characteristic "Muslim" to "probably Muslim" and "legal residence" to "probably legal residence." After two other changes addressing data providers, a final profile was developed. This profile eliminated "probably Muslim" and "probably legal residence" as their data providers had difficulties with these vague criteria. Thus, the criteria of the first profile were:

- male;
- born between January 1960 and October 10, 1993 (as was the case with the Hamburg cell);
- coming from a list of 28 countries or stateless or nationality not defined (this replaced "probably Muslim").

Justice Initiative interview, Berlin, March 2006. The 8.3 million figure is widely cited in German media and academic reports.

330. These criteria were established by the "Sub-Working Group Grid" of the Coordination Group on International Terrorism (KG IntTE). The KG IntTE was set up pursuant to a decision of a Working Group (AK II) of the Interior Ministers' [of German states] conference (IMK); it is chaired by the BKA and includes the subcommittee on leadership, operations and fight against crime (UA FEK), AG Krip, Federal Border Guards, Foreign Intelligence Service, internal intelligence service, chief public prosecutor and army representatives. Martina Kant, "Nothing doing? Taking stock of data trawling operations in Germany after 11 September 2001," *Statewatch Bulletin*, Vol. 15, Nos. 3–4, August 2005.

331. Entries in the sleeper database by state: Baden-Württemberg: 3,800; Lower Saxony: 2,588; Bavaria: 2,053; North-Rhine Westphalia: 11,004; Berlin: 710; Reinland Pfalz: 1,792; Brandenburg: 333; Saarland: 416; Bremen: 546; Sachsen: 1,317; Hamburg: 811; Sachsen-Anhalt: 1,292; Hessen: 3,739; Schleswig-Holstein: 534; Mecklenburg; Vorpommern: 895; Thuringia: 158; Total: 31,988. These figures are listed in Martina Kant, "Nothing doing?".

332. "They included personal data on people holding flight licenses, flight students, users of flight simulators, members of flying associations and even the customer database of a company distributing aeronautical supplies. The Goethe Institutes also delivered data because many foreign students receive their German language certificate required for their studies there. Data from license holders authorised to transport dangerous goods and airport employees, nuclear power stations, 24 chemical companies, the German railway, biological laboratories and research institutes were collected. Alongside police data gathered from the INPOL system [5] information gathered from police searches of the "Taliban offices" in Frankfurt/Main on February and June 2001 was used as well." Kant, *Taking Stock*.

333. Ibid.

334. Ian Johnson and David Crawford, "Germany's Terrorist Hunt Spurs Corporate Defiance," *Wall Street Journal*, August 9, 2002. Martina Kant, "Nothing doing?".

335. Justice Initiative interview with Mr. Wolfgang Wieland, Green Party Member of German Bundestag (Mitglied des Deutschen Bundestages, Sprecher für Innere Sicherheit), Berlin, March 2006.

336. Justice Initiative interview with Mr. Sebastien Müller, Researcher, Berlin, March 2006.

337. Justice Initiative interview with Alexander Dix, Berlin, March 2006. Several persons with ties to the Hamburg cell were arrested in the months after 9/11, including Mounir al-Motassadek and Ramzi Binalshibh. Profiling played no role in these arrests. They were identified and arrested on the basis of personal connections, such as sharing an apartment, and other intelligence on bank accounts allegedly used to pay for visas and flight training. "Profile: Mounir al-Motassadek," available at http://news.bbc.co.uk/2/hi/europe/2223152.stm.

338. David Cole, "Are We Safer?" *The New York Review of Books*, Vol. 5, No. 4, March 9, 2006.

339. Martina Kant, "Nothing doing?".

340. One German analyst noted that: "The court [that struck down the practice] decided as well that especially the analyzed method of data screening could have a *"stigmatisierende Wirkung"* (stigmatizing impact) on those effected and thus 'increase the risk of being discriminated against in working and everyday life.' After all, the measure was specifically aimed against immigrants of Muslim faith: reproducing prejudices is a side effect hardly avoidable when recording members of a religious community generally." Gabriele Kett-Straub, "Data Screening of Muslim Sleepers was Unconstitutional," *German Law Journal*, Vol. 7, No. 11, November 2006, available at http://www.germanlawjournal.com/print.php?id=770.

341. Full-text of decision available at: http://www.bundesverfassungsgericht.de/pressemitteilungen/bvg06-040.html.

342. http://www.bundesverfassungsgericht.de/pressemitteilungen/bvg06-040.html. See also G. Kett-Straub, "Data Screening of Muslim Sleepers Unconstitutional," at 967, 970–71.

343. "Trawling for data illegal, German court rules" Reuters/Associated Press, May 24, 2006.

344. Ibid.

345. Bundestagsdrucksache 16/10121; amended by the Committee for Interior of the German Parliament as Bundestagsdrucksache 16/10822; with a second amendment in Drucksache 971/08 of the "Vermittlungsausschuss." The First Instance Court in Wiesbaden, the legal location of the German Federal Police, will be the only court that can review legal challenges to such an operation, instead of courts in each German state. Justice Initiative telephone interview with Heiner Busch, MitarbeiterInnen, Institut für Bürgerrechte & öffentliche Sicherheit e.V., November 2008. § 20 v para 1, Bundestagsdrucksache 16/10121.

346. "... In Germany's view, computerized profile searches both for criminal prosecution purposes and in order to avert dangers constitute a proper and necessary tool in the fight against international terrorism. However, in view of the fact that members and supporters of terrorist groups are known to roam across Europe, the measure would be much more effective if it were applied by all EU Member States." Council of European Union, Brussels, German proposal to Article 36 Committee, March 8, 2002 (doc 6403/2, ENFOPOL 27). R. Kleine, "Schily calls for data mining across Europe," *Bild-Zeitung*, (March 27, 2004), cited in Daniel Moeckli, "Discriminatory Profiles: Law Enforcement after 9/11 and 7/7," in *European Human Rights Law Review*, 2005.

347. Justice Initiative interview with Mr. A.B., French counterterrorism official, Paris, February 2006.

348. Council of the European Union, Draft Council Recommendation on the development of terrorist profiles, Brussels, October 14, 2002 (11858/1/02, REV 1 LIMITE ENFOPOL 117).

349. Question Time on July 2, 2003, London: Hansard, House of Commons, Vol. 408, Part No. 420.

350. EU network of independent experts in fundamental rights, CFR–CDF, First Report, May 2003. The elements of the profiles identified in the document include nationality, travel document, method and means of travel, age, sex, physical distinguishing features (e.g. battle scars), education, choice of cover identity, use of techniques to prevent discovery or counter questioning, places of stay, methods of communication, place of birth, psycho-sociological features, family situation, expertise in advanced technologies, skills at using non-conventional weapons (CBRN), attendance at training courses in paramilitary, flying and other specialist techniques. Draft Council Recommendation on the development of terrorist profiles. The references to nationality and place of birth among the criteria raise red flags for concerns that this undertaking could drive ethnic profiling.

351. Question Time on July2, 2003, London: Hansard, House of Commons, Vol. 408, Part No. 420.

352. See the extensive work on these issues by Statewatch, a U.K.-based NGO that monitors civil liberties in Europe, available on their web site at http://www.statewatch.org/.

353. The Visa Information System or VIS was created to support coordination of data between EU consular officials, immigration, asylum and border authorities for the 134 countries that require EU entry visas. The VIS was proposed by the European Council in February 2004 and legally established by a June 8, 2004 Council of Ministers Decision 2004/512/EC (see OJ L 213, 15.6.2004, at 5). Reportedly the VIS will store the personal and biometric data (digitized photos and fingerprints) of approximately 20 million Schengen visa applicants annually; some 70 million sets of fingerprints may be stored at any one time. (Comment on database dimensions by participant at "Ethnic Profiling and Ethical Approaches to Security and Counter-Terrorism," a meeting co-hosted by the European Policy Center, the King Badouin Foundation and the Open Society Justice Initiative, Brussels, May 31, 2007.) On March 7, 2005, the council recommended granting internal security authorities access to the VIS in order to "achieve fully the aim of improving internal security and the fight against terrorism." The European Commission has made a proposal for a Decision on access for consultation of the VIS by law enforcement authorities (COM (2005)600). Both proposals have been discussed by the council and the parliament and endorsed by plenary vote of the European Parliament on June 6, 2007; publication in the official journal is pending. Information provided by email by the office of MEP Sarah Ludford, November 2007.

354. The Schengen Information System (SIS I and SIS II) is a secure database used by 15 European countries to support the free movement of persons following the abolishing of border controls under the 1985 Schengen Agreement. SIS I and SIS II maintain and distribute information for border security and law-enforcement purposes. According to the newly agreed regulation on SIS II, biometrics will be inserted in the SIS II following a quality check, though for the time being will be used only for verification purposes (as opposed to identification purposes). Article 22; OJ L 381 of 28 December 20056, at 4.

355. The Eurodac is a fingerprint system created to coordinate asylum applications across EU member states. Discussions about giving law enforcement authorities access to Eurodac are ongoing, following the explicit call of the European Council to permit such access at a June 2007 meeting. June 12–13, 2007 Justice and Home Affairs Council meeting. Eurodac reportedly has some 350,000 entries. Comment at "Ethnic Profiling and Ethical Approaches to Security and Counter-Terrorism," Brussels, May 31, 2007.

356. Ibid., para. 41. In addition to European Union databases, the Prüm Treaty, signed on May 27, 2005 by seven European Union countries, will facilitate the exchange of data from DNA and fingerprint databases to produce improved cross-border cooperation, particularly in combating terrorism, cross-border crime and illegal migration. See Fausto Correia, *Prüm Treaty will allow EU27 to exchange DNA data to fight crime*, (Brussels: Challenge Project report, adopted by the European Parliament, June 19, 2007), available at http://www.libertysecurity.org/article1498.html.

357. See Commission's Communication on interoperability: Com (2005) 597 Final of 24.11.2005.

358. Council Decision 2008/633/JHA of 23 June 2008 concerning access for consultation of the Visa Information System (VIS) by designated authorities of member states and by EUROPOL for the prupose of the prevention, detetction and investigation of terrorist offenses and of other serious criminal offenses.

359. "The rapporteur also has doubts as to the proportionality of the individual measures. The ends do not justify the means, as the measures are neither appropriate nor necessary and are unreasonably harsh toward those concerned." European Parliament Draft Report on the proposal for a Council framework decision on the protection of personal data processed in the framework of police and judicial co-operation in criminal matters. Committee on Civil Liberties and Home Affairs. Rapporteur: Martine Roure. Provisional 2005/0202(CNS). Amendment 15, Article 5, paragraph 1 a (new). Almost identical concerns are raised in the European Parliament Draft Report on the proposal for a regulation of the European Parliament and of the Council on the Visa Information System (VIS) and the exchange of data between Member States on short-stay visas. (COM(2004)0835–C6-0004/2005–2004/0287(COD)) Committee on Civil Liberties, Justice and Home Affairs, Rapporteur: Sarah Ludford, Amendment 14, Article 1 (c).

360. Art 4.4 is too broad allowing that law enforcement need only believe that having the personal data would make it easier to prevent, investigate, detect and prosecute crime; rather the standard should be that law enforcement can demonstrate a need and show that less intrusive measures are not available. Opinion of the European Data Protection Supervisor on the Proposal for a Council Framework Decision on the protection of personal data processed in the framework of police and judicial co-operation in criminal matters (COM(2005) 475 final), December 19, 2005.

361. Peter Hustinx, *Third Opinion of the European Data Protection Supervisor on the Proposal for a Council Framework Decision on the protection of personal data processed in the framework of police and judicial cooperation in criminal matters*, (Brussels: August 27, 2007) 17. See also, Opinion of the European Data Protection Supervisor for a Council Decision concerning access for consultation of the Visa Information System (VIS) by the authorities of Member States responsible for internal security and by Europol for the purposes of the prevention, detection and investigation of terrorist offenses and other serious criminal offices (COM (2005) 600 final). (2006/C 97/03). This opinion

specifically raises concern with the risk of profiling of travelers through access to information such as "purpose of travel."

362. Council Framework Decision 2008/977/JHA of November 27, 2008 on the protection of personal data processes in the framework of police and judicial cooperation in criminal matters. Criticisms fo this instrument are discussed in Commissioner for Human Rights, *Protecting the Right to Privacy In the Fight Against Terrorism*, Strasbourg: Council of Europe, November 17, 2008, CommDH/IssuePaper(2008)3, para. 5.4.

363. Ibid., at Article 1 (4).

364. Council of the European Union, Interinsitutional File: 2007/0237 (CNS), CRIMORG7, AVIATION 3, DATAPROTECT2, Brussels, January 23, 2009.

365. The European Union Directive on the protection of individuals with regard to the processing of personal data and on the free movement of such data (Data Protection Directive 95/46/EC, of October 24, 1995) expressly exempts from its application anonymous statistical information of the kind needed to document and prove racial discrimination. Paragraph 26 states that: "the principles of protection must apply to any information concerning an identified or identifiable person"; and "the principles of protection shall not apply to data rendered anonymous in such a way that the data subject is no longer identifiable." Article 2 defines "personal data" as "any information relating to an identified or identifiable natural person ('data subject'); an identifiable person is one who can be identified, directly or indirectly, in particular by reference to an identification number or to one or more factors specific to his physical, physiological, mental, economic, cultural or social identity." Moreover, even if the data at issue are "personal data" under the terms of the directive, processing of that data would still be permissible where "d) the processing relates to data which are ... necessary for the establishment, exercise or defense of legal claims." Thus, the directive does not bar the collection of race or ethnic data necessary to challenge ethnic discrimination—including ethnic profiling—in court. The Council of Europe's Convention for the Protection of Individuals with Regard to Automatic Processing of Personal Data (1981) is in accord. Art. 2(a) states that: "'personal data' means any information relating to an identified or identifiable individual. The Explanatory Report on the Convention, in paragraph 28 states that: "'Identifiable persons' means a person who can be easily identified: it does not cover identification of persons by means of sophisticated methods". (Recommendation No. R(97) 18 of the Committee of Ministers Concerning the Protection of Personal Data Collected and Processed for Statistical Purposes (1997), preamble.) The recommendation further distinguishes in the preamble between "personal" and "anonymous" data (as to which "identification requires an unreasonable amount of time and manpower"), and in paragraph 58 notes that "statistical results ... are not personal data, as they are not linked to an identified or identifiable natural person." Finally, Article 6 also makes clear that "sensitive data"—including "personal data revealing racial origin"—may be processed automatically where domestic law provides for the data to be 'collected in such a way that the data subject is not identifiable.'" (Appendix, Principle 4(8); Exlpanatory Memorandum to Recommendation No. R(97) 18, para. 76(a)).

366. See Jean-Patrick Courtois, "Law on the fight against terrorism providing diverse dispositions for the border controls and security," (Paris: Report on behalf of the Commission on Laws, Ordinary session 2005–2006, Annex to the Senate session record of December 6, 2005), available at http://www.senat.fr/rap/l05-117/l05-1177.html. See also, Piotr Smolar, "Anti-Terrorism, according to the head of the RG," *Le Monde*, November 24, 2005, "When businesses hide clandestine prayer halls," Agence France-Presse, September 26, 2005.

367. The monitoring activities carried out by the regional centers to combat radical Islam are discussed in detail below.

368. "Created at the end of January 2005, the police have been placed under the authority of the prefects. The principle is to use all the resources of the administrative police in order to disrupt the small businesses and meeting places used by radical militants... ." Piotr Smolar, "Disruption of the locations where radical Islam is spread," *Le Monde,* April 11, 2006: "The aim is to destabilize radical Islam in the very early stages, without disturbing the actions or framework of the intelligence services nor interfering with Republican Islam, explains the head of the intelligence services, Pascal Mailhos."

369. Piotr Smolar, "Disruption of the locations where radical Islam is spread," *Le Monde*, April 11, 2006. Smolar reports that the judicial charges are typically deportations or restraining orders (interdiction d'exercer une activité), while others are administrative charges on grounds such as sanitation or tax matters.

370. Ibid., and "The French lesson, Europe and terrorism," *The Economist*, August 13, 2005.

371. Jean Chichizola, "Radical Islam: the greater Paris area police increases its discoveries," *Le Figaro*, May 18, 2005.

372. Justice Initiative interview with Samy Debah, Paris, July 2006.

373. Ibid.

374. Article 78.1 of the Code of Criminal Procedure sets out a general obligation for anyone found on national territory to accept to undergo a police identity check pursuant to the conditions established therein. Article 78.2 al. 2–5 establishes four distinct grounds for stops. When the police officer is not satisfied with the identity documents provided, they may take the person for a verification of identity (*vérification d'identité*) which entails taking them into the police station for a formal document check where the person may be held for up to four hours.

375. Official statements have singled out Salafist Muslims as examples of those who may be subject to controls. Newspapers reports indicate that Tabligh Muslims have also been targeted. See Jean Chichizola, "Radical Islam invests in teen fashion," *Le Figaro*, September 7, 2005. "When businesses hide clandestine prayers halls," Agence France-Presse, September 26, 2005, available at http://www.acb54.com/breve.php3?id_breve=17.

376. Justice Initiative interview with A.B., Paris, July 2006.

377. Ibid.

378. "Officially they are sanctioned because they employ illegal workers, the fridge doesn't work or another reason ... but in essence they find pretexts to force them to close." Justice Initiative interview with Boualam Azahoum, DiverCité spokesperson, Lyon, July 2006.

379. Justice Initiative interview with Mr. H.L., Paris, July 2006.

380. Comments at a meeting of Islamic organizations attended by Justice Initiative staff, Paris, July 2006.

381. "Airlines Terror Plot Disrupted" BBC News Online, August 10, 2006, available at http://news.bbc.co.uk/2/hi/uk_news/4778575.stm.

382. The raid involved sites in cities in fourteen provinces: Bari, Bologna, Cagliari, Catania, Florence, Genoa, Milan, Naples, Palermo, Reggio, Calabria, Turin, Venice and Rome. AGI, "Interior Ministry, 40 Arrests in Italy," Special Service by AGI on behalf of the Italian Prime Minister's Office, August 11, 2006, available at: http://www.agi.it/english/news.pl?doc=200608112053-1270-RT1-CRO-0-NF82&page=0&id=agionline-eng.italyonline.

383. "Italy Arrests 40 in Security Crackdown," Associated Press, August 11, 2006. Massimiliano di Giorgio, "Italy Arrests 40 in Security Swoop," Reuters, August 11, 2006; and "Interior Ministry, 40 Arrests in Italy."

384. AGI, "Interior Ministry, 40 Arrests in Italy." "Italy Arrests 40 in Security Crackdown," Massimiliano di Giorgio, "Italy Arrests 40 in Security Swoop.

385. Ibid., "Italy Arrests 40 in Security Crackdown."

386. European Monitoring Center on Racism and Xenophobia, *The Impact of 7 July 2005 London Bomb Attacks on Muslim Communities in the EU*, (Vienna: EUMC, November 2005), available at http://eumc.eu.int/eumc/material/pub/London/London-Bomb-attacks.pdf#search=%22eumc%20impact%20of%20london%20bombings%22; "Italian Police Arrest 141," Associated Press, August 15, 2005.

387. "Italy Questions Thousands in Extremist Crackdown," *ABC.net.au*, July 17, 2005; European Monitoring Center on Racism and Xenophobia, *The Impact of 7 July 2005 London Bomb Attacks*. Nick Morris, "Italy terror attack risk remains elevated after 141 arrested and more than 700 are questioned," *The New Criminologist*, August 16, 2005, available at http://www.newcriminologist.co.uk/news.asp?id=1124189253.

388. These individuals were charged with "unauthorised stay or failure to obey a previous expulsion order or illegal use of the stay permit," European Monitoring Center on Racism and Xenophobia, *The Impact of 7 July 2005 London Bomb Attacks.*

389. "Italian Police Arrest 141 in Anti-Terror Raids," Associated Press, August 15, 2005.

390. Nick Morris, "Italy terror attack risk remains elevated."

391. "Italy launches nationwide sweep on suspected militants," *Euronews*, July 14 2005, available at http://euronews.net/create_html.php?page=detail_info&article=299106&lng=1; "Italy detains 174 people in anti-terror sweep,"Reuters, July 14, 2005, available at http://www.nzherald.co.nz/section/story.cfm?c_id=2&objectid=10335764.

392. "Italy detains 174 people in anti-terror sweep,"Reuters.

393. Ibid.; "Anti-terror raids in Italy," *World News Australia*, July 14, 2005, available at http://www9.sbs.com.au/theworldnews/region.php?id=115867&region=3.

394. Daniel Williams, "Italy Stages 'Maxi-Blitz' Raids after London Attacks," *Washington Post*, July 14, 2005; "Italy detains 174 people in anti-terror sweep,"Reuters.

395. Justice Initiative interview with L.S. and Mr. V.W., Desio, May 2006.

396. Justice Initiative interview with N.R., Milan, May 2006.

397. Justice Initiative interview with S.M. Arshad, Milan, May 2006.

398. Justice Initiative interview with N.R., Milan, May 2006.

399. Ibid.

400. Justice Initiative telephone interview with S.S., November 2008.

401. Information provided by Udo Enwereuzor, Cooperazione per lo Sviluppo dei Paesi Emergent (COSPE), November 2008. Corte Costituzionale Sentenza 350/2008 del 22/10/2008.

402. Justice Initiative interview with Mr. S.S., November 2008.

403. "Milan Mosque to be 'closed down,'" *BBC News,* July 7, 2008, *BBC News,* available at http://news.bbc.co.uk/1/hi/world/europe/7493756.stm.

404. "Evicted Milan Muslims pray at stadium 'mosque'", *Europe News,* July 18, 2008. "Italy: Police guard makeshift Milan Mosque for Friday prayers," *Adnkronos international Italia,* July 18, 2008.

405. Information provided by Walter Citti, acting executive secretary of Associazione Studi Giuridici sull'Immigrazione, December 2008; see also Stephen Brown, "Italy's right to curb Islam with mosque law," *Reuters,* September 16, 2008.

406. See Rachel Donadio, "Italy: Mosque Moratorium Plan," *The New York Times,* December 4, 2008. "Mosque ban criminalizes Muslims: Italian groups," December 5, 2008. Al Arabiya news channel, available at http://www.alarabiya.net/articles/2008/12/05/61430.html.

407. Dr. Oliver Maor, German Ministry of the Interior, comments made at "Ethnic Profiling and Ethical Approaches to Security and Counter-Terrorism," a meeting co-hosted by the European Policy Center, the King Badouin Foundation and the Open Society Justice Initiative, Brussels, May 31, 2007, and subsequent email exchange.

408. "Police Raid Islamic School in Frankfurt," *Deutsche Welle,* July 12, 2004; "German Police investigate mosque preaching hatred to children," *Associated Press* , July 12, 2004; Richard Bernstein, "Raid on 'holy war' mosque'," *New York Times,* July 14, 2004.

409. "The Battle for German Muslim Minds," *Deutsche Welle,* July 27, 2004.

410. Siddik and Harburg, "The Ghosts that I Awoke."

411. Comment of Ahmed Ayaou, executive board member of the mosque, cited in Bureau of Democracy, Human Rights and Labor, *International Religious Freedom Report 2005: Germany,* (Washington, D.C.: United States Department of State, 2005).

412. Richard Bernstein, "Raid on 'Holy War' Mosque,'" *New York Times,* July 14, 2004.

413. Sarah Plass, "World Briefing Europe: Germany: Raids Aim at Islamic Radicals," *The New York Times,* September 29, 2005.

414. Justice Initiative interview with Burhan Kesici, Vice President of the Islamic Federation in Berlin, Berlin, March 2006.

415. Ibid.

416. Sarah Plass, "World Briefing Europe: Germany: Raids Aim at Islamic Radicals," *The New York Times,* September 29, 2005.

417. Simone Kaiser, Marcel Rosenbach and Holger Stark, "Operation Alberich; How the CIA Helped Germany Foil Terror Plot," *Spiegel Online,* September 10, 2007, available at http://www.spiegel.de/international/germany/0,1518,504837,00.html.

418. "Germany arrests three terror suspects," Associated Press, November 25, 2008.

419. Decision of the first instance administrative court of Gelsenkirchen, # Az: 17 K 524/05, November 22, 2007, in the case of "The police action was an encroachment on the fundamental right of the Islamic Cultural Association as a representative of the Khaled Mosque to the undisturbed exercise of religion (Art. 4 Abs. 2 GG)." The court ruled that "The police measure constituted an infringement of the fundamental right to association of the "Islamischen Kulturverein e.V." responsible for the Khaled Mosque and of the freedom of religion as guaranteed by Law (Art 4 Abs. 2 GG). http://www.igmg.de/nachrichten/artikel/gericht-erklart-polizeiaktion-fur-rechtswidrig. html.

420. Seven men faced trial on terror charges and five were found guilty as a result of Operation Crevice Seven, an investigation of several months that culminated in coordinated raids on March 30, 2004. See BBC News, "Timeline: Operation Crevice," available at http://news.bbc.co.uk/1/hi/ uk/6207348.stm and Elaine Sciolino and Stephen Grey, "British Terror Trial Traces a Path to Militant Islam," *The New York Times*, November 26, 2006.

421. Cited in "The French Lessons, Europe and Terrorism," *The Economist*, August 13, 2005.

422. EUROPOL, *TE-SAT Report 2007*, at 14, reports that in 2006 European member states arrested 257 Islamist terrorism suspects (of 706 arrests on suspicion of terrorism—the largest group is separatist terrorists). There are no data yet on the outcomes of those arrests in terms of charges, releases, and convictions.

423. Describing patterns predating 9/11, a French immigration activist told the Justice Initiative: "For many years counterterrorist operations involved massive arrests (*rafles*) involving hundreds of people. I remember one raid on Rue Myrha [a street in Paris] where around 200 people were arrested and then they weeded out a few. In the end about 2 or 3 cases actually went to trial. But many individuals spent months in prison. This caused a bit of a scandal at the time. There are no longer such massive arrests. The last occurred around 1998. Today they occur on a smaller scale, but this still means dozens of individuals." Justice Initiative interview with a representative of the Mouvement de l'Immigration et des Banlieues (MIB), Paris, June 2006.

424. Article 421-2-1 of the French Penal Code designates as an "act of terrorism" participation in "any group formed or association established with a view to the preparation, marked by one or more material actions, of any of the acts of terrorism provided for under the previous articles...." "Previous articles" identify conduct considered to constitute acts of terrorism "where they are committed intentionally in connection with an individual or collective undertaking the purpose of which is seriously to disturb public order through intimidation or terror." Official English translation available on "legifrance" at http://195.83.177.9/code/liste.phtml?lang=uk&c=33&r=3794#art16569].

425. A detailed inquiry report discussing the implementation of AMT provisions in France, published by the International Federation of Human Rights Leagues comments:

"It is particularly noteworthy that, in the last couple of years the "anti-terrorist" authorities of the 14th Section have chosen to charge the overwhelming majority of those arrested on suspicion of involvement of terrorist activities with participation in such associations. The way in which the offense has been defined and indeed interpreted is especially interesting:

The offense continues to consist of preparatory participation: participation in a group or an understanding, preparation of a subsequent or ecological act of terrorism. The association therefore remains independent of the actual commission of the offenses, which are its object. This is significant, since it means that, as long as it is sufficiently realized, the preparation alone is enough to constitute the punishable offense.

[...] The intention of the Article is quite clear: the investigating and prosecuting authorities ... are statutorily absolved from any duty to link the alleged participation with any actual execution of a terrorist offense or even a verifiable plan for the execution of such an offense."

Michael McColgan and Alessandro Attanasio, *International Mission of Inquiry France: Paving the Way for Arbitrary Justice* (Paris: International Federation of Human Rights Leagues, March 1999), at 9; citing Yves Mayaud, *Le Terrorisme*, (Paris: Dalloz, 1997), at 29.

426. Even before 9/11, French prosecutors often relied upon weak and tenuous evidence to charge individuals suspected of terrorist sympathies. The International Federation of Human Rights Leagues (FIDH), which published in-depth research on AMT detentions in 1999, observed:

> What is striking about the cases we have enquired into is the paucity of real evidence about intended acts of terrorism, coupled with questionably relevant evidence as far as large numbers, possibly the majority, of those accused are concerned. [...] [O]ur reading of a considerable number of case papers confirms what so many defense lawyers have told us: that the evidence against many of their clients at the time they are arrested is so insubstantial as not to merit arrest and detention at all, let alone prosecution for terrorist activities.

McColgan and Attanasio, *France: Paving the Way for Arbitrary Justice*, at 10 and 14.

427. Piotr Smolar, "French Jails Contain 358 Persons Detained for Activism," *Le Monde*, September 9, 2005.

428. Justice Initiative interview with Emmanuel Guittet, doctoral student in political science at Université Paris X, Nanterre Researcher, ELISE consortium (European Liberty and Security), Paris, January 2006. Justice Initiative interview with Piotr Smolar, journalist and security specialist at *Le Monde* newspaper, Paris, April 2006.

In a report to the French Senate on behalf of the Commission on Laws, Senator Jean-Patrick Courtois, explained: "According to M. Jean-Louis Bruguière [France's leading antiterrorism investigative judge], this new form of terrorism involves dispersed cells, that are atomized, which renders all modeling impossible. [...] In order to communicate and coordinate, these groups work in networks. This translates particularly into the massive use of electronic means of communication, especially the Internet. It is essential to reconstruct the history of each individual, the person's personal itinerary, in order to map out the networks of contacts. [...] Access to a greater number of information sources is important for the counterterrorist services, because this makes it possible to reconstruct the crossed paths and personal itineraries. The objective evidently is not to put in place a generalized surveillance of the population. It means gathering the maximum amount of information about individuals that have already been spotted or persons in contact with these persons."

Jean-Patrick Courtois, "Projet de loi relatif à la lutte contre le terrorisme et portant dispositions diverses relatives à la sécurité et aux contrôles frontaliers," (Paris: Report on behalf of the Commission on Laws, Ordinary session 2005–2006, Annex to the Senate session record of December 6, 2005), available at http://www.senat.fr/rap/l05-117/l05-1177.html. Justice Initiative translation, original French on file.

429. Justice Initiative interview with L.L., senior French police officer, Paris, May 2006. Justice Initiative interview with Mr. A.B., senior French counterterrorism official, Paris, February 2006.

430. Mr. Henri Leclerc, a prominent member of the French Human Rights League, recently commented: "AMT allows for the arrest in too broad a fashion of enormous numbers of people

including a significant number of innocent individuals who will be freed, either after non-suits or discharges. And this is generally after many months of provisional detention." Patricia Touran-cheau, "For the judges, it is the intent of the networks that matters," *Libération*, October 26, 2005, available at http://www.minorites.org/article.php?IDA=15733.

431. Justice Initiative interview with A.B., Paris, July 2006.

432. Tabligh, or Tablighi Jamaat, is a missionary Muslim movement with roots in South Asia. It is generally viewed as apolitical and nonviolent.

433. Justice Initiative interview with L.L, Paris, May 2006. (Emphasis added.)

434. Justice Initiative interview with William Bourdon, Paris, May 2006.

435. Justice Initiative interview with Q.C., Paris, July 2006.

436. Justice Initiative interview with Q.C., Paris, July 2006.

437. Isabelle Coutant-Peyre, who has defended numerous individuals charged with AMT offenses, commented that at least half of the questions asked when in police detention are about how individuals practice their religion. Justice Initiative interview with Isabelle Coutant-Peyre, Paris, June 2006. Several other defense lawyers interviewed by the Justice Initiative commented on the amount of questioning about religion during interrogations.

438. Justice Initiative interview with Jacques Debray, Paris, July 2006.

439. Justice Initiative interview with Nisar Sassi, Lyon, July 2006.

440. Justice Initiative telephone interview with G.H., June 2006.

441. "Arrest of an iman in an investigation of terro financing," Agence France-Presse, June 20, 2006. Jean Chichizola, "Inquiry into the iman of Clichy-sous-Bois," *Le Figaro*, July 5, 2006. "Concern follows the arrests of suspected associates," Union des Associations Musulmanes de la Seine-Saint-Denis, June 21, 2006, available at http://lekhalidien.over-blog.com/article-3075513.html.

442. Justice Initiative attendance meeting of Muslim nongovernmental organizations, Paris, July 2006.

443. According to Privacy International, "in 2003 alone there were over 70 antiterror arrests, and these figures were heralded by the Interior Minister, Giuseppe Pisanu as 'evidence of the commitment of Italian police forces in the face of Muslim terrorism.'" Gus Hosein, "European Anti-Terrorism Discrimination and the Threat of Indiscriminate Policy," *Privacy International*, September 20, 2005.

444. Professor Salvatore Pallida, who has been systematically documenting arrests, commented, "there were 208 arrests between 2001 and today... With respect to these arrests, Mr. Berlusconi said we saved Italy from terrorism. In reality of these 208 persons, in almost every case they were released ... Most of these arrests had nothing at all to do with terrorism; they were street vendors, simple migrants, people who really had nothing to do with terrorist activities." Justice Initiative interview with Professor Salvatore Pallida, University of Genoa, Genoa, May 2006.

445. Justice Initiative interview with Carlo Bonini, security specialist and journalist at *La Repub-blica*, Milan, May 2006.

446. Justice Initiative interview with Professor Salvatore Pallida, Genoa, May 2006. Justice Initiative interview with Professor Alessandro dal Lago, University of Genoa, Genoa, May 2006. Justice Initiative interview with Carlo Bonini, Milan, May 2006.

447. Justice Initiative interview with Carlo Bonini, Milan, May 2006. "Italy Arrests Egyptians for U.S. War Cemetery Plot," Reuters, May 19, 2002, available at http://www.freerepublic.com/focus/news/763507/posts.

448. "Italy acquits 'terror plotters,'" BBC News, April 31, 2004, available at http://news.bbc.co.uk/2/hi/europe/3674501.stm.

449. "Italy Arrests Egyptians for U.S. War Cemetery Plot," Reuters, May 19, 2002. "Italy acquits 'terror plotters,'" BBC News.

450. "Italy acquits 'terror plotters,'" BBC News.

451. Justice Initiative interview with Mr. Carlo Bonini, Milan, May 2006. The case is discussed in Carlo Bonini, Mercato de la paura, (Rome: Editore Einaudi, 2006).

452. Gill Donovan, "Police arrest four in alleged terrorist plot against basilica," National Catholic Reporter, August 30, 2002. "Italy arrests men over 'church plot,'" BBC News, August 20, 2002.

453. "Italy Frees Fresco Suspects," New York Times, August 22, 2002.

454. Hadia Messia, "Sicily police hold terror suspects," Agence France-Presse, September 12, 2002. "Sicily police hold terror suspects," CNN News, September 12, 2002, available at http://archives.cnn.com/2002/WORLD/europe/09/12/sicily.arrests/index.html. "Italian police arrest terror suspects," BBC News, September 12, 2002.

455. "15 detainees charged as possible terrorists," The Washington Post, September 13, 2002. "15 Al Qaeda suspects arrested in Italy," Agence France-Presse, September 13, 2002, available at http://www.khaleejtimes.co.ae/ktarchive/130902/theworld.html.

456. "Italian police arrest terror suspects," BBC News, September 12, 2002. "15 Al Qaeda suspects arrested in Italy," AFP, September 13, 2002. "15 detainees charged as possible terrorists," The Washington Post, September 13, 2002. Hadia Messia, "Sicily police hold terror suspects," Agence France-Presse, September 12, 2002.

457. "Italy releases 15 Pakistanis," Agence France-Presse, June 24, 2003.

458. "Burney meets 15 Pakistani prisoners in Italy jail," Syrian Arab News Agency, undated, available at http://www.ansarburney.com/news4.htm#5.

459. In 2005, Italy adopted Law Decree 144/2005, converted into Law 155/2005 ("Pisanu Law"), on "emergency measures to combat international terrorism." Law 155/2005 allows the minister of interior, or under his delegation, the prefects to order expulsions, for the purpose of preventing acts of terrorism. Further legislation, Law Decree 249/2008 on expulsion and removals on grounds relating to terrorism and public security, was passed in January 2008. See Memorandum by Thomas Hammarberg Commissioner for Human Rights of the Council of Europe following his visit to Italy on 19–20 June 2008; Strasbourg, July 28, 2008, CommDH(2008)18.

460. Ibid., and Justice Initiative telephone interview with Carlo Bonini, November 2008.

461. Rohit Jaggi, "Police gain extra time to question suspects," The Financial Times, August 9, 2004. Terror policing brings many arrests but few charges, (London: Institute of Race Relations, March

5, 2003). *The Impact of Anti Terrorism Powers on the British Population*, (London: Liberty, June 2004). *Anti-terrorism legislation: A handbook on how to alienate Muslim communities*, (London: Liberty, Spring 2003). International Helsinki Federation for Human Rights, *Intolerance and Discrimination against Muslims in Selected EU Member States, Report to the OSCE Conference on Tolerance and the Fight against Racism, Xenophobia and Discrimination*, (Brussels: International Helsinki Federation for Human Rights, September 13–14, 2004).

462. Hamed Chapman, "Most terrorist convictions are non-Muslim," *The Muslim News*, August 27, 2004.

463. "New study highlights discrimination in use of anti-terror laws," Institute of Race Relations (IRR), September 2, 2004.

464. The Muslim Council of Britain, *A response to the government discussion paper "Counter-Terrorism Powers: Reconciling Security and Liberty in an Open Society."* (London, MCB, August 2004), at 30–31.

465. Tariq Panga and Martin Bright, "Man U bomb plot probe ends in farce," *The Guardian*, May 2, 2004. Duncan Campbell, Richard Norton-Taylor and Vikram Dodd "Words of warning backed by little clear evidence," *The Guardian*, April 23, 2005.

466. "'Regret' at Kurd terror raid link," *BBC News*, May 9, 2004.

467. Home Office Statistical News Release, Statistics on Terrorism Arrests and Outcomes: Great Britain, 11 September 2001 to 31 March 2008, (London: Home Office, May 13, 2009).

468. Home Office Statistical Bulletin, *Statistics on Terrorism Arrests and Outcomes: Great Britain, 11 September 2001 to 31 March 2008*, (London: Home Office, May 13, 2009), at 2. The non-terror related cases faced charges such as forgery, theft, misuse of drugs or other, unspecified criminal offenses.

469. Ibid., at 3.

470. Ibid., see chart at 4.

471. Ibid., at 6.

472. *France Confronts Terrorism: Government White Paper on Internal Security in the Face of Terrorism*, (Paris: La documentation Française, 2006).

473. Justice Initiative interview with L.L., French police officer, Paris, May 2006. See also Laurent Bonnelli, "Quand les services de renseignement construisent un nouvel ennemi," *Le Monde Diplomatique*, April 2005.

474. Justice Initiative interview with L.L., Paris, May 2006.

475. In a recent article, a French security expert comments that AMT "allows for the use of what professionals call the strategy of the 'net' or the 'kick in the anthill.' It consists of arresting in an extremely broad manner any individuals that they think may be linked in one way or another to radical networks. It relies on the belief in the method's capacity to destabilize the networks and disrupt logistics. And it doesn't matter if a significant part of those arrested are let off after having spent a year or two in preventive detention. As a general rule, as concerns 'Islamist' terrorism, the ratio between the number of arrests, charges and guilty findings is totally disproportionate." Laurent Bonnelli, "An 'anonymous and faceless enemy,': The Intelligence Services, exception and suspicion

after September 11, 2001," *Cultures & Conflicts,* No. 58 (2005), 101–129, available at http://www. conflits.org/document1818.html (original French text on file).

Lawyer William Bourdon clearly summed up this way of thinking: "Some judges and police officers are very well aware that there are innocent individuals amongst those that they place in police celss (*garde-à-vue*). They want to disrupt the networks, cut their wings and create a strong dissuasive effect. They also want to make people speak, obtain information and reassure public opinion... This, they think, can require raking large. So what if they catch fish who have done absolutely nothing? There is collateral damage, but so what? And no-one cares that this is going on..." Justice Initiative interview with William Bourdon, Paris, May 2006.

476. Communication from the Commission to the European Parliament and the Council concerning Terrorist recruitment: addressing the factors contributing to violent radicalization, Brussels, 21.9.2005, COM(2005) 313 final. The European Union Strategy for Combating Radicalisation and Recruitment to Terrorism, Council of the European Union, Brussels, November 24, 2005, 14781/1/05 Rev 1, Limite, JAI 452 / ENFOPOL 164 / COTER 81. In a meeting held on August 16, 2006, the urgency of work on radicalization was emphasized. See Ministers of U.K., Finland, Germany, Portugal, Slovenia, France and the Vice-President of the European Commission, "Informal London Meeting on Counter-Terrorism August 16, 2006," Joint Press Statement, available at www. statewatch.org/news/2006/aug/eu-joint-press-statement-london.

477. Rick Coolsaet, "Between Al-Andalus and a failing integration: Europe's pursuit of a long-term counterterrorism strategy in the post-Al Qaeda era," *IRRI–KIIB,* (Brussels: Academia Press, May 2005), at 9.

478. Director General of the Security Service, Dame Eliza Manningham-Buller, at Queen Mary's College, London, November 9, 2006, "The International Terrorist Threat To The UK," available at http://www.mi5.gov.uk/output/Page568.html.

479. Alan Travis, "MI5 report challenges views on terrorism in Britain," *The Guardian,* August 20, 2008.

480. While radicalism can pose a threat it is extremism, and particularly terrorism, that ought to be our main concern since it involves the active subversion of democratic values and the rule of law. In this sense violent radicalization is to be understood as socialisation to extremism which manifests itself in terrorism. Ibid., at 7.

481. The International Crisis Group comments: "In this 'slippery slope' view of extremism, dreams of 'kingdom come' place the highly religious just a notch or two from the potentially violent on a continuum of radicalization." International Crisis Group, *Islam and Identity in Germany; Europe Report,* No. 181, (New York: International Crisis Group, March 14, 2007), at 15.

482. Rita Breuer, "Islamist educational and social organizations: One element in the radicalization process? "The radical enemies and processes, elements and instruments of political extremism," (Germany: Bundesministerium des Innern, June 2005), at 111.

483. E.S.M. Akerboom, Director Democratic Legal Order General Intelligence and Security Service of the Netherlands (AIVD) 24/04/2007, *Counter-Terrorism in the Netherlands,* available at http:// english.nctb.nl/publications/reports/.

484. Justice Initiative interview with Mr. A.B., Paris, July 2007.

485. Saimir Amghar is a Ph.D. student completing his doctoral thesis at *L'École des hautes études en sciences sociales* (EHESS). His research has included interviews with hundreds of Muslim youth in Belgium, France, Netherlands, Spain, Switzerland, and the United Kingdom. Justice Initiative interview, Paris, August 2007.

486. Justice Initiative interview with Robert Lambert, head of the MPS Muslim Contact Unit, Washington, D.C., June 14, 2007; Briggs, Fieschi, and Lownsbrough, *Bringing It Home*, at 75–6. See Chapter V for further discussion of the work of the Muslim Contact Unit.

487. In a recently published guide aimed at local authorities, the National Coordinator for Counterterrorism (NCTB) states that radicalization is, "a growing willingness to strive for and/or support radical changes in society which are at odds with the democratic legal order and/or which involve the use of undemocratic means." National Coordinator for Counterterrorism, *Counterterrorism at Local Level: A Guide*, at 61, available at http://english.nctb.nl/publications/reports/nctb/.

488. "Radicalism is an attitude of mind. We use this term to indicate the preparedness to accept the extreme consequences of a philosophy and turn them into actions. These actions may result in situations where contrasts that—in themselves—are manageable, can escalate to a level at which they disrupt society. This may be because violence is involved, or because other behavior is encouraged that deeply wounds people or affects their freedom, or because entire groups distance themselves from society. But at the same time we are also dealing with a philosophy, and in a multiform and free society like ours we want it to be possible for people to freely discuss their ideas..." Ministry of Justice Directorate of General Judicial Strategy, "Policy memorandum on radicalism and radicalization to the Speaker of the Lower House of the States General," (August 19, 2005).

489. Dutch Minister of Justice, "Broad-based approach against radicalism and radicalization," September 30, 2005, available at http://english.nctb.nl/press_and_publications/Press_releases/ Press_releases_2005/Press_release_050930.asp. In a communication, the Ministry of Justice further explained its approach: "Combating radicalization is, in practice, to a large extent a matter of the timely recognition of the manifestations of radicalism and a targeted approach to sources of potentially violent radicalization. Dealing with radicalism and radicalization is therefore an area where local and national government need each other and complement each other. Decentralized authorities must take the lead in recognizing manifestations of radicalism, as they are best able to generate an accurate picture through their contacts with, among others, the local (ethnic) community and on the basis of information from, for instance, the police, Social Affairs, community centers and clubs, and educational institutes. Municipalities can be expected to take charge, on a local basis, of measures like establishing a system for early recognition of manifestations of radicalism and the implementation of administrative measures to counteract radicalism and extremism. The preventative aspects of the approach and the connection to the local integration policy also deserve attention. In this context it is heartening to see that municipalities like Amsterdam and Rotterdam have taken the initiative in the implementation of measures and policies with respect to tackling radicalization at the local level. We refer to the memorandum entitled '*Meedoen of achterblijven*' (Join in or get left behind) published by the municipality of Rotterdam and the Amsterdam action an entitled '*Wij Amsterdammers*' (We, the citizens of Amsterdam)."

490. Ibid., at 64.

491. Justice Initiative interview with Mr. Y.W., National Coordinator on Counterterrorism, the Hague, April 2006.

492. A municipal institution established to oversee the program.

493. "Radicalization in Rotterdam," Report Information Switchpoint, January 2006, at 17. Justice Initiative telephone interview with Wil van der Schans, Buro Jansen and Janssen (Dutch media bureau specializing in security issues), Amsterdam, April 2006. We understand, but were not able to verify, that no legal actions resulted from these alerts; rather individuals were referred to counseling, tutoring, or flagged for additional attention from social services. Justice Initiative interview with Mr. Y.W., National Coordinator on Counterterrorism, The Hague, April 2006.

494. Justice initiative interview with E.F., Dutch anti-radicalization expert, December 2008; Justice Initiative telephone interviews with local Muslim representatives.

495. See for instance, *"What steps can your company take to counter terrorism?" Guide for Companies by the National Coordinator for Counterterrorism*, December 24, 2006.

496. Justice Initiative telephone interviews with Muslim representatives, November, December 2008.

497. Justice Initiative interview with Colin Mellis, Amsterdam switchpoint, December 2008.

498. See for example, "Polarization and radicalization action plan 2007–2011," available at http://www.nyidanmark.dk/NR/rdonlyres/E9353925-A523-41C6-94F1-643EACF826CC/0/minbiz007_actieplanukv3.pdf.

499. Blick, Choudhury and Weir, *The Rules of the Game*, at 33–34.

500. Dr. Farhad Khosrokhavar, describing research based on interviews with radical Muslims in jail in England and France, conference on Muslims in Europe post 9/11, Saint Anthony's College and Princeton University, April 25–26, 2003, Oxford, U.K., available at http://www.sant.ox.ac.uk/princeton/pap_khosro.shtml.

501. Blick, Choudhury and Weir, *The Rules of the Game*, at 23.

502. International Crisis Group, *Islam and Identity in Germany*.

503. Paddy Hillyard, *Suspect Community; People's Experience of the Prevention of Terrorism Act in Britain,* (London: Pluto Press, 1993).

504. Paddy Hillyard, "The "War on Terror"; lessons from Northern Ireland," *European Civil Liberties Network, Essays for Civil Liberties and Democracy in Europe,* (London: ECLN, 2005), available at http://www.ecln.org/essays/essay-1.pdf.

505. A search of Finsbury Park Mosque, in north London, led to the discovery of forged passports, CS gas, knives, and guns, among other items. "Mosque raid findings revealed," *BBC News*, February 7, 2006, available at http://news.bbc.co.uk/1/hi/uk/4689816.stm. The iman of the Finsbuary Park Mosque at the time of the 2003 raid was Abu Hamza al-Masri, a person well known to intelligence services who suspected him of financing terrorism. The intelligence services of "France, Spain, Germany, Italy, Belgium and the Netherlands all accused Abu Hamza of being the ringmaster of a terrorist operation," according to an exhaustive account of the history of the Finsbury Park Mosque and Abu Hamza's leadership. Quoted in Sean O'Neill and Daniel McGrory, *The Suicide Factory: Abu Hamza and the Finsbury Park Mosque* (London: Harper Perrenial, 2006). "The Untouchable: How Abu Hamza was allowed to preach hate as authority looked the other way,"*The Times*, June 1, 2006.

506. See BfV website: http://www.verfassungsschutz.de/en/en_fields_of_work/islamism/.

507. Justice Initiative interview with Wolfgang Wieland, Green Party MP, Berlin, March 2006.

508. Stefan Nicola, "German Muslims feel sidelined," UPI, July 15, 2005. "Greater Surveillance of German Muslims," *Deutsche Welle*, July, 14, 2005. Ahmed Al-Matboli, "Germany Mulls Spying on all Mosques," *IslamOnlinenet*, July 18, 2005.

509. Matboli, "Germany Mulls Spying on all Mosques."

510. *"Mehr als 2500 Islamische Gotteshäuser auf Islamistische Umtriebe hin untersucht,"* March 22, 2003. Justice Initiative interview with Melanie Kamp, Berlin, March 2006. Justice Initiative interview with Sebastian Müller, German Institute for Human Rights, Berlin, March 2006. In an interview with Dr. Kai Andreas Otto, advisor to Mr. Wolfgang Bosbach, Deputy Chairman, Parliamentary Faction of CDU/CSU, confirmed that, according to his conversations with a representative of the Office of the Protection of the Constitution, 39 mosques are under surveillance. Justice Initiative interview with Kai Andreas Otto, Berlin, March 2006.

511. Burhan Kesici, vice president of the Islamic Federation of Berlin, told Justice Initiative researchers that it became clear during a controversy over expulsion procedures against the imam of the Mevlana mosque in Berlin that the BfV had taped all of the imam's speeches for some time, and tapped his telephone. As the BfV did not announce which mosques and prayer halls have been placed under surveillance, it is unclear whether the Mevlana mosque figures amongst the 39 "critical" sites. Justice Initiative interview, Berlin, March 2006.

512. Justice Initiative interview with Mr. R.J., Berlin, March 2006.

513. Justice Initiative interview with Mr. Burhan Kesici, Berlin, March 2006.

514. The BfV describes this distinction on its website: "Islamism—in particular its terrorist form—has developed into a major threat posed to the internal security of the Federal Republic of Germany, too. Islamism is a political, mostly socio-revolutionary movement—heterogeneous in itself—which is supported by a minority of the Muslims. With reference to the original Islam of the 7th century, its adherents—the Islamists—are calling for the "reinstitution" of an "Islamic order," [...] ... the various Islamist organizations can be distinguished by the methods and means used to achieve their objectives.... It has to be clearly emphasized that Islam as a religion is not being monitored by the Offices for the Protection of the Constitution, neither is the Muslims' personal faith nor their religious practice which is protected by the basic right to religious freedom as part of the free democratic basic order which is laid down in Art. 4 of the German Grundgesetz (the German Constitution)." See BfV website, available at http://www.verfassungsschutz.de/en/en_fields_of_work/islamism/. A 2007 BfV paper on Islamism stated that: "Neither the Federal Office for the Protection of the Constitution nor its federal state counterparts monitor Muslim milieus as such, they neither deal with Muslims nor with Islam, but with Islamism as a form of political extremism and with Islamist terrorism. The only relevant aspects are Islamist efforts or activities of Islamist organizations. Only about one percent (about 32,000) of the Muslims living in Germany have joined Islamist organizations. It cannot be emphasized strongly enough that the vast majority of the Muslims living in Germany practice their belief in the framework of our legal order." Federal Office for the Protection of the Constitution, *Integration as a means to prevent extremism and terrorism: Typology of Islamist radicalisation and recruitment*, (January 2007), at 3, available at www.verfassungsschutz.de.

515. Ibid.

516. Ibid.

517. Hamas (or *Harakat al-Muqawama al-Islamiyya* or Islamic Resistance Movement) is a Palestininan Sunni militant organization, currently governing the Gaza Strip. GIA is *Groupe Islamique Armé (al Jama'ah al-Islamiyah al-Musallaha* in Arabic or the Armed Islamic Group) that seeks to create an Islamic state in Algeria. It is considered a terrorist group by Algeria, France, and the United States. Several GIA members were convicted in 1999 in France for bombings carried out in 1995 in that country. Hezbollah or Hizb Allah—the "Party of God"—is from Lebanon, and follows a Shia stream of Islamism originating in Iran.

518. Werner Schiffauer, "Enemies within the Gates—The Debate about the Citizenship of Muslims in Germany," in *Multiculturalism, Muslims and Citizenship: A European Approach,* (London: Routledge, 2006), at 6–7. The BfV describes this categorization in its annual reports. See for example, *Annual Report 2005 on the Protection of the Constitution,* at 188–190, and also *Annual Report 2004 on the Protection of the Constitution,* under the section "Activities by Extremist Foreigners that Endanger the Security of the State," at 179–182. This classification is also explained in brief on the website of the BfV available at http://www.verfassungsschutz.de/en/en_fields_of_work/islamism/.

519. Milli Görüs, or the "National Vision," is an Islamic movement of Turkish origin that challenged Turkey's secularist state, calling for distance from Europe, independent development, and stronger ties with Muslim countries. It has a strong following among Turkish migrants in Europe. The Muslim Brotherhood is a Sunni Islamist group that originated in Egypt. It has spread widely, and is the largest opposition group in a number of countries, including Egypt, Syria, and Jordan.

520. *Annual Report 2005 on the Protection of the Constitution,* at 199. For a description of groups considered by the BfV to be Islamist, see *Annual Report 2005 on the Protection of the Constitution,* at 205–222.

521. Petra Follmar-Otto, researcher at the German Institute of Human Rights (*Wissenschaftliche Mitarbeiterin Schwerpunkt Menschenrechte im Inland*) explained that the authorities rely on paras. 10, 11, 37 and of the Citizenship Law in order to check a person's background with the BfV. Para. 10 requires an applicant to declare that he or she has not in the past and does not at present participate in structures or organizations against the Federal Democratic Order. Para. 11 provides that the authorities processing naturalization claims are to ask the BfV for information when they have suspicions that the person does not support democratic aims. Para. 37 stipulates that the authorities are to cooperate with state and federal level BfVs.

522. Justice Initiative interview with Kenan Kolat, *Turkischer Bund,* Berlin, March 2006.

523. "Islamists stripped of German nationality," *Deutsche Welle,* May 19, 2005.

524. Article 54 of the German Aliens Law provides that an individual may be expelled if he is a threat to the Federal Republic of Germany. According to Sebastian Muller of the German Institute for Human Rights, this vague formulation could, for example, be met if an individual is considered to be a member of Milli Görüs.

525. Professor Schiffauer has documented five or six such cases. The individuals received letters saying their residency permits will not be extended because they are members of Milli Gorus. Justice Initiative interview with Werner Schiffauer, Berlin, March 2006.

526. The individual has a period of 7 days to launch a single appeal to the highest administrative court. The relevant provision is article 58(a) of the Aliens Law. According to Mr. Sebastian Muller, to date expulsions have occurred under the normal provisions provided for by articles 54(5) and 55(a). Amnesty International has recently criticized Germany's new deportation provisions: "Following the attacks on March 11, 2004 in Madrid the anti-terror measures within the German Immigration Act were again expanded, resulting in the introduction of a number of clauses facilitating deportation. The new immigration Act entered into force in January 2005. A deportation order can now be issued on the basis of an 'evidence-based threat prognosis,' i.e. if there are fact-based reasons to suspect that the person might be a threat to national security. Proof that someone committed a crime is not needed, the suspicion based on facts suffices for deportation. In cases where deportation would result in suspects facing torture or the death penalty in their home country, they would be allowed to stay in Germany under tight restrictions, limiting freedom of movement and the right to communication. Breach of these restrictions would be heavily penalized. The new Act gives discretionary power to the authorities to expel so-called 'intellectual incendiaries' or leaders publicly inciting hate, violence and terrorist acts." *Counter-terrorism and Criminal Law in the EU*, (London: Amnesty international, EUR 45/020/2005).

527. Justice Initiative interview with Kai-Andreas Otto, Berlin, March 2006. Justice Initiative interview with Melanie Kamp, a doctoral student currently writing a thesis on Islamic organizations in Germany, Berlin, March 2006. Justice Initiative interview with Petra Follmar-Otto and Sebastian Müller, German Institute for Human Rights, Berlin, March 2006.

528. The 2007 BfV annual report details the breakdown of support for organizations considered to be "Islamist": "The number of supporters of the 30 Islamist organizations (in 2006 the number was 28) active in the Federal Republic of Germany has risen to 33,170 (from around 32,150 in 2006). With around 27,920 supporters (27,250 in 2006), Turkish groups have the largest following. The largest organization, with around 27,000 members, is still the Turkish *Islamische Gemeinschaft Millî Görüs* (IGMG, Islamic Community Milli Görüs). The number of supporters of Arab Islamist groups rose to 3,390 from 3,350 in 2005. The Muslim Brotherhood (MB) remains the largest group, with around 1,300 supporters. Membership of the second-largest group, the Lebanese Hezbollah (Hizb Allah, "Party of God"), remained steady at 900." The report states that: "No exact figures are available as regards followers of international mujahidin networks living in Germany." *BfV Annual Report 2007*, at 168.

529. *BfV Annual Report 2005*, at 189–190.

530. This point was made by journalists, academics, and politicians, as well as the organizations themselves.

531. The BfV did not respond to repeated requests for an interview. United States State Department, "Human Rights Report: Germany," (Washington, D.C.: Department of State, 2004). Justice Initiative interview with Sebastian Müller, Berlin, March 2006.

532. Justice Initiative interview with V., Berlin, March 2006. V. was unable to say with certainty whether the OPC has collected information about all of Milli Görüs's members. However, he believes that the security services have collected data about every person that he knows in Milli Görüs.

533. Justice Initiative telephone interviews with Muslim representatives and academics, November and December 2008.

534. See Section 3(1)1 and Section 4(1), *Act Regulating the Cooperation between the Federation and the Federal States in Matters Relating to the Protection of the Constitution and on the Federal Office for the Protection of the Constitution* (Bundesverfassungsschutzgesetz—BverfSchG) of December 20, 1990, last amended June 21, 2005 (Federal Law Gazette I), 1818.

535. Justice Initiative interview with Dr. Tânia Puschnerat, Berlin, July 2007.

536. Professor Werner Schiffauer writes: "The distinction between real Islam ('religion') and Islamism ('ideology') is drawn primarily by German politics and the German *Verfassungsschutz* [BfV]. Muslim authorities are hardly referred to when making this distinction. In fact, only Muslims supporting this distinction are accepted as partners in the debate. *Ulema* (Muslim scholars) questioning it would immediately and by this very act qualify themselves as Islamists and be deemed partisan. The self-confidence with which German politicians and intellectuals judge what is or is not Islamic is one of the debate's most striking features." Werner Schiffauer, "Enemies within the Gates—The Debate about the Citizenship of Muslims in Germany," in *Multiculturalism, Muslims and Citizenship: A European Approach* (London: Routledge, 2006), at 6–7.

537. Justice Initiative interview with Professor Werner Schiffauer, Europa Universität Viadrina, Berlin, March 2006.

538. International Crisis Group, *Islam and Identity in Germany; Crisis Group Europe Report No. 181* (March 14, 2007), at 17.

539. Justice Initiative interviews, Rotterdam, Utrecht, and Amsterdam, December 2005, March 2006.

540. "The radicalization processes among the minority of the total Muslim population and some converts in the Netherlands is highly dynamic. This is manifested in a number of ways, including the further advance of *Salafism* in some mosques. It is now also becoming increasingly clear that the major *Salafist* centers in the Netherlands are actively trying to exert an ideological influence on mosques elsewhere in the country, in part by organizing lectures in a large number of small Dutch towns. In addition to this ideological influence, the *Salafists* are also, in some instances, actively trying to take over moderate mosques," U.S. National Coordinator for Counterterrorism. "Fourth Progress Report on Counterterrorism," *Report to the President of the House of Representatives*, June 7, 2006.

541. "Besides these mosques which can be characterised as explicitly *Salafist*, there are several others (probably up to several dozen) that are less easy to typify as such, but which also receive financial support from Saudi charities, private benefactors or government bodies. Although not explicitly *Salafist*, as a result of the very orthodox message propagated these mosques attract certain groups of Muslims that can be characterised as *Salafist*, a designation which they often use themselves." AIVD, "Saudi influences in the Netherlands: Links between the *Salafist* mission, radicalization processes and Islamic terrorism," January 6, 2005, at 4. (Translation of paper *Saudi influences in the Netherlands*, AIVD, March 2004, available at https://www.aivd.nl/actueel-publicaties/aivd-publicaties/saudi_influences_in).

542. Justice Initiative interview with K.D., The Hague, June 2007. The Hofstadt group was identified by Dutch officials as a network of Dutch jihadists, one of whose members murdered Dutch filmmaker and columnist Theo van Gogh on November 2, 2004.

543. "Home-Grown Terrorism and Radicalization in the Netherlands: Experiences, Explanations and approaches," Testimony by Lidewijde Ongering, Deputy National Coordinator for Counterterrorism, before the United States Senate Committee on Homeland Security and Governmental Affairs, June 27, 2007.

544. Justice Initiative interview with Brahim Bursic, Rotterdam, December 2005.

545. Justice Initiative interview with S.N, Amsterdam, June 2007.

546. General Intelligence and Security Service, *From Dawa to Jihad: The various threats from radical Islam to the democratic legal order*, (The Hague: AIVD, December 2004).

547. General Intelligence and Security Service, *From Dawa to Jihad*.

548. Justice Initiative interview with S.N., Amsterdam, June 2007.

549. "Terrorism is the ultimate consequence of a development starting with radicalization processes. These processes may manifest themselves in various ways and also involve other than terrorist threats (for example, interethnic tensions). For the AIVD, combating terrorism starts by countering radicalization processes. Preventing, isolating or curbing radicalization are important means to combat terrorism with a long-lasting effect. Simultaneously, traditional investigations into terrorist organizations and networks are continuing unabatedly. But traditional counterterrorism without a focus on radicalization processes and prevention will prove to be less effective in the long run." AIVD, *From Dawa to Jihad*.

550. National Coordinator for Counterterrorism, *Counterterrorism at Local Level: A guide*, (The Hague: AIVD, June 2006). The guide states that: "Intervention in hotbeds of radicalism involves the coordinated use of existing powers and instruments of central and local government under the direction of the National Coordinator for Counterterrorism Organizations such as the intelligence and security services, the National Police Services Agency (KLPD), the Immigration and Naturalization Service (IND), the Public Prosecution Service, the Fiscal Information and Investigation Service/Economic Investigation Service (FIOD–ECD), the Minorities Integration Policy (Coordination) Department of the Ministry of Justice (DCIM), the Education Inspectorate, the Royal Military Constabulary, the regional police and the municipalities are closely involved."

551. AIVD, *From Dawa to Jihad*.

552. Ibid.

553. Justice Initiative interview with Professor Salvatore Pallida, Genoa, May 2006.

554. Justice Initiative interview with S.M. Arshad, Milan, May 2006.

555. Justice Initiative interview with Professor Salvatore Pallida, Genoa, May 2006; Justice Initiative interview with Carlo Bonini, Milan, May 2006.

556. Justice Initiative telephone interview with R.J., December 2008.

557. For more information on the evolution of this monitoring see Laurent Bonnelli, "When the intelligence services construct a new enemy,'" *Le Monde Diplomatique*, April 2005.

558. According to French journalists and counterterrorism officers, the RG's dense network is spread thickly across the country. They have long made it their business to monitor all collective movements that play a role in the country's social and political life, including human rights organizations, political parties, unions, and religious sects. Justice Initiative telephone interview with

Laurent Bonnelli, June 2006; and Justice Initiative interview with A.B., senior French counterterrorism official, Paris, July 2006. "Collecting information about Jihadists has become one of the priorities of the administrative police. Their reports feed the files of the investigators of the judicial police. 'The RG have a deep knowledge of the Muslim community,' believes Alain Chouet, former head of the General Directorate of External Security (DGSE). 'Their grassroots work provides 80 percent of the information.'" Olivier Talles, "Confronting terrorism: The French model," *La Croix*, October 24, 2005.

A representative of a Muslim nongovernmental organization described his contact with the RG: "Often the RG services phone and say 'we need to see you.' Or they phone and say, 'Mr. X., we would like to see you.' … They knew when I joined the association. And once they asked, 'is the young lady still working with you?'" Justice Initiative interview with S.D., CCIF, Paris, July 2006.

559. "Some twenty mosques in France in the hands of radical Islamists according to the RG," Associated Press, July 22, 2005. "Some twenty mosques in France in the hands of radical Islamists according to the RG," Agence France-Presse, July 24, 2005.

560. Piotr Smolar, "Anti-terrorism, according to the head of the RG," *Le Monde*, November 25, 2005.

561. Justice Initiative interview with Yamin Makri, Lyon, July 2006. Yamin Makri was a co-founder of the Collective of Muslims of France, a nongovernmental organization representing several dozen Muslim organizations from across the country.

562. See Courtois, *Projet de loi*. An article in the French newspaper *Le Monde* similarly stated that: "According to the estimates of the French intelligence services, salafism in France now has 5000 members, 500 activists and 30 places of worship." Piotr Smolar, "Salafism extends its reach to medium-sized cities," *Le Monde*, February 22, 2005.

563. Cited in "Counter-terrorism, the French method," *Le Nouvel Observateur*, No. 2154, February 16, 2006.

564. Courtois, *Projet de loi*.

565. The European Network on Liberty and Security (ELISE), a network of experts funded by the European Commission, commented: "It is striking to see the effect of the *continuum* of insecurity created by different narratives justifying the idea of connections between terrorism, organized crime, illegal migration, and (some) foreigners especially from Muslim origin, even if they have been living for a long time inside Europe. Stigmatization of some groups by establishing profiles along dubious correlations is the result of this restrictive norm creating a misleading hodgepodge of different notions." ELISE, *Synthesis Report 1—Report on Security and Civil Liberties; The extent to which there is an emergence of a common set of European values in matters of security and civil liberties*, available at http://www.libertysecurity.org/elise/article111.html#nb2.

The final report of the ELISE network discussed the Italian context: "In the Italian case, claims about difference are mainly linked to the role of the country as southern "limit" of Europe. Whether in journalistic discourse, political debate, or the common knowledge of Italian prosecutors, the so-called 'invasion' of 'illegal migrants' is frequently translated into terms that are synonymous with terrorist dangers. Two local factors are involved here: the traditional criminalization of migrants as dangerous aliens, and the alleged weakness of Italian borders to terrorist infiltration. Although there is no evidence of connections between terrorism and illegal migrations, it has now become normal to search for terrorist among migrants, especially those coming from Muslim countries.

This tendency has led to several trials in which people have been charged but eventually acquitted." ELISE, *Security Issues, Social Cohesion and Institutional Development of the European Union; Elise Final Synthesis Report*, para. 5.5, available at http://www.libertysecurity.org/IMG/pdf/ELISE_FINAL_SYNTHESIS_REPORT.pdf.

566. Daniel Wagman, *Ethnic Profiling by Police in Spain*, (Madrid: GEA21, 2006).

567. A leader of Milli Görüs (IGMG), cited in the International Crisis Group, *Islam and Identity in Germany; European Report No. 181*, at 17.

568. At a meeting of Muslim associations from the Paris suburbs, one representative commented: "We are all afraid here. I am afraid. The officials can come at 5.00 a.m. and stick any label on us. They can ruin our lives." Justice Initiative participation in meeting of Muslim associations, Paris, July 2006.

569. Justice Initiative interview with Omeyya Seddik, Paris, June 2006. Justice Initiative interview with Boualam Azahoum, Lyon, July 2006. Yamine Makri, pointed to the Minguettes neighborhood of Lyon as an example of where Islam in France is headed: "Fear, disappointment and individualism... the social fiber is destroyed... There is a climate of suspicion. No one has confidence in anyone. So no one can build something with anyone else. Even from the same family people are suspicious of each other...Everyone is afraid of everyone. People withdraw into themselves. That is why community movements that involve a withdrawal from society are flourishing... People want to keep relations with society at a strict minimum." Justice Initiative interview with Yamine Makri, Lyon, July 2006.

570. Justice Initiative interview with S.M. Arshad, Milan, May 2006. Spanish researcher Jose Maria Ortuño noted that when a petition was circulated to request respect of the presumption of innocence for a group of individuals detained on terrorist related charges, many Muslims were afraid to sign the petition.

571. Justice Initiative interview with B.A., Lyon, July 2006.

572. European Commission against Racism and Intolerance, *Second Report on Italy*. (Strasbourg: ECRI, April 2002).

573. Information from Luciano Scagliotti, vice president of the European Network against Racism (ENAR), to the IHF per email August 23, 2004.

574. Sara Cerretelli, *ENAR Shadow Report 2003: Italy* (Brussels: European Network Against Racism, 2003), at 30, available at http://www.enar-eu.org.

575. EUMC, *Second Report on Italy*.

576. European Monitoring Center on Racism and Xenophobia (EUMC), *Anti-Islamic reactions within the European Union after the acts of terror against the USA: Italy* (prepared by the Cooperative for the Development of Emerging Countries (COSPE),May 2004), available at http://www.eumc.at; *ENAR Shadow Report 2003: Italy*, at 26.

577. EUMC, *Anti-Islamic reactions within the European Union after the acts of terror against the USA: Italy*.

578. Justice Initiative interview with H.K., Utrecht, December 2005. The deputy chief of the Amsterdam police expressed his own concerns about stigmatizing individuals singled out: "Two Muslim youngsters were in a train preparing a prayer. People found this strange; it worried them.

Two passengers made a call to the police in a panic. We responded with the most intense level of police response. It was worse than a SWAT team really. When I look back it was just strange behavior of two young guys in *djellabas*–what was all the fuss about? I wouldn't like it if we contribute to a state of suspicion or aggression against everyone in different clothing or of a different religion. And that is really what could happen if we focus too much on specific appearance that you see and name as risky." Justice Initiative interview with B.W., Amsterdam, March 2006.

579. Justice Initiative interview with Werner Schiffauer, Berlin, March 2006.

580. Mustafa Yoldas, Hamburg, cited in the International Crisis Group, *Islam and Identity in Germany, European Report No. 181*, at 17.

581. Cited in IHF, *Intolerance and Discrimination against Muslims in Selected EU Member States*, at 13–14.

582. This raid is described in detail in Chapter IV, Section C.

583. Telephone interview with Mr. Udo Enwereuzor, representative of the Italian non-governmental organization Cooperazione per lo Sviluppo dei Paesi Emergenti (COSPE), April 2006.

584. Justice Initiative interview with D.K. Berlin, March 2006.

585. "In the aftermath of September 11 many NGOs reported on increasing xenophobia in Germany, especially against Muslims or persons with an Arab appearance. Complaints ranged from vandalism and bomb threats against mosques, to verbal abuse, discrimination and violent attacks. While German politicians condemned intolerance and hostility towards Muslims, critics made counterterrorism measures partly responsible for creating prejudice. Indeed, a great part targets foreigners, either wishing to enter or living in Germany. Regarding the latter, there are problems with various human rights: again, the right to privacy, but also freedom of religion and the prohibition of discrimination." Verena Zoller, "Liberty Dies by Inches," *German Law Journal*, Vol. 5, No. 5.

586. See *The Impact of 7 July London bomb attacks on Muslim Communities in the EU*, (Vienna: European Union Monitoring Centre, November 2005); International Helsinki Federation, *Intolerance and Discrimination against Muslims in Selected EU Member States*.

587. International Helsinki Federation, *Intolerance and Discrimination against Muslims in Selected EU Member States*.

588. *ECRI, Third report on France*, (Strasbourg: ECRI, 2005), at 3. See also other ECRI reports on Western European countries for a description of racism and discrimination directed at Muslims.

589. EUMC, *Anti-Islamic reactions within the European Union after the acts of terror against the USA: Italy*. See also see the chapter on "hate crimes and discriminatory policies" in IHF, *Anti-Terrorism Measures, Security and Human Rights* (Vienna: IHF, April 2003), available at http://www.ihf-hr.org.

590. Information from Udo C. Enwereuzor, European Racism and Xenophobia Network (RAXEN), coordinator with the COSPE branch in Florence, via email, March 2003.

591. UN Committee on the Elimination of Racial Discrimination, *Concluding Observations: Italy*, August 8, 2002, available at http://www.unhchr.ch.

592. Information from Luciano Scagliotti to the IHF, August 23, 2004.

593. Open Society Institute, *Monitoring Minority Protection in EU Member States: The Situation of Muslims in France*, (New York and Budapest: Open Society Institute, 2002), at 89.

594. Information from the French Association against Islamophobia to the IHF, September 10, 2004.

595. Several decades after his tenure as the British secretary of state, when he was responsible for the 1974 Prevention of Terrorism Act (PTA) that restored the exceptional powers in Northern Ireland, Roy Jenkins reflected that: "At the time, like everybody, I thought that these powers were justified; I still think this. But I thought that they would be temporary and that after the two years foreseen, we would return to normal, in other words the protection of freedoms. I am now horrified to know that these exceptional powers are still in force and if I had been told this at the time I would have refused to believe it, and if I had believed it, I would have refused to apply them." The PTA was authorized by the British Parliament, with almost no dissent, in the wake of the November 21, 1974 Birmingham pub bombings that killed 21 and injured 184 persons. Roy Jenkins, *A Life at the Centre*, (London: Macmillan, 1991), at 397.

596. Metropolitan Police Authority (2007) *Counter-Terrorism: The London Debate*, (London: MPA, 2007); Black Londoners Forum, *Stop and Searches under Section 44 of the Terrorism Act 2000* (London: Black Londoners Forum, 2004); John Vidal and Helen Pidd, "Police to use terror laws on Heathrow climate protesters," *The Guardian*, August 11, 2007.

597. In a 2005 debate of the French Senate on new terrorist measures, Eliane Assassi said: "I fear, in this respect, that the new exceptional regime for terrorist infractions, which already has a natural tendency to extend to other infractions—like police detention for four days, the presence of a lawyer only after the seventy-second hour [of detention], the special first instance criminal courts, or the possibility to carry out search warrants at night, which are now also applied drug cases—will soon extend to other areas." Mme. Eliane Assassi, "Lutte contre le terrorisme, Discussion d'un projet de loi déclaré d'urgence," Séance du 14 décembre 2005, Sénat français. (Translation by the Justice Initiative.) Henri Leclerc, former president of the French League for Human Rights commented on this same problem: "Each time, exceptional laws are enacted in the name of the danger of terrorism, for a short period, and then they are extended. For example, the police detention period of four days with the right to see a lawyer at the 72nd hour, now applied to cases of drugs; the special assizes courts to judge these crimes, search warrants conducted at night, etc." cited in Patricia Tourancheau, *Pour les juges*. Leclerc has also commented that "Laws of circumstance may respond to popular anxiety, but they also create it. They reduce freedoms in a durable way without their effectiveness ever being proven." Henri Leclerc, "Libertés immuables," *Web de l'humanité*, October 18, 2001. Italian journalist Carlo Boninni observed that the extension of counterterrorism measures has already begun to take place in Italy. He noted that an investigation was underway of the former security chief of Telecom Italy on suspicion of gathering personal data on thousands of Italian citizens. "The Italian Parliament has suddenly realized that something weird happened. In the name of national security, the fundamental defense of democracy was in some way breached. Officially his actions had been justified by the 'international terrorist threat.'" Justice Initiative interview with Carlo Boninni, Milan, May 2006.

598. Bernard E. Harcourt, "Muslim Profiles Post-9/11: Is Racial Profiling an Effective Counter-Terrorist Measure and Does It Violate the Right to be Free from Discrimination?" In Benjamin Jervis Gold and Liora Lazarus (eds.), *Security and Human Rights*, (Oxford: Hart Publishing, 2007).

599. EUROPOL, *EU Terrorism Situation and Trend Report 2007, TE-SAT 2007*, (The Hague: EUROPOL, March 2007).

600. Observation modeled on Livingston and Gross: "it could simultaneously be true that 90 percent of major cocaine traffickers on I-95 are black and Hispanic, and that 99.9 percent of black and Hispanic motorists on that highway are not drug traffickers." Samuel R. Gross and Debra Livingston, "Racial Profiling Under Attack," *Columbia Law Review*, Vol. 102 (June 2002) at 5.

601. NYPD Police Commissioner Ray Kelly, cited in Malcolm Gladwell, "Annals of Public Policy: Troublemakers: What Pit Bulls Can Teach Us about Profiling," *The New Yorker*, February 6, 2006.

602. Rapport d'information déposé par la délégation de l'Assemblée nationale pour l'Union européenne sur l'Union européenne et la lutte contre le terrorisme, présenté par M. Christian Philip, deputé. No. 2123, March 2, 2005, at 52.

603. Sageman distinguishes between three Al Qaeda groupings: the "core Arabs" (Saudi and Egyptian), the South-East Asian cluster, and the Maghreb Arab group, which is the most common in European terrorism. Sageman notes that the Maghreb Arab group is the poorest and least educated of the three Al Qaeda networks he identifies, and that European jihadists also differed from jihadists in other parts of the world in that they tended to drift toward violence alone or under the influence of friends rather than through formal ties to global extremist groups. Marc Sageman, *Understanding Terror Networks*, (Philadelphia: University of Pennsylvania Press, 2004).

604. "The most extensive research projects focused on former German and Italian terrorists from the 1970s. These studies concluded that there was no psychological profile for terrorism." Marc Sageman, *Understanding Terror Networks*, at 91. This was also EUROPOL's conclusion, as discussed above.

605. Edwin Bakker, *Jihadi Terrorists in Europe: Their characteristics and the circumstances in which they joined the jihad: An exploratory study*, (The Hague: Clingandael Security and Conflict Programme, January 30, 2007).

606. See detailed discussion of the report above at Chapter IV, Section E.

607. Sean O'Neill and Daniel McGrory, "Detectives Draw Up New Brief in Hunt for Radicals," *The Times*, December 28, 2005.

608. *Report of the Official Account of the Bombings in London on 7 July 2005*, Return to an Address of the Honorable House of Commons (11 May 2006), at 31. It had earlier been reported that British investigations into the bombings had "forced Scotland Yard to throw away the existing intelligence profile of a terrorist because none of the bombers fitted the model." Daniel McGrory, Alice Miles and Sean O'Neill, "Police 'betrayed' over cash to fight terrorism," *The Times*, December 28, 2005.

609. In the policing context, profiling involves a dynamic form of prediction—the profiling itself alters the behaviors of the people being profiled and the people who are not profiled. The success of profiling depends on two factors: a) identifying a stable group trait that correlates with higher offending, and b) how comparatively responsive profiled and non-profiled groups are to the targeted law enforcement and whether they engage in forms of substitution. In the long term, counterterrorist profiling will succeed only if the profiled group of young, male Muslims are at least equally likely as others to respond to the increased risk of detection by curtailing their activities. If not, then terrorists will be able to recruit non-Muslims or Muslims who do not fit the profile well (elderly,

white, female, etc.) as substitutes at least as frequently as profiled Muslims are deterred from committing terrorist acts.

610. "Bush details foiled 2002 al Qaeda attack on L.A.," CNN, February 9, 2006, available at http://www.cnn.com/2006/POLITICS/02/09/bush.terror/index.html.

611. New York City Police Commissioner Raymond Kelly cited in Malcolm Gladwell, "Annals of Public Policy: Troublemakers," *The New Yorker*.

612. Bernard E. Harcourt, "Muslim Profiles Post-9/11: Is Racial Profiling an Effective Counter-Terrorist Measure and Does It Violate the Right to be Free from Discrimination?" In Gold and Lazarus (eds.), at 10.

613. "At first suicide terrorists [in Israel] were all religious, militant young men recruited from Palestinian universities or mosques. In early 2002, however, the profile began to change as secular Palestinians, women and even teenage girls volunteered for suicide missions. On March 29, 2002, Ayat Akhars, an 18-year-old Palestinian girl from Bethlehem who looked European and spoke Hebrew, blew herself up in a West Jerusalem supermarket, killing two Israelis. Suicide bombers have also sought to foil profiling efforts by shaving their beards, dyeing their hair blond, and wearing Israeli uniforms or even the traditional clothing of Orthodox Jews." Counterterrorism expert Jonathan Tucker quoted in Bernard Harcourt, *Muslim Profiles Post-9/11*, at 18–19.

614. Craig Whitlock, "Terrorists Proving Harder to Profile: European Officials Say Traits of Suspected Islamic Extremists Are Constantly Shifting," *The Washington Post*, March 12, 2007.

615. The history of counterterrorism provides a cautionary tale. Installation of metal detectors in airports in 1973 reduced the number and rate of airplane hijackings worldwide, but, according to one analysis, resulted in a sharp and proportionally larger increase in bombings, assassinations and hostage-taking incidents. Harcourt, *Muslim Profiles Post-9/11*.

616. Ibid., at 9: "But on this central question, we have absolutely no reliable data. As an empirical matter, we do not know whether profiling will work in the counterterrorism context or on the contrary cause more terrorist attacks."

617. Ibid., at 10.

618. "Terror swoops 'persecuting' Muslims," *The Guardian*, August 5, 2004. According to the Islamic Human Rights Commission (IHRC), many Muslims also felt that police did not respond adequately to anti-Muslim attacks during the first backlash after September 11, which negatively influenced their perception of police practice and their readiness to turn to police. Information from Arzu Merali, research director, IHRC, via email, December 2002 and February 2003.

619. "Rise in police searches of UK Asians," *Daily Times*, August 24, 2004, available at http://www.dailytimes.com.pk/.

620. Cited in Jane Perlez, "British Police Criticized in Shooting After Terror Attack," *The New York Times*, August 2, 2007.

621. *Reconciling Security and Liberty in an Open Society—Liberty Response* (London: Liberty, August 2004).

622. "Islamophobic policing alienating young Muslims: UK government," *Rediff.com*, July 3, 2004, available at http://www.rediff.com/news/.

623. The opinion notes that: "This constitutes the first condition for such discriminatory practices to be effectively combated. Indeed, proving discrimination may be difficult were a victim is obliged to put forward elements demonstrating, beyond a reasonable doubt, that a discriminatory motive has been underlying a particular behavior, if the victim cannot rely on such statistics."

624. See, for example, ECRI, *Third Report on Germany* at para 85 and the OSCE, *Recommendations on Policing in Multi-Ethnic Societies.*

625. For example, France responded to ECRI's recommendation that they include the collection of statistics broken down by ethnicity, that collection of such data is "inconceivable." European Commission against Racism and Intolerance, *Third Report on France* (Strasbourg: ECRI, 2004), at appendix, available at http://www.coe.int/T/E/human_rights/Ecri/1-ECRI/2-Country-by-country_approach/. Greece also asserted that: "In particular, some aspects of the program concerning adoption of ways to reduce the racist discrimination during the police action, such as collection and process of specific data, is contrary to Greek legislation on protection of personal data," July 4, 2005 letter to the Open Society Justice Initiative from the head of staff of the Greek Ministry of Public Order.

626. The Open Society Justice Initiative is also working in partnership with police in Bulgaria, Hungary, and Spain to develop data gathering practices to monitor stops and ethnicity.

627. See, for example, "Gypsies march to protest racism," Associated Press, March 23, 2000: "In the last five days, [Romanian] police have raided Bucharest's seediest areas, in a crackdown on violent crime. Of 2,000 people arrested, police have said, most of them were Roma."

628. There remain concerns about police singling out Roma in special police databases in Germany. The annual report for 2000 of the United Nations Special Rapporteur on Racism noted information from Germany "that Sinti and Roma minorities are being specially registered in the databases and records of the Bavarian police as Roma/Sinti type, gypsy type or the old Nazi term *Landfahrer* (vagrant)." See E/CN.4/2000/16, (February 10, 2000), para. 37. Similar databases existed in Finland until at least 1995. Finland Report of the UN Convention Against Torture, UN Doc. CAT/ C/25/Add. 7, para. 120; cited in the E.U. Network of Independent Experts on Fundamental Rights, "Ethnic Profiling," Ref: CFR–CDF, Opinion 4, 2006; December 2006.

629. In October 2006, the London Metropolitan Police Service introduced Operation Pennant, an internal accountability system aimed at improving the effectiveness of stops and searches and reducing disproportionality by holding poorly performing London boroughs to account using a range of criteria. The system makes use of a self-assessment questionnaire completed by both the police and community representatives (participants in Independent Monitoring Groups) to highlight policy and practice that may be having a disproportionate impact on local communities. In the first six months, the system improved effectiveness of various aspects of stops and searches, and significantly reduced disproportion of stops of minorities in a number of boroughs. For further information about Operation Pennant please see Metropolitan Police Service website, available at http://www.met.police.uk/stopandsearch/com_engagement.htm.

For other examples of policy audits aimed at addressing police discrimination please see: The Open Society Justice Initiative's STEPSS project, which included a policy audit of existing legislation, policy, practice, and training in the use of police powers to check IDs, and conduct stops and searches, aimed at identifying areas in which these may have a disproportionate impact on ethnic minorities and immigrant communities in Bulgaria, Hungary, and Spain. Further information about the STEPSS project and assessment framework can be found at: www.justiceinitiative.org.

The U.K. Home Office's Stop and Search Action Team's Practice Orientated Package, which was primarily designed to determine the reasons for the disproportionate use of stops and searches conducted under PACE and is based on a systematic assessment of polices and practices surrounding stops and searches. Information can be found at http://police.homeoffice.gov.uk/news-and-publications/publication/operational-policing/PACE-SSAT-POP.pdf.

The Romanian Police Strategic Initiative conducted by OSCE–ODIHR, European Dialogue and the Romanian Police, which aims to deliver a model for the assessment of policing policy and practice in relation to the Roma in compliance with the European Convention on Human Rights (ECHR). Information can be found at http://www.europeandialogue.org/.

630. Community consultation on issues of disproportionate policing of minority communities is a critical element of an effective policy audit. Communities need to be involved in setting the parameters and questions for the audit, in discussions of the findings, and in shaping recommendations and proposals for action. It is also important that audits focus on different rank levels and relevant practices at each level of policing (policy setting, training, resource deployment, supervision, street patrol); and that they encompass a range of quantitative and qualitative data, going beyond a review of policy standards to assess actual practice and scrutinize areas where policy standards may not be followed or respected in practice.

631. European Commission Network of Independent Experts in Fundamental Rights, *Opinion 4. 2006: Ethnic Profiling*, at 20. The opinion questions whether the breadth of these powers "may constitute a violation of the requirement according to which any interference with the right to respect of private life should be in accordance with law: this not only means that such interference should be in accordance with the national legislation applicable, but also that the law should be sufficiently accessible and precise, so as to offer an adequate protection against arbitrariness." Ibid., at 20.

Differences in suspicion standards can be charted along a "discretion continuum," bracketed on one end by the virtual absence of any suspicion standard governing stop-and-search operations, providing officers with near-total discretion in the use of their powers. Of all the EU member states, Hungary appears to enjoy perhaps the highest margin of officer discretion: Hungarian law allows stops and searches of practically anyone at practically any time. Article 29 of the 1994 Act on Police gives the police full authorization to stop and request identification of "anyone whose identity needs to be established" with no requirement that this action be based on any suspicion of criminal activity. Cited in Open Society Justice Initiative, *"I Can Stop and Search Whoever I Want."* The United Kingdom lies at the other end of the spectrum with its highly regulated stop-and-search procedures with clearly articulated grounds for suspicion and officer actions, including explicit prohibitions on the use of race and ethnicity. It should be noted that, as of March 2008, a reform to the Hungarian police law proposed a new requirement that officers inform the person stopped of the reason for the stop.

632. The Europe Union's counterterrorism strategy is based on the four-pronged approach of "prevent, protect, disrupt and respond." "(1) To prevent people from turning to terrorism by tackling factors and root causes which can lead to radicalization and recruitment, in Europe and internationally. (2) To protect citizens and infrastructure and reduce vulnerability to attack. (3) To pursue and investigate terrorists across our borders and globally; to impede planning; to disrupt support

networks; to cut off funding and bring terrorists to justice. (4) To prepare ourselves to manage and minimize the consequences of a terrorist attack." Council of the European Union, Brussels, 15 November 2005; 14469/05 Limite.

633. Eric Herren, "Tools for Countering Future Terrorism," August 15, 2005, available at http://www.ict.org.il/articles/articledet.cfm?articleid=547. . CBS News quoted Michael Sheehan, head of the New York Police Department's Counter-Terrorism Bureau, "'What we do in the counter-terrorism bureau is try to define what the threat is [...] and understand the threat. That drives everything that we do'. Sheehan acknowledges the NYPD has its own informants working undercover in the city. 'The key to counter-terrorism is intelligence,' he says, 'and the key to intelligence are informants.' "The value of the information they find, says one member [of the bureau], is priceless. 'You cannot put a price tag on intelligence.' Just how priceless, the police say, has been shown twice a year and a half ago when a tip from an NYPD informant uncovered a plot to bomb the subway station outside Macy's Department store, and once before in 2003, when a plot to blow up the Brooklyn Bridge by al Qaeda operative Iyman Farris was uncovered." Ed Bradley, "Inside the NYPD's Anti-Terror Fight," March 19, 2006, *CBS News (60 Minutes)*, available at http://209.157.64.201/focus/f-news/1600505/posts.

634. Elaine Sciolino and Stephen Grey, "British Terror Trial Traces a Path to Militant Islam," *The New York Times*, November 26, 2006, at 1 and 14.

635. A vital third source of intelligence, particularly in the age of global terror networks, is through international cooperation between intelligence agencies—as borne out by the Operation Crevice Seven trial described above.

636. Justice Initiative interview with Mr. L.L., Paris, May 2006.

637. Remarks made at "Ethnic Profiling and Ethical Approaches to Security and Counter-Terrorism," a meeting co-hosted by the European Policy Center, the King Badouin Foundation and the Open Society Justice Initiative, Brussels, May 31, 2007. A U.K. academic study published in 1998 found that the police, working alone, only identify five to ten percent of crimes; 90 to 95 percent are reported by the public. Similarly, the study finds that less than five percent of crimes are solved (detected) through the use of forensics, 95 percent rely on evidence from crime victims and witnesses. Rod Morgan and Tim Newburn, *The Future of Policing*, (Oxford: Clarendon Press, 1998), at 117–118.

638. Blick, Choudhury and Weir, *The Rules of the Game, Terrorism, Community and Human Rights*, at 34.

639. Italian counter-terrorist investigative judge Maurizio Romanelli explained: "We start with one piece of information. Sometimes information that comes from the base... new persons are in contact with a known individual... it is very difficult to investigate—these are areas that are difficult to enter... if the first piece of information is solid we can work from there. Not in 10 minutes, it takes time... it is not easy." Justice Initiative interview, Milan, May 2006.

640. German counterterrorism official F.W. said: "One person is sometimes enough to give a whole department work. We found out we have whole group of people just in our state and most have contact with each other... It is enough just to get one person: most cases this will lead to other persons, societies or mosques. This is the good thing in this matter: most know each other ... For example, we may get information that there is an imam who is preaching against the western world.

This information is enough to step further into investigation. You have to have a judge that gives you authorization to listen to phone calls, etc. A judge always wants a certain level of information and that means you need to investigate further..." Justice Initiative telephone interview with F.W., July 2006.

641. William Finnegan, cited in "How Is the N.Y.P.D. Defending the City?" *The New Yorker*, July 25, 2005, at 58.

642. Jean Chichizola, "Derrière Richard Reid se cachait un réseau al-Qaida en France," *Le Figaro*, April 10, 2005.

643. Briggs, Fieschi, and Lownsbrough, *Bringing It Home*, at 32.

644. Comment of Danish participant, "Ethnic Profiling and Ethical Approaches to Security and Counter-Terrorism," a meeting co-hosted by the European Policy Center, the King Badouin Foundation and the Open Society Justice Initiative, Brussels, May 31, 2007. Summary meeting report available at http://www.kbs-frb.be/files/db/EN/xxx.pdf.

645. The Muslim Safety Forum is an umbrella organization made up of national and regional Islamic organisations including: MAB, IHRC, IFE, MCB London Affairs Committee, YMO UK, Muslim College, FAIR, Amal Trust, The London Central Mosque, London Muslim Centre, Muslim Parliament, FOSIS, ISB, Muslimaat UK, Avenues School, Somali Muslim Community, UKIM, MPAC, Stop Political Terror, Muslim Directory, Ershad Centre, BanglaMedia, Iqra Trust, Association of Muslim Police, Al-Khoei Foundation, UMO, Muslim Welfare House, Women's Relief. The MSF is the key advisory body for the Police Service and has signed a working protocol with the Metropolitan Police to build better police–community relations. It has been advising the police on matters of safety and security from the Muslim perspective for four years now. It meets on a monthly basis with senior representatives of ACPO and the MPS, the Metropolitan Police Authority, Home Office and the Independent Police Complaints Commission amongst others. From Muslim Safety Forum press release, March 2, 2005.

646. The Rotterdam Charter recommends that police acknowledge that inaccurate reporting and stereotyping by the media has a harmful effect on community relations, and recognize that police must take particular care in interactions with the press to avoid perpetuating stereotypes in descriptions of minority ethnic communities. It recommends introducing a code of conduct with specific guidance on when circumstances warrant reference to the national or ethnic origin of a crime suspect or convicted person. In most cases, there is no reason to mention the ethnicity of persons arrested or charged with crimes. This would not apply when police are seeking a particular person for a particular crime—here ethnic appearance is a valid aspect of a suspect description or suspect profile that police may choose to release to the press in an effort to secure public cooperation in identifying the person. The Rotterdam Charter, October 1997, available at http://www.rotterdam-charter.nl/read/2465.

647. As explained by the head of the review process in August 2007, MPS Commander Rod Jarman: "We have had a press push over the last two weeks—we have spoken to a lot of the ethnic press and have also spoken to every local newspaper and this past week there has been all the media coverage around the levels of searches after attempted bombings in July [2007]. The way that it has been reported has been immensely positive and the debate has been about what we are doing and what we hope to achieve. Part of this is about getting the message very clear; making sure that

the public understands that terrorists travel and so on and that we are using [Section 44 stop and search powers] to disrupt this, so that we can all work together to make it a hostile environment for terrorists. If you are stopped, of course you will want to know 'why me?' This is about ensuring that officers can respond effectively with information and they do so. That they feel confident to explain how the power is being used and why it is necessary." Justice Initiative interview with Commander Rod Jarman, London Metropolitan Police Service, London, August 7, 2007.

648. Organization for Security and Cooperation in Europe (OSCE), "Recommendations on Policing in Multi-Ethnic Societies," (Warsaw: OSCE, February 2006). See also, the Council of Europe human rights and policing programme; and the Rotterdam Charter, October 1997, available at http://www.rotterdamcharter.nl/read/2465. The Rotterdam Charter resulted from the work of a multi-national steering group, and a working conference on "Policing for a Multi-Ethnic Society: Principles, Practice, Partnerships" held in Rotterdam on May 30–June 1, 1996. The conference was attended by more than 120 delegates, representing 17 countries, drawn from police, elected authorities, and civil society. The charter sets out principles of good practice in various areas, noting that police most frequently have contact with people in troubled circumstances, most often in response to emergency calls or other negative situations. One result of this is an increased risk of "opposed and biased thinking" about minorities. The charter set out recommendations in five areas: recruitment and retention; training; effective implementation of anti-discrimination law; building bridges between ethnic minorities and police; migrant participation in crime versus police participation in criminalizing migrants.

649. This issue has been the focus of extensive debate and controversy in the U.S., where immigration law was used for counterterrorism efforts. In the U.S., immigration enforcement is a federal rather than a local police duty, though recent changes to the law have greatly expanded local police powers in this area. Police departments vary greatly in their policies around immigration enforcement. The NYPD has taken pains to tell local communities that it is not an immigration department and that they should not be afraid of having contact with the police and sharing information. See "How Is the N.Y.P.D. Defending the City?" *The New Yorker*, July 25, 2005, at 58. Two studies in the U.S. both found that America's Muslim communities want better relations with the police, and that the use of immigration law to round up Muslims for questioning after 9/11 and fear that such practices will continue constituted the single largest impediment to improving police-community relations. *Nicole J. Henderson, Christopher W. Ortiz, Naomi F. Sugie, and Joel Miller, Law Enforcement and Arab-American Community Relations after September 11: Engagement in a Time of Uncertainty*, (New York: Vera Institute of Justice, June 2006); Deborah Ramirez et al., *Developing Partnerships between Law Enforcement and American Muslim, Arab and Sikh Communities: A Promising Practices Guide*, (New York and Boston: OSI and Northeastern University, 2004).

650. Two U.S. studies examined police relations with Arab-American communities in the wake of 9/11. The issue of immigration enforcement was particularly prominent in the U.S. because the Federal Bureau of Investigation (FBI) made extensive use of immigration enforcement as a counterterrorism tool after 9/11. The studies found that Arab-American communities were more concerned about being targeted by government policies than they were about hate crime, and that immigration enforcement was the most troubling. Both studies also found that Muslim communities want better relations with the police. Their recommendations emphasized the importance of good communication, and commitment to work together, as well as the need for both police and communities to dedicate resources to the effort. Deborah A. Ramirez, Sasha Cohen O'Connell

and Rabia Zafar, *A Promising Practices Guide, Developing Partnerships between Law Enforcement and American Muslim, Arab and Sikh Communities*, (New York and Boston: Northeastern University, Open Society Institute and The Whiting Foundation, 2004), and Nicole J. Henderson, Christopher W. Ortiz, Naomi F. Sugie, and Joel Miller, *Law Enforcement and Arab American Community Relations after September 11, 2001: Engagement in a Time of Uncertainty*, (New York: Vera Institute of Justice, June 2006).

651. Rachel Briggs, Catherine Fieschi, Hannah Lownsbrough, *Bringing it Home: Community Based Approaches to Counter-Terrorism*, (London: DEMOS, December 2006), at 26–28.

652. Briggs, Fieschi, and Lownsbrough, *Bringing it Home*, at 15.

653. See discussion of radicalization and categorizing groups in Chapter III.

654. The report recommends that authorities and police should take the following actions to improve the way they tackle racist crime and violence: authorities need to examine their legal framework and make sure that it is adequate in defining racist crimes and creating mechanisms for reporting, recording and prosecuting them; police leaders should make a public commitment to encourage reporting and recording of racist crime; police should work with civil society and communities to encourage reporting; police officers should be given clear guidance and training in how to address racist crime, and police should create specialist officers at the local level with backing from a national office on hate crime; police should prioritize the needs of the victims and assure they have access to victim support services. Robin Oakley, *Policing Racist Crime and Violence: A Comparative Analysis*, (Vienna: EUMC, September 2005), at 4, available at http://fra.europa.eu/fra/material/pub/PRCV/PRCV-Final.pdf.

655. *Migrants' Experiences of Racism and Xenophobia in 12 EU Member States: A Pilot Study*, (Vienna: EUMC, May 2006).

656. David Weisburd and John E. Eck, "What Can Police Do to Prevent Crime, Disorder and Fear," in *The Annals of the American Academy of Political and Social Science* (2004, Vol. 593, No. 1, at 42–65); David A. Harris, *Profiles in Injustice: Why Racial Profiling Cannot Work* (New York: New Press, 2002); Rachel Tuffin, Julia Morris, and Alexis Poole *An Evaluation of the Impact of the National Reassurance Policing Programme*, (London: Home Office, 2006).

657. See for example, OSCE, *Recommendation on Policing in Multi-Ethnic Societies*, and the European Code of Police Ethics, at B. 25. Council of Europe, Recommendation Rec(2001)10.

658. It should be recalled that human rights must not be derogated and must also be respected in emergency situations and in times of emergency (Article 4, section 2, International Covenant on Civil and Political Rights and Article 15, section 2 ECHR). See discussion in: Wolfgang S. Heinz and Jan-Michael Arend, "The International Fight against Terrorism and the Protection of Human Rights," German Institute for Human Rights, August 2005.

659. Martin Scheinin, Special Rapporteur on the promotion and protection of human rights while countering terrorism, "Profiling in counter-terrorism," presentation to the UN Working group on people of African descent, Geneva, January 31, 2007.

Open Society Justice Initiative

The Open Society Justice Initiative, an operational program of the Open Society Institute (OSI), pursues law reform activities grounded in the protection of human rights, and contributes to the development of legal capacity for open societies worldwide. The Justice Initiative combines litigation, legal advocacy, technical assistance, and the dissemination of knowledge to secure advances in the following priority areas: anticorruption, equality and citizenship, freedom of information and expression, international justice, and national criminal justice. Its offices are in Abuja, Brussels, Budapest, London, New York, and Washington DC.

The Justice Initiative is governed by a Board composed of the following members: Aryeh Neier (Chair), Chaloka Beyani, Maja Daruwala, Anthony Lester QC, Jenny S. Martinez, Juan E. Méndez, Diane Orentlicher, Wiktor Osiatyński, Herman Schwartz, Christopher E. Stone, Abdul Tejan-Cole, and Hon. Patricia M. Wald.

The staff includes James A. Goldston, executive director; Robert O. Varenik, program director; Zaza Namoradze, Budapest office director; Kelly Askin, senior legal officer, international justice; David Berry, senior officer, communications; Sandra Coliver, senior legal officer, freedom of information and expression; Rebekah Delsol, project officer, ethnic profiling; Indira Goris, program officer, equality and citizenship; Julia Harrington, senior legal officer, equality and citizenship; Ken Hurwitz, senior legal officer, anticorruption; Katy Mainelli, director of administration; Rachel Neild, senior advisor, equality and citizenship; Chidi Odinkalu, senior legal officer, Africa; Martin Schönteich, senior legal officer, national criminal justice; and Rupert Skilbeck, litigation director.

www.JusticeInitiative.org

Open Society Institute

The Open Society Institute works to build vibrant and tolerant democracies whose governments are accountable to their citizens. To achieve its mission, OSI seeks to shape public policies that assure greater fairness in political, legal, and economic systems and safeguard fundamental rights. On a local level, OSI implements a range of initiatives to advance justice, education, public health, and independent media. At the same time, OSI builds alliances across borders and continents on issues such as corruption and freedom of information. OSI places a high priority on protecting and improving the lives of marginalized people and communities.

Investor and philanthropist George Soros in 1993 created OSI as a private operating and grantmaking foundation to support his foundations in Central and Eastern Europe and the former Soviet Union. These foundations were established, starting in 1984, to help countries make the transition from communism. OSI has expanded the activities of the Soros foundations network to encompass the United States and more than 60 countries in Europe, Asia, Africa, and Latin America. Each Soros foundation relies on the expertise of boards composed of eminent citizens who determine individual agendas based on local priorities.

www.soros.org